"Jennifer Barrick has a contagious faith, and we have prayed for her fervently since the day of the accident. The pages of this book reveal the greatness of our God and how He supernaturally ministered to the entire Barrick family. *Miracle for Jen* will take you on a journey of experiencing God's help, hope, and healing power in a whole new way."

TIM AND BEVERLY LAHAYE
Bestselling authors

"Jen's story exemplifies how a battle can be turned into a beautiful life that glorifies God."

SHERI ROSE SHEPHERD
Bestselling author of *His Princess*

"In a world full of hurting and broken people, *Miracle for Jen* will astound you and bring healing to your soul. If you have ever questioned how God could turn a tragedy into triumph, you need this book."

DR. TIMOTHY CLINTON
President, American Association of Christian Counselors

"Jen Barrick is an inspiration. What a wonderful living example of perseverance! This story is a must-read for anyone facing the unexpected storms of life."

VERNON BREWER
President, World Help

miracle for Jen

a tragic accident,

a mother's desperate prayer,

and heaven's extraordinary answer

Linda Barrick

TYNDALE
MOMENTUM™

The nonfiction imprint of
Tyndale House Publishers, Inc.

Visit Tyndale online at www.tyndale.com.

Visit Tyndale Momentum online at www.tyndalemomentum.com.

Visit the Barrick family website at www.miracleforjen.com and ministry website at www.hopeoutloud.com.

Library of Congress Cataloging-in-Publication Data

Barrick, Linda.
  Miracle for Jen : a tragic accident, a mother's desperate prayer, and heaven's extraordinary answer / Linda Barrick.
      p. cm.
  Includes bibliographical references.
  ISBN 978-1-4143-6119-2 (hc)
  1. Barrick, Jennifer—Religion.   2. Brain damage—Patients—Rehabilitation.   3. Traffic accident victims—Rehabilitation.   4. Traffic accident victims—Religious life. I. Title.
  BV4910.B37 2012
  248.8'60922—dc23
  [B]   2011041689

ISBN 978-1-4143-7263-1 (International Trade Paper Edition)
ISBN 978-1-4143-6120-8 (sc)

Printed in the United States of America

23 22 21 20 19 18 17
 9   8   7   6   5   4   3

To our "army of helpers"—
hundreds of people who went into action
and thousands who prayed for us in our darkest hour.
You brought hope to our hearts.

Contents

Acknowledgments

I would like to extend a heartfelt thank-you to the publishing and marketing team at Tyndale House. I remember thinking, *I can't believe God wants me to write a book*. I think God has a sense of humor. He delights in using us to accomplish what we're incapable of because He wants to receive all the glory and praise! I am grateful for the opportunity to work with such amazing and talented editors as Kim Miller, Kathy Olson, and Bonne Steffen. Stephen Vosloo did a spectacular job during our photo shoot; one of his portraits of Jen appears on the cover.

I also want to express my appreciation to Wolgemuth and Associates, Joe Musser, Dawn Emeigh, and Stephanie Schneider, who helped make this book a reality.

Literally hundreds of people went into action when they heard about our accident. Our family refers to them fondly as our "army of helpers." I was told that, thanks to e-mail, there were thousands of people all around the world praying for us within minutes of the accident. I truly believe those prayers kept us alive through the night and brought us strength in the months that followed.

For months, our army of helpers were scheduled 24/7 to bathe us, watch over our kids, feed us, clean our house, and help in more ways than we could ever imagine.

Job 25:3 says, "Who is able to count [God's] heavenly army?" That's how I feel about the army of volunteers God called together to help us on earth. While I could never mention every name without frustrating my readers or leaving someone out, here's my attempt to at least mention the groups who became our hands and feet when our bodies were broken. . . .

Our incredible families, my childhood girlfriends, the Lynchburg General Hospital staff, the UVA Children's Hospital ICU staff, Liberty University staff and alumni, our Thomas Road Baptist Church family, my Mountain Blend Bible study girls, out-of-state-friends who traveled to help us, neighbors, Andy's basketball team, the Fellowship of Christian Athletes, and Liberty Christian Academy's extended family. We are especially grateful for the local volunteer rescue workers and firemen on the scene of the accident, the special education school teachers from Jefferson Forest High School, the staff and therapists at Kluge Children's Rehabilitation Center, and the nurses who volunteered to help us once we were home.

Finally, to my husband (who is more like Jesus than anyone else I know), to my daughter (who praises God and bows her desires to His plan every day), and to my son (who is an amazing, selfless servant leader). I am so proud of who each of you is becoming. In the early days of the tragedy, I thought it would have been easier if we had all just gone to heaven. But I truly cherish each moment we have together here on earth to live for the Lord and glorify God with our lives.

Before You Begin . . .

My life is on display. Whether it's the child studying my wheelchair, the couple in the store smiling sympathetically, or the waiter eyeing me as I use my bent spoon to eat slippery spaghetti, I'm aware that people are watching. Some watch out of pity, some out of admiration. But all watch with unspoken questions.

A front-seat passenger in an accident that almost took the lives of her whole family, Linda Barrick has watched her daughter, Jennifer, face the same thing. But this fresh-faced, beautiful teenager chooses to think that people are curious for good reasons. Like me, she knows she is called to be on display (as any Christian is)—she is exhorted to smile from the inside out, showcasing God's strength through her physical limitations. Believe me, Jennifer does that so *well.* One look into her bright eyes tells you this girl's love for Jesus is utterly unique. When she shares her happy-hearted and winsome affection for her Savior, people can't help but watch and think, *How great her God must be to inspire such joy in Him!*

Jennifer does not mind being on display—she relishes it! Despite the horrible accident in which she suffered a serious head injury, Jennifer knows God is up to something big.

I have had the joy of meeting this dear family. Dad and mom,

Andy and Linda, and their children, Jennifer and Josh. Their love for Jesus and each other is clearly visible. They stand strong together. I watched Jennifer on the campus of Liberty University . . . the way she speaks ever so naturally about her Lord with total strangers is truly remarkable. She discovered something special about Him while she was unconscious from her head injury, something sweet from the inner sanctum of sharing in the fellowship of His sufferings, and I confess, even *I* am curious about her unique and otherworldly faith. You'll be curious too, once you spend just a few minutes with Jennifer through the eyes of her mother on these pages—and what a story it is!

Finally, in a world that is splitting apart at the seams, we need to hear from courageous people who "fall in love with God" in the midst of terrible trials. The Barricks do that . . . and more. In these pages, you will discover a young woman and her family who are very ordinary, yet so surprising. And like me, you will think, *If Linda is able to look up and trust Jesus and if Jennifer is able to overcome her limitations by the grace of God, I can too.*

But I'm getting ahead of myself. And so are you. There is so much more to discover in the chapters ahead. Trust me; this book is definitely a surprising read. *Miracle for Jen* will inspire you, challenging your very concept of what it means to know God, as well as to trust Him. You will see the miraculous—often mysterious—way He weaves the strangest of circumstances into a life plan one wouldn't trade for the world. Just ask Linda. Just ask Jennifer. You'll see.

Joni Eareckson Tada
AGOURA HILLS, CALIFORNIA

CHAPTER 1

ALMOST PERFECT

You saw me before I was born. Every day of my life was recorded in your book. Every moment was laid out before a single day had passed.

PSALM 139:16

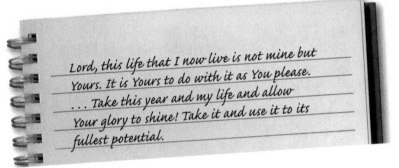

Lord, this life that I now live is not mine but Yours. It is Yours to do with it as You please. . . . Take this year and my life and allow Your glory to shine! Take it and use it to its fullest potential.

Jen's journal, three months before the crash

MY CELL PHONE WAS RINGING.

My brain reacted automatically. I knew I should reach down toward my feet and fish the phone out of my purse. But my body wasn't moving. I had no feeling anywhere, only a sensation of being restricted as if I were wrapped in a steel blanket.

I opened my eyes. My face was smashed against a windshield of crushed glass. *How did I get here? Is this a dream? Wasn't I just sitting with my husband and son watching our fifteen-year-old, Jen, sing in the choir at her school's fall concert?*

I reached down with my right hand to touch my leg, and when I lifted my hand up again it was covered with blood.

This can't be real. Lord, please wake me up!

"Mom? Mom?!"

I heard Josh calling for me from the backseat. I couldn't turn around to see him, but I answered anyway. "Josh! Josh!"

"Mom!"

"Is this real?!" I asked. "Is it a dream?" I didn't hear an answer so I said again, "Is this real?"

"Yes, Mom, this is real."

In anguish, I cried out, "Lord Jesus, please *help* us! Come to our rescue! Save us!"

Josh and I both began to pray out loud. "Father, please don't let Jen and Andy die! Oh, God, help us! Please don't let them die! You are all powerful. You can do anything! We need a miracle!"

Then my husband, Andy, started to stir. "Where are we?" he asked groggily. "What's happening?"

He was in shock and didn't answer any of our questions, but at least he was alive. Jen remained silent and still in the seat behind Andy's.

As a mom, I wanted with every molecule inside me to hug Josh and touch him and make him feel better. I wanted to hold Jen in my arms and tell her that I loved her. But I couldn't move. The crushed metal and broken glass encased my body like a giant, sinister glove.

The only thing I could do was pray.

Only an hour earlier, I had been sitting in our church sanctuary as music washed over the audience in waves, filling the room with sounds of praise and the pulsing energy of young hearts on fire for Christ.

For the first few verses, the choir stayed in the background as the soloist sang about the awesome and inexpressible love of Jesus. Then with a swell of strings and a kick of the drums, the choir stepped into the musical spotlight, each singer moving to the rhythm of the orchestra, swaying with the beat, some lifting their hands as they joyfully praised their incredible, all-powerful Savior:

Wonderful, glorious, holy, and righteous,
Victorious conqueror, triumphant and mighty,
Healer, deliverer, shield, and defense,
Strong tower and my best friend,
Omnipotent, omnipresent, soon-coming King,
Alpha, Omega, Lord of everything,
Holy, holy, holy is your name![1]

Of all the singers from Liberty Christian Academy onstage that night, one stood out especially to me: a beautiful, auburn-haired sophomore who seemed transformed by the words and music surrounding her, completely focused on conveying her passion for Christ to the audience. Maybe it was because the video monitors flanking the stage kept showing her face, beaming with enthusiasm. Maybe it was because she was on the end of a row and had room to move a little, while most of the students stood shoulder to shoulder on banks of risers.

Or maybe it was because I'm her mother.

Jennifer had been anticipating this fall concert for weeks, looking forward to the privilege of singing in the Sunday night church service for more than three thousand people. It was her first performance with the high school choir, and Jen always loved new experiences. I was a little surprised she wanted to be in the group since, for all her many gifts and talents, Jen did not have what I'd call a fabulous voice. God had blessed her in so many other ways—she was a straight-A honor student, varsity soccer player, and nationally ranked varsity cheerleader—and she hadn't seemed that interested in choir before. However, in typical Jen fashion, what she lacked in natural ability she made up for in enthusiasm and hard work.

Sophomore year was shaping up to be her best yet, part of an incredible season of transformation taking place right in front of me. It seemed like just yesterday she was running around in a baseball cap and mud-stained clothes, spitting sunflower seeds. I would often have to beg her to comb her hair. Now she was blossoming into a beautiful young lady. The braces had come off after two years, revealing a dazzling new smile. Just recently she'd gotten her first formal dress to wear to the junior-senior banquet. I'd scarcely recognized the glamorous, elegant woman who had come out of Jen's bedroom when her date arrived to pick her up.

Only two nights before the concert I'd been at the football game to watch her cheer. She was so exuberant and full of life, going all out with every jump like she always did, her face glowing with energy and excitement. Now here she was onstage, just as intent on doing her best with the choir as she was with the soccer team or the cheering squad. I could not have been more proud of my precious daughter. Her life seemed almost perfect!

Music was good for Jen because it was a fresh way to express her faith. She was such a friendly, popular girl, yet all her life she had held her thoughts inside. Spiritually and emotionally she was a very private person. She didn't talk much to me or to anybody else about what was on her mind and heart. As deeply committed to Christ as Jen was, and as much as she wanted her friends to know Christ the way she did, it wasn't a natural thing for her to witness one-on-one. When her youth group went door-to-door sharing God's love with strangers, she was always the one standing quietly in back, never saying a word.

In fact, one of my prayers for Jen that year had been for boldness. She'd asked me to pray for her to find a way to express her private relationship with God out loud. Music gave her a tool to shout out her love. That's why I think she sang with a special radiance that night at her musical debut.

The song she was performing heightened her sense of excitement even more. "Lord, You're Holy" was one of her favorites, especially the part in the middle where the choir takes the lead, describing the unbelievable, unfathomable depth and richness of God's love. She'd sung those lyrics around the house all week.

I didn't know it at the time, but that very afternoon Jen had written about the upcoming concert in her journal. The pages of her daily journals were the one place where the deep, tender spirit of Jennifer Barrick was fully revealed. There, in goofy, unassuming spiral notebooks decorated with polka dots or cartoon characters, she wrote letters to Jesus like He was her best friend. Only hours earlier, anticipating this moment onstage, she had told Him:

Lord, the only way I feel worthy to sing this song is on my face before You! This song can't even describe You to Your true fullness! Mere words cannot express You! Lord, I love this song b/c it helps put things in perspective! It lifts Your name on high! You are worthy of all my praise! And the only one deserving all my worship!

The music rocked to a big finish. Before the last note sounded, the audience of parents, friends, and church members rose as one, their cheers and applause roaring through the spacious sanctuary of Thomas Road Baptist Church, home of Liberty Christian Academy and partners in ministry with Liberty University, where my husband, Andy, was director of alumni relations. He was beside me in the audience that night, along with our son, eleven-year-old Josh. Like his dad, Josh loved sports and would probably not have put a choir concert first on his list of favorites for a family outing. But he obviously enjoyed seeing his sister onstage.

Andy and Josh had slipped into the performance just in time. Jen and I came to church by ourselves that afternoon because the guys were on their way home from a baseball tournament Josh played over the weekend. They were with our friend Dr. Tim Clinton and his son, Zach, who was also in the tournament. Tim's daughter, Megan, sang in the concert that night too, so the ballplayers stopped by our house for a quick shower and then came to church in Tim's car. That way Andy, our kids, and I would be able to ride home together. It would be great to spend the time catching up on each other's adventures. Besides, as Andy knew, I hated driving in the dark.

Once the applause tapered off and the crowd sat down, the speaker for the evening took his place at the lectern. My father, Dr. Ed Hindson, preached that night on prophecy. I've heard Dad, a distinguished professor at Liberty University, speak thousands of times since I was a little girl. His insights, based on years of study and teaching from the book of Revelation, have inspired untold numbers of people. On this particular night, I sensed that his preaching was especially anointed. By the end of his sermon the entire audience seemed stirred. More than a hundred came forward to pray.

After the closing prayer, the audience stood, buzzing with pent-up energy and moving toward the exits. Outside it was crystal clear with an autumn snap in the air, unseasonably cold for early November in Virginia. Josh wore only a T-shirt and jeans, but we'd be home in no time so it didn't really matter. Heading toward the parking lot, Andy and I made a point of reminding several couples that they were invited to our house for an impromptu postconcert supper and to watch football on TV.

I saw Jen talking—let's be honest, flirting—with her boyfriend,

Brandon. Curly-haired and blue-eyed, he was a handsome young man. He was a senior and had just turned eighteen, which initially had my motherly antennae on high alert. However, over the months they'd been dating he had proven himself to be a Christian gentleman in every way. I'd even relaxed my "no riding with teenage drivers" rule to let Jen ride with him. Since the rest of his family would be coming to our house in a few minutes anyway, I decided to let him drive her home.

"Did you drive tonight?" I asked him.

"No, ma'am," he answered with his unfailing Southern manners. "I rode with my parents."

For a second I considered letting Jen go with the Knight family. Then I realized that between Josh's baseball and Jen's cheerleading events, it had been three weeks since we'd been in the car at the same time. So I didn't offer. I was looking forward to the four of us being together again, even for the short trip home.

We climbed into our 2003 Toyota van with Andy at the wheel, me beside him, Jen behind Andy, and Josh behind me. Some of our company would probably beat us home, but that was okay; they could talk in the yard for five minutes until we got there. We were expecting my parents, Andy's mom and dad, Andy's brother, John, and his two kids, Brandon and his family, and our friends Robb and Paula Egel. Ever the thoughtful husband, Andy suggested we swing by KFC for fried chicken instead of trying to whip up something so late at the house. The kids added their "yes" votes from the backseat, and I wasn't going to turn down a trouble-free party dinner with no dishes afterward.

We had to go a little out of our way to get the food, so we didn't take the usual route home from church. Andy parked and went in to pick up our order while the rest of us waited in the van. After what seemed like a long time, Josh asked if he could go inside to see what the holdup was. I said he could and he jumped out, ignoring the cold despite his thin T-shirt, and walked purposefully inside as only an eleven-year-old going to check on his father can do.

In another five minutes, my two men came back carrying their bounty: four big buckets of just-fried KFC. Andy put his two on the floor beside me, and Josh put his on the seat between him and Jen. She was busily texting Brandon, despite the fact that she had seen him ten minutes before and expected to see him again in another five. I could feel the heat from the containers at my feet. Our meal would still be piping hot by the time we arrived home.

Andy's cell phone rang. It was his brother, John. "Where are you guys?" he asked, three-fourths teasing, one-fourth annoyed. "We're waiting in your driveway, along with the rest of your company! Are you on your way?"

"Yeah," Andy assured him. "The guy at KFC had to fry some extra chicken to fill our order, but we'll be home in five minutes."

Andy turned onto Waterlick Road, a narrow, two-lane street we both traveled dozens of times a week that ran within a mile of the house. It was an old-fashioned country lane with open drainage ditches on both sides, leaving scarcely a car width of shoulder between pavement and drop-off. I'd noticed those ditches in the past—the neighborhood was outgrowing its old rural roads—but didn't give them a moment's thought now. It was a quiet, clear Sunday night, the moon etched bright against the dark sky. Not much traffic.

I was thinking ahead to a house full of friends and warm fellowship only a few turns away. I'd put on some coffee, and Andy would get the fire going in the fireplace and turn on the football game. Josh was eager to tell us about his big plays at the baseball tournament and how they won the championship game. The in-laws looked forward to a visit with each other, and we'd all celebrate a wonderful concert and an inspired sermon.

But that's not what happened. Jen didn't see Brandon, Josh didn't tell us about his ball game, Andy and I didn't visit with our friends, and no one ate any chicken.

Instead, within a matter of seconds, our lives would change forever.

As we were all sitting in church watching Jennifer sing, a man I'll call "Carl Johnson," though that isn't his real name, was sitting in a restaurant across town ordering one drink after another. Carl was twenty-six and had a long history of drinking and driving. In fact, on that night he didn't have a valid driver's license or auto insurance. Since Carl had more than twenty traffic violations, his license had been revoked. He had been convicted twice for DUI and arrested for a third, which upon conviction would mean mandatory jail time. That charge was still pending; otherwise, Carl would have been locked up and off the street that night.

Carl paid for his drinks and staggered outside to his 1979 Chevy truck. He stabbed his key at the ignition switch, started the engine, and careened onto Timberlake Road, barely missing other cars that honked and swerved to get out of the way. Within seconds he was barreling down the road and sideswiped a Ford Explorer going in the same direction.

Fortunately, that driver, whom I'll call Don, had seen Carl in his rearview mirror and prepared as much as possible in the split second before impact. He corrected the skid and followed Carl, calling 911 as he drove.

"We've been hit by a truck . . . and he's not stopping!" Don reported. He continued to follow the weaving truck and feed information to the 911 dispatcher. "He's heading down Waterlick Road toward [Highway] 811."

"This guy's gotta be drunk," Don reported. "He's over in the other lanes and runs off the road on both sides."

We later learned from state police reports that Carl's blood alcohol level measured 0.33 percent at the crash site, *four times* the legal threshold for driving after drinking. Don's mother and girlfriend, passengers in the SUV, began to pray that God would protect whomever was down the road as the battered pickup raced away. The next victim might not be so fortunate.

Don followed Carl onto a residential dead-end street. After a minute, Carl made a U-turn and drove back to the intersection of Highway 811 and Waterlick Road. He passed out at the wheel and sat through several green lights. The truck was still running and in gear, with only Carl's foot on the brake to keep it from drifting out into the middle of the intersection. It had been over twenty minutes since Don had first called 911, and he wondered what he should do.

Finally, a police officer arrived on the scene and quickly opened the pickup door. He reported seeing a white male subject with his head on the steering wheel and a strong smell of alcohol coming from the vehicle. The officer depressed the parking brake and woke Carl up. He then ordered him to put the truck in park, turn off the ignition, and hand him some identification.

Don, still on the line with the 911 dispatcher, reported that the man was getting out of his truck.

"So he's talking to the deputy now?" the dispatcher asked.

"Yes," Don replied.

After a couple of minutes, the officer ordered Carl to get back inside his truck and stay there.

Not a day goes by that my mind doesn't revisit that moment. Why didn't the officer handcuff Carl and lock him in the back of his cruiser? Or at the very least, take his keys? Obviously the suspect was drunk out of his mind. Had the policeman stopped him from driving anymore, the future for the Barrick family would have turned out very differently.

Having told the reckless driver to stay put, the officer walked over to the Explorer to get Don's account of the incident. He stood at the driver's side window while Don began his statement, then stepped back to wave a passing car around.

Suddenly, Carl fired up the engine of his truck and sped away with a squeal of tires and burning rubber. He ran through the light at 811 and headed back up Waterlick Road—going eighty miles an hour, with his headlights off in the dark night.

Straight at us.

If we hadn't been to the concert that night, hadn't decided to stop for chicken, or hadn't had to wait longer than usual for our order, we would not have been driving down Waterlick Road at that moment. But there we were, headed in the opposite direction from Carl about three-fourths of a mile from home. Just minutes earlier on his way to our house, Andy's brother, John, had actually seen Carl's pickup, lights off, sitting through a green light. He figured some poor guy had dropped something on the floor of his car and was reaching down to get it. Now John, with his children Amanda and Andrew, was in our driveway with our other guests waiting for us to get there with the house key and the chicken.

Andy slowed the van to take the familiar curve just before the intersection of Waterlick and 811, where we would turn left to go into our neighborhood.

I had turned around toward the backseat and was talking to Jen, who was a little nervous that Brandon's whole family was coming to our house for the first time. She was calling a neighborhood girl-friend named Kelsey to invite her to the party as well.

"She's not there," Jen said. "Should I leave a message?"

I never had a chance to answer. Suddenly Andy yelled, "Watch out!"

I heard no impact, felt no collision, no pain, nothing. The world simply went black.

CHAPTER 2

"WHERE ARE WE?"

Do not be afraid or discouraged. For the LORD your God is with you wherever you go. JOSHUA 1:9

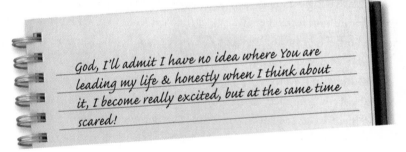

God, I'll admit I have no idea where You are leading my life & honestly when I think about it, I become really excited, but at the same time scared!

Jen's journal, two months before the crash

I HEARD MY CELL PHONE CHIRPING AWAY, but I was powerless to reach it. I wondered if one of the friends we'd invited to our house was trying to call.

In fact, our friends Paula and Robb Egel had driven by our accident just minutes after it happened. As they passed, Paula noticed a pile of crushed silver metal in the brush about twenty-five yards off the road. Immediately, she got a sick feeling in her stomach.

"Robb, what if that was Andy and Linda?" she wondered aloud. "They have a silver van."

"Oh, Paula, don't worry," Robb assured her. "I'm sure they're home by now, and besides, that mess didn't look anything like a van."

The two of them had continued to survey the scene as the police waved them slowly through the one open lane. Paula then called my cell phone, and I listened helplessly as it rang. Next Robb called my husband's brother, John, asking if he'd heard from Andy.

"I got tired of waiting and I needed to get the kids home, so we left before Andy arrived," John told them. Robb briefly described the accident scene on Waterlick Road.

"I talked to Andy about thirty minutes ago," John replied. "He was just leaving KFC and said he was only minutes away. I haven't heard from him since then. Maybe he had car trouble . . ." The words trailed off. The mass of metal in the wreck had been silver, like our minivan, and neither Andy nor I had answered our phones. Deep down, Robb and John were beginning to wonder if the worst could actually have happened.

"Where'd you see this?" John asked. His tone alarmed his wife, Gina, and the kids. They watched wide-eyed from across the room, waiting for some sign of what was going on.

"About a mile from Andy's on Waterlick, where the road curves past that big brown building."

"Go check it out again and call me right back," pleaded John.

Neighbors for half a mile in every direction had heard the crash as the drunk driver drilled us head-on going eighty miles per hour. His pickup truck hit with such force that its V-8 engine was ripped out and dropped in the middle of the road as he literally ran over the top of us. Our van became a launching pad for the truck as it flew into the air and landed upside down. Carl, who wasn't wearing a seat belt, was thrown clear of the wreckage into a ditch somewhere behind us. According to the time stamp on the 911 transcript marking when the accident was called in, it was thirty-three seconds past 8:25 p.m. on Sunday, November 5, 2006.

After the collision, Josh woke up first. Momentarily disoriented, he shook bits of glass and metal out of his hair and looked around. His first impression was of fried chicken and baked beans all over the place, even inside his shoe. There was a horrible smell of gasoline, chicken, burnt rubber, and blood all mixed together. To his left in the backseat was his sister, still unconscious. Her body was completely motionless, so he couldn't tell whether she was alive or dead. Then he saw me, still strapped into the seat in front of him. My whole left side was covered with blood. He yelled for me, but I was still unconscious. He looked over at Andy, bleeding and unconscious in the driver's seat, and thought at first the steering wheel had cut him in two.

Josh didn't know what to think. He screamed for help, but no one came. Was his whole family dead? Despite the destruction all around him, he remained remarkably calm. An unexplainable peace came over him, and he could sense that God was with him and he was not alone. He started to recall the events of the day, which had begun with such promise. His team had won their championship game! Now Josh remembered how he had helped carry the team to victory. He made it to third base his last at bat, and his dad was so proud of him.

He was jerked back to the present when he saw me start to stir in response to my ringing cell phone. As the rescue team began working all around us, Josh and I prayed out loud. Drifting in and out of consciousness, the last thing I could remember was seeing Jennifer leaning against her van door dialing Kelsey's number. She was the only one still unconscious, hanging limp, dangling from her seat belt. Because my body was turned toward Andy, I was able to steal a glance at my daughter behind him.

Except for a cut over her left eye, Jen's face seemed to be serene and almost glowing. It was the face of an angel. At that moment the

Lord gave me a peace that even though she still hadn't come to, she would live. God somehow protected me from the actual scene, the horrible sight of her bleeding face and a gash that was so deep you could see part of her brain. Amazingly, months later Josh confirmed that he had seen the same angelic image of Jen that night in the wreckage. What a miracle! Somehow God protected us both from "seeing" what Jen really looked like and gave us another image to focus on instead. What an act of mercy!

The steering wheel had shattered Andy's pelvis. Both of us were pushed up against the broken windshield and only a fraction of an inch from a wall of steel debris that seemed to have molded around our bodies, as though some invisible barrier had miraculously stopped it from crushing us to death. I could imagine that angels had formed a protective shield around us in that fraction of a second. No one ever came up with a better explanation.

Still fading in and out, I realized I was covered with tiny pieces of glass. They were in my hair, my eyes, my mouth, and my clothes, and stuck to my skin. A policeman was trying to ask Andy questions, but Andy's only concern was getting us out of the wreckage. "Please help my family first! Help my family! Can you get them out?" he kept repeating. Josh tried to answer the policeman's questions for him, telling the officer how old he was, how many people were in the car, and other basic information.

"Can you get out, son?" the officer asked. Josh said he could and climbed out through a door. He was freezing, so the officer wrapped him in a blanket. Josh had a broken nose and his face was bleeding, but he could still walk.

Just then, an EMT rushed toward them.

Even in the flickering searchlights, Josh and the paramedic recognized each other. Kristi Vann was a referee at Josh's basketball games.

"Josh, let me look at you! Who is with you?"

Josh was relieved to see someone he knew. "I'm with my family. They're still in the van, and they're hurt really bad. Please take care of them, Mrs. Vann."

Kristi approached the wreckage and couldn't tell it had been a van until she looked inside and saw the rows of seats. She started wiping the blood and glass off Jen's face and assessing our injuries. I heard her tell another rescue worker that Jen had "severe head injuries and is unresponsive. . . . She appears lifeless." She described me as "semiconscious and in shock" with "obvious broken bones in her left arm and foot." Andy had "possible internal injuries" and "broken bones in his shoulder, pelvis, and hip . . . in shock and barely responsive."

It didn't take Kristi long to realize that Jen was the most seriously injured, and she started working at once to find a pulse. Meanwhile, a firefighter cut Jen's seat belt, and she fell into Kristi's lap. She looked at Jen's face, which was covered in blood, and saw the horrific gash in her head running from her left eye into her hairline. The flesh was split open to the bone, and the skull was bashed in from the force of impact. *Andy and Linda have lost their little girl,* Kristi thought. Finally, to her surprise and relief, Kristi was able to find a faint pulse.

"Jen's alive! I got a pulse!"

Her words penetrated through the chaos and shock. My daughter was still alive!

Jen wasn't trapped in the van like Andy and I were, so it didn't take long to get her out.

Four male EMTs were there immediately with a backboard. They strapped Jen's body to it and ran with her to the nearest ambulance. When Jen's left leg slid off the board and dangled to the side, Kristi noticed that the laces of her elegant, black high-heeled shoe were still strapped around her ankle. At that moment, Kristi wondered if Jen had taken her last breath. She later told me that every time she closed her eyes for months afterward, that image haunted her.

By now the traffic was so backed up on that narrow country road that the ambulance had to park hundreds of yards from the scene. The ambulance rushed Jen to a soccer field nearby, where a medevac helicopter could land. Jen used to play her games on that same grassy turf, which lay across from our neighborhood.

As he approached the field, the helicopter pilot saw what looked like a war zone, with pieces of vehicles scattered everywhere. He said later that it was the worst accident site he had ever seen. Once they were on the ground, he and the flight nurse quickly brought Jen on board and took off.

Andy and I remained trapped in our vehicle. I could move my head a little, but that was all. Then I felt something tighten around me, and my surroundings started going dark. I was dizzy and claustrophobic. Was I dying now? I began to call out, struggling to breathe.

"Linda!" Kristi's voice cut through the fog. She had just enough room to get an oxygen mask on me and cover me with a blanket. "The firefighters have to break out the windshield to get to you and Andy! The blanket is to protect you from flying glass."

Once the windshield was bashed out, I can't really remember what happened next. To keep me alert, Kristi kept asking me for our mutual friend Julie Clinton's phone number, but I couldn't seem to tell her what it was. I was sure I knew it, but the numbers kept floating around in my head and I couldn't say the words.

To get Andy and me out, firefighters would also have to cut the top off our van. They set to work with power saws, cutting through one twisted window post and roof support after another until they could lift the top in one piece and set it off to the side on the grass. That allowed them to get me onto a stretcher and into an ambulance, but Andy was still trapped by the steering wheel and pieces of the front of the van that were jammed through the fire wall and into the passenger compartment.

Andy had lost so much blood by this time that getting an IV in him was critical. The rescue team, most of whom were volunteers, was doing an incredible job under very tough circumstances, but it would still be a while before Andy was loose. Seemingly out of nowhere, a man in street clothes walked up and saw the critical situation. The man recognized that Andy needed fluids immediately and offered to try to start an IV. Everyone at the scene was working feverishly to handle multiple emergencies at once; now God brought in one more pair of experienced hands at just the right moment.

Kenny Turner was an off-duty fireman who happened to be in the area because he had to pick up a real estate contract. He soon succeeded in getting an IV line in Andy's vein to administer a large volume of liquids quickly. Had that man not come along when he did, Andy may well have died at the scene. Even then, God was orchestrating every detail. Add one more to the miracles list.

It would be another half hour before Andy was freed from the driver's seat with hydraulic jacks that bent hundreds of pounds of jagged metal out of the firemen's way. Andy's healthy lifestyle—regular workouts and lots of basketball—had helped save his life. As I was carried to the ambulance, I could hear Andy crying out to God for help. "Deliver us, Lord! Help us! Save us!"

Josh had begged to stay and wait for his family, but the rescue workers insisted he go to the hospital. They put a neck brace on him as a precaution and made him lie flat on a gurney as the ambulance raced to the nearest emergency room.

Josh and I were taken to Lynchburg General Hospital in separate ambulances. Jen was being flown there by helicopter. Before the night was over, Josh and Jen would both be sent to other hospitals. When Andy was finally extricated from the van, he was flown to Carilion Roanoke Memorial Hospital since Lynchburg already had our three emergencies to deal with.

As I was en route to the ER, Kristi had a chance to take a closer look at my injuries. My whole left side was injured—my leg was gashed and my foot badly broken; my arm was shattered and my left hand hung limp. I had also suffered broken ribs and serious facial lacerations, and my left eyeball had been dislodged from its socket. Gently yet relentlessly she kept massaging and working on my face, trying to ease the eye back into position. Eventually she succeeded.

As Kristi worked on me, I remember begging her to pray with me. I felt such an urgency to pray for Jen. I knew her life depended on it. Exasperated at Kristi's apparent lack of attention and still in shock, I grabbed her by the collar and pulled her down to me.

"Kristi, we need to pray *right now*! Please pray with me!"

"I want to, Linda, but right now I'm trying to save your life." I had no idea that my left lung had just collapsed. What a blessing that it happened in the ambulance and not while I was still trapped in the wreckage.

Kristi said later that our short conversation in the ambulance that night—the idea of going straight to God first of all in a moment of terrible crisis—changed her life forever.

It would be more than two weeks before I saw Andy or Jen again. By then God would have completely transformed all of us, both as individuals and as a family, and completely rewritten our future. I didn't know it yet, but even though I was still alive, the old Linda Barrick was dead. And a new Linda was beginning the agonizing, exhausting, and ultimately triumphant process of being born.

CHAPTER 3

A LIFE IN THE BALANCE

Let all that I am praise the LORD. . . . He redeems me from death.

PSALM 103:2, 4

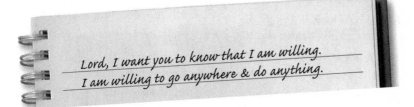

Lord, I want you to know that I am willing.
I am willing to go anywhere & do anything.

Jen's journal, two months before the crash

WHILE WAITING TO HEAR BACK FROM ROBB EGEL, Andy's brother, John, and his wife, Gina, heard a helicopter fly low overhead, then moments later a second one. The blare of sirens seemed to be coming from every direction. What in the world was happening?

When his cell phone rang, John grabbed it, expecting to hear Andy's voice. Instead it was Robb Egel.

"It's them! It's them!" Robb shouted. "It's Andy and Linda! It's really bad! I mean *really* bad!"

John bolted for the door. Gina and the children fell to their knees, crying and praying.

Andy's parents, Al and Fran Barrick, were already at the accident scene. Emergency workers kept them from the van so they wouldn't see the carnage inside. Standing in the street beside the pickup engine, Fran was weak in the knees and about to pass out as she fell into her husband's arms. She was so distraught that the only sound she could make was a loud moan. Finally, she managed to form the word, "Mercy!" Over and over, she cried, "Mercy! God have mercy!" It was all she could say. Robb found Al and Fran and took them to John's house.

Meanwhile, John arrived at the crash site and found a spot as close as possible to the rescue activity, on the soccer field where the helicopters had landed. From there he could phone in updates to the rest of our friends and family.

John and Gina's house became the gathering place where everyone waited for news of our condition and where we would go for treatment. Andy's lifelong friend Jonathan Falwell arrived. Andy worked at Liberty University where Jonathan's father, Dr. Jerry Falwell, was chancellor. Jen's boyfriend, Brandon, was at the house too, along with his parents, Andy's parents, the Egels, and other close friends.

In God's providence, Dr. Falwell was already at Lynchburg General, where his wife was recovering from surgery, when he got a call with news of the accident. He sent Jonathan to help us, then immediately called my parents, who'd gone home to change clothes before coming to our house. They had taken a different route because of the huge traffic jam on Waterlick.

With an edge to his booming voice, Dr. Falwell declared, "Ed, your family has been in a terrible accident." My dad could tell by the tone that something truly horrible had happened, and he began to shake. My mom ran from across the room to help him sit down. Dr. Falwell continued, "The good news is Linda and Josh are alive." Dropping the phone, my dad began to weep, thinking by what he'd heard that Andy and Jen were dead. By God's grace, my parents had friends visiting from California who could take them to the hospital, since they were in no shape to drive.

Within an hour, Dr. Falwell sent out an e-mail to the entire Liberty University community—over 100,000 strong—with information about the crash and a request for prayer.

Meanwhile, John and Gina were getting a flood of information and questions. Cell phones were ringing constantly. Friends and family were praying and weeping, waiting for what seemed like an eternity. Finally, John called from his observation point to say he'd seen me loaded into an ambulance. "Linda is awake," he reported. "I could see her talking. She's going to Lynchburg General. Josh will be okay, but he's going to the hospital too, to get checked." Andy was still trapped behind the steering wheel. There was no word on Jen, which made everyone hope she was relatively okay since she and Josh had been sitting side by side in the backseat.

In the Lynchburg ER, doctors were busy assessing my injuries and stitching up Josh's eyebrow when my parents arrived. Josh had a broken nose, a cracked orbital bone above his left eye, a bruised sternum, a scratched spleen, and some cuts and bruises. Some of the players and dads from his baseball team were already there to cheer him up. Just hours earlier they had all been playing in the championship game. Josh seemed to be in good spirits, laughing and joking with his friends.

My parents looked in briefly on Jen. They could tell that she was breathing but couldn't see much because she was surrounded by doctors and tubes and machines. When they came to me, my face was so bloody and disfigured that they hardly recognized me. I'm not sure what I said to them or what they said to me. All I could think of was my family and how desperately I wanted God to spare them. The doctors decided to move Josh to the pediatric unit at Carilion Roanoke Memorial, the hospital where Andy had been taken. Dr. Tim Clinton and his son, Zach, were in the ER with Josh. A psychologist, Tim insisted that Josh have a chance to see his mother before he left.

A nurse wheeled Josh into the ER bay where doctors were still working to stop my bleeding and get the glass out of my face. Since both of us wore neck braces, we couldn't see each other even when our gurneys were side by side. I felt his little fingers on my uninjured right arm and reached out to hold his hand in mine.

"Mommy loves you so much," I said. "I'm so proud of you. Everything is going to be okay. God is with you and will never leave you."

Through his tears Josh answered, "I love you, too, Mom." There wasn't a dry eye in the room. Then off Josh went to Roanoke, with Tim accompanying him in the ambulance. Since Andy couldn't go with him, there wasn't anyone we'd rather have assume a fatherly role for Josh at this frightening time than Tim, Andy's dear friend and coaching partner.

Jennifer was still unconscious. Though I didn't know it, her prospects for survival were very, very poor. She had multiple skull fractures and severe brain damage. Yet before the long night was over, God would work a fresh series of miracles to begin the transformation of her young life into a powerful new voice for His message.

One of the first steps for medical rescue teams in the field is to give injured patients a Glasgow Coma Scale rating. This is a standardized way to register a person's level of consciousness on a scale from 3 to 15, with 15 indicating the normal response of a fully awake person, 8 indicating serious brain injury or coma, and 3 indicating deep unconsciousness or death: no eye movement, no verbal response, no physical response. Jen was a 3.

Jen had been flown to Lynchburg General because the helicopter pilot, Sam Bryant, and the flight nurse, June Leffke, had made a split-second decision that she looked like she was at least twenty-one years of age. When Jen arrived, Lynchburg was ready immediately to administer a specialized medicine to help lower Jen's blood pressure quickly and take pressure off her brain. Brain swelling was one of the most serious of the many threats she faced in those first critical hours. The medicine wasn't on the helicopter because it has to be stored under pressure and then be prepared just before it is administered. As soon as she landed they gave her this drug, then did a brain scan. In addition to the other injuries, the scan showed pockets of blood at the base and top of her brain.

Along with her massive injuries, the CT scan of her brain also revealed that Jen was younger than the treatment team had thought—certainly not twenty-one. This meant, according to protocol and legal requirements, she was supposed to be treated at a pediatric facility. The chopper should have taken her to the pediatric unit at the University of Virginia hospital in Charlottesville. But if they had, she would almost certainly have died en route. That was seventy miles from Lynchburg, and it would have taken much longer to get there; yet only the pressure-reducing medicine at Lynchburg had kept her alive. I have no doubt that God's hand was in that chopper pilot's decision to go where he did. His "mistake" saved Jen's life.

As doctors prepared Jen for transfer to UVA, they doubted she would live through the night. She was still comatose. Her pupils were dilated and fixed. Her blood pressure was increasing, and her heart rate was dropping. Before leaving with Josh in the ambulance for Roanoke, Tim Clinton had gone into the waiting room in Lynchburg, which was filled to overflowing with friends and family waiting for updates. He signaled for attention, and the room went silent.

"Anyone who wants to see Jen Barrick alive better get to Charlottesville tonight. They're flying her there now, and they don't think she'll make it until morning."

Our friends divided their forces to help the four of us scattered among four different intensive care units. Roanoke is an hour west of Lynchburg, and Charlottesville is an hour and a half northeast. That meant Andy was two and a half hours away from Jen. Tim stayed with Josh at the Roanoke pediatric unit. Andy's brother and his parents went to be with Andy at Roanoke. My cousin Heidi Foster and my friends Pam Foster and Julie Clinton stayed in the ER and later in the ICU with me all night at Lynchburg.

Gina, my sister-in-law, who had also been my best friend since sixth grade, knew exactly what I would want her to do: go to Jen and not leave her side. So Jonathan Falwell drove Gina, Robb and Paula Egel, and Lisa Bryant, a friend who was also a nurse, to Charlottesville. Brandon Knight; Jennifer's best friend, Kaelynn Queen; and many others also went to Charlottesville for what they thought would be a final good-bye to our precious Jen.

One of the ER doctors had put more than thirty stitches in the cuts on my face. My bleeding was under control by this time, and my vital signs were stabilizing. They kept giving me sedatives, hoping I'd fall asleep, but I was thinking too much about Jen. I knew this was spiritual warfare. Satan had tried to take my family down, and there was no way I was going to lie there helplessly and let him claim victory as long as God gave me the strength to pray!

I was still in shock and couldn't make sense of anything. Even so, I had an overwhelming sense of *urgency* to pray for Jen. I was praying for Andy and Josh too, but something in my soul told me that Jen's very life depended on our prayers. My motherly instinct kicked in, and no matter how much morphine I had, I never went to sleep and never stopped praying out loud all night.

"Lord, please save my family," I begged. "God, please don't let Jen die. She loves You with all her heart. God, You are all-powerful! Nothing is impossible for You!"

In only a few hours I had seen one miracle after another: The fact that the metal from the front of the van stopped inches from Andy and me, even formed to the shape of our bodies, yet gave the EMTs just enough room to reach us. Josh being only slightly hurt, with no injury that would keep him from the sports he loved so much. The seemingly random appearance of the off-duty firefighter who got Andy's IV in and saved his life. Jen being airlifted to Lynchburg instead of Charlottesville. It was unexplainable why any of us were alive! Although my left lung had collapsed, Andy and I had no other injuries to major organs. If we had, surely we would have died while trapped in the van for so long.

However clear these thoughts were in my head, I was too sedated and too injured to express them. All I could say to Heidi, Pam, and Julie was, "Are you praying? Keep praying! Are they praying at UVA? Are they on their knees? Please tell everyone in the waiting room to get on their knees."

As the doctors worked on me, Heidi stood beside me picking glass out of my hair, mouth, scalp, and back. It would take days for the countless tiny pieces of windshield embedded in my skin to work their way to the surface.

I asked Pam if she thought Jen was going to die. As I did, a tear rolled down my cheek.

"No, Linda," Pam lied, "I think Jen's going to be all right."

All I could think about was surrounding my family with the power of God through prayer. In my painkiller-induced fog I kept wondering if the doctors and other people running around every-where knew of that power. "Do they know Jesus? Do these nurses know Jesus?" I kept asking Heidi and Pam. I'd start to doze off—to the relief of my friends and the medical staff—then come to with the feeling that I had to keep reminding everybody to pray.

"Who's in the waiting room?" I demanded groggily time and again. "Tell them to get on their knees and pray!"

Dutifully Heidi and Pam trudged down to the waiting room packed with friends keeping their faithful vigil.

"Linda says to get on your knees and pray."

And they did.

Heidi came back to say that members of Jen's cheerleading squad were in the waiting room. I led devotions for those girls every week and knew some of them were struggling. Maybe now they would realize that Christ was the answer to any problem, no matter how big or small.

One reason I was so obsessed with prayer that night was that it was my only weapon. There was nothing else I could do. I knew the power of prayer from years of leading Bible studies and moms' prayer groups. Praying out loud and surrendering on your knees to God is incredibly powerful. Every morning for the past three years I'd gotten on my knees in the kitchen while the coffee was brewing and given my day to the Lord. That simple act of obedience had changed my life. Now I was calling on that strength in my moment of crisis.

God was already using this tragedy for His purposes, transforming people's lives forever. One of my ER nurses, Kim Bishop, e-mailed me much later: "I have wanted to thank you for what you taught me that night. I will never forget your faith and strength in the face of fear: asking for readings aloud from Psalms; being in your room as we prayed for Jen, having no clue if she was even alive. It was one of the most worshipful experiences of my life, and witnessing your faith has greatly affected the growth of mine."

As I was praying through the night, Jen was fighting for her life in Charlottesville. My sister-in-law Amanda, who is very forceful and to the point, called the hospital from her home in Atlanta and insisted on speaking to the doctor treating Jennifer Barrick. After a moment, Dr. John Jane Jr., a renowned pediatric neurosurgeon, came on the line.

"What will Jennifer's recovery look like?" Amanda insisted.

"*Recovery?*" Dr. Jane replied, taken by surprise. "Right now we're just hoping she will live until morning."

Dr. Jane and the treatment team were most concerned about the pressure in Jen's brain. The doctor had drilled a hole into her skull and then inserted a bolt into the opening. When John's wife, Gina, arrived later, he explained to her that the procedure would release cranial pressure and relieve swelling of the brain. A nurse compared it to the valve on a pressure cooker. "But it's only a temporary measure," Dr. Jane advised. "When she's a little more stable we'll have to do a craniotomy." A craniotomy is the surgical removal of a section of skull. Once the risk of swelling was past, the hole would be covered with a titanium plate screwed in place.

The doctor's final words kept ringing in Gina's head: "This is a *global* injury to the brain. Just pray that she survives through the night."

Gina and the others hoped and prayed that Jen's reading would go down so she wouldn't have to have the surgery. Her intracranial pressure was still more than thirty millimeters of mercury (mm Hg), and the doctor wanted it at no more than sixteen. The normal range is between one and fifteen mm Hg. Paula, Lisa, and Gina prayed that the pressure would go down on its own. Only minutes before Jen was scheduled to be wheeled in for surgery, the pressure dropped, and Dr. Jane decided to wait and see if it would stay down. The pressure built again, and the surgeon prepared for the craniotomy a second time. Once again the pressure dropped and the surgery was canceled.

I'd made Gina promise to call me with progress reports. It was 4 a.m. before the doctors allowed her to see Jen. Nothing could have prepared her for the sight of her beautiful niece. Her hair glistened with hundreds of glass fragments; her face, hair, and body were caked with blood. Most alarming of all was the bolt in her head. Then there were the tubes going in and coming out everywhere, plus a bright blue ice blanket completely covering her along with a machine blowing cold air onto her body to fight her soaring temperature. Her left eye was swollen shut below a deep gash and an indention in her skull above that eye. Now that she had survived this long, the next seventy-two hours would be the most critical. The doctors still had no confidence that she would pull through.

"Jen looks beautiful," Gina assured me over the phone. She didn't want to upset me or raise my already sky-high blood pressure. "The doctors are keeping her asleep for now."

"Promise me something, Gina," I said. "Promise me you will have everyone in Charlottesville get down on their knees and pray for Jen. And keep a Bible open in her room at all times, because God's Word is alive and powerful."

"Don't worry, Linda, I promise," she answered. "We're all praying for Jen and for you, too."

As focused as I was on Jen waking up, my heart was also with Josh at the hospital in Roanoke. When he'd gotten there, he'd had the chance to see his father briefly. Andy's surgery was delayed because he still wasn't stable enough. He was sedated, and the doctors had given him local anesthetics while they worked on his injuries.

Andy was in the trauma unit when Josh and Tim arrived by ambulance. They wheeled Josh into Andy's room in the ICU, and just as during his good-bye to me in Lynchburg, he and his dad were unable to look at each other because they both wore neck braces. Josh reached out his hand, but Andy couldn't lift his to take it. Numb and groggy as he was, Andy kept trying until somehow he grabbed Josh's hand. He told Josh how much he loved him and was proud of him, then assured his son, "Daddy's going to be fine."

Later, in Josh's hospital room, Tim prayed with Josh for God to save his family. He could see the fear and pain in Josh's eyes, so he tried to get Josh's mind off of the trauma of the night and even had him laughing as they rated the nurses on a scale of 1 to 10 as to which one Josh thought was the prettiest.

Andy's brother, John, faced a more serious task, sitting by Andy's side all night as he moaned and cried out in excruciating pain. Through the long hours his anguish never diminished. *Just how much can one person take?* John thought. At one point John cried as he prayed, "Jesus, if your suffering on the cross was more than this, I can't even begin to fathom it."

Andy's parents, along with other friends who had gathered in the waiting room, circled together and prayed relentlessly every hour on the hour for God's healing and mercy and for Him to save Andy, Jen, and me.

On Monday afternoon, November 6, I had my first round of surgery. Doctors put a plate in my left arm to help the bones heal, though because of nerve and tendon damage my arm was still almost useless and my hand hung limp. They also put two temporary plates in my left foot and taped my broken ribs. My left eye remained swollen shut, and no one would let me look at myself in the mirror for the first several days after the accident because they didn't want me to scare myself.

My sister, Christy, drove all night from Atlanta to be with me. She walked into my room with tears streaming down her face and quoting John 11:4: "[This] sickness will not end in death. No, it happened for the glory of God so that the Son of God will receive glory from this." I clung to that promise and repeated it out loud for Jen's sake. I felt an assurance that God was going to spare her for some great work He had planned just for her.

That same day we had another wonderful visitor. LeeAnn Miller had been one of my dearest friends since we were children. Gina, my sister-in-law, was another member of that childhood group. Our friendships had survived college, moves, marriages, parenthood, and all the other busyness of life. LeeAnn had heard about the accident and called Gina for the details. As soon as she got the whole story, she left her husband and family in Ohio and drove to be with Jen in the hospital. By this time Gina hadn't slept since Saturday night and was physically and emotionally exhausted.

Though Gina tried to prepare LeeAnn for the sight, she was still shocked to see Jen swollen and disfigured—stitches in her face, a bolt in her head, tubes coming out everywhere from under her ice blanket—and not moving or making a sound. Gina didn't want to leave Jen's side at first, but LeeAnn finally convinced her to lie down on a couch in the waiting room. Gina explained my instructions about praying continually and keeping an open Bible in the room. LeeAnn promised to take care of everything and said she'd call if there was any change.

By God's grace and against all odds, my daughter was still alive.

The Liberty University e-mail blast had inspired thousands of people to pray for her. Liberty Christian Academy held a special hour-long chapel service and prayer meeting for our family that day. Dr. Falwell encouraged the whole university community to pray. Students clustered in groups in the hallway at school, crying, praying, consoling each other. The question on everyone's lips was the same: How could this happen to somebody like Jennifer? She was so beautiful, so sweet, so talented, so on fire for the Lord! It was impossible to imagine they might never see her again this side of heaven.

That night LeeAnn sat watching Jen sleep, softly reading the Bible aloud. Later she told me that as she read, she felt the presence of evil. She knew the angel of death was in the room with them. At the same time, LeeAnn felt God's presence in a way she'd never felt it before. There was a spiritual battle going on in that room all around her—a battle for Jen's life. "Suddenly God was completely real to me," LeeAnn explained. "He was right there in the room. It was indescribable."

Falling to her knees, LeeAnn began a prayer that lasted more than eight hours. It was the prayer of a lifetime, a prayer for Jen's life to be spared. Nurses walked around her through the night as she poured out her heart to God. "I can't explain it, but I just knew in my heart that Jennifer's very life depended on my prayers and the prayers of countless others to spare her."

At one point she felt God saying to her, *No. Not now. She will not die.* Looking up, LeeAnn sensed a shining protective barrier around Jen's body. She recited Bible verses from memory, and even sang a children's song that begins, "My God is so big, so strong and so mighty; There's nothing my God cannot do!" Through the night LeeAnn never felt tired or afraid, only energized and empowered.

The experience changed LeeAnn's life. She realized that she had become complacent in her spiritual walk and that the passion and burden she felt for Jen in that moment was something she should feel for all those around her who were lost and spiritually dying. Something happened that night that she couldn't put into words. She felt a personal sense of God's power in the room. He was real. He was there beside Jen, comforting her and protecting her, filling her with His goodness and mercy.

It may be that LeeAnn Miller was the first person God spoke to through Jen Barrick. That night in a quiet hospital room, unconscious and clinging to life, my formerly very private daughter, who always kept her spiritual thoughts to herself, became the mouthpiece of the Creator of the universe. God's presence was there. LeeAnn's heart was transformed. Though she had come to minister to Jen, God had ministered through Jen to her.

Had the Lord taken Jen home that very night, she would already have led one soul to a renewed relationship with Him. But He wasn't finished with her yet. Not by a long shot.

CHAPTER 4

THE WAGES OF SIN

We ourselves are like fragile clay jars containing this great treasure. This makes it clear that our great power is from God, not from ourselves. We are pressed on every side by troubles, but we are not crushed. . . . We are hunted down, but never abandoned by God. We get knocked down, but we are not destroyed. 2 CORINTHIANS 4:7-9

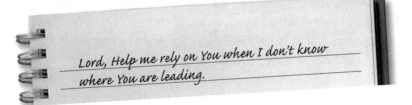

Lord, Help me rely on You when I don't know where You are leading.

Jen's journal, three months before the crash

THE DAY AFTER MY SURGERY a flood of people came to visit. "We had a hundred people claim to be your best friend," the nurses joked. I have asthma and allergies, which meant perfume from well-meaning visitors or the truckload of flowers I received could set off a fit of coughing—devastating for someone with broken ribs. But I never coughed once. Fortunately someone began to intercept the flowers, take pictures of them for me to enjoy, and then give them to other patients.

Meanwhile, friends continued to gather in the waiting room at UVA, praying mightily for Jennifer to wake up and be healed. My sister, Christy, headed to UVA to be with Jen as well. Soon after she arrived at her niece's bedside, Christy naively asked a nurse how long it would be before Jen was back to normal.

"Oh, honey, she'll never be back to normal," the nurse said bluntly. "With a brain injury like that, she'll never be the same." Christy was shocked at the news. Based on the nurse's statement, she feared that maybe the doctors were giving up on Jen. Christy thought if Jen could hear her mother's voice maybe that would get some kind of response. She called me and held her phone to Jen's ear so I could talk to her. Even though I knew she was in a coma, I was secretly praying that somehow she would be able to hear me.

"Jennifer, this is Mommy," I said, fighting back tears. "I love you so much. You are so beautiful, and I'm so proud of you. Keep fighting, sweetheart, and don't give up! God is with you. He is going to heal you. Please hold on. Mommy and Daddy and Josh love you so much. We will always be here for you. I will never stop praying for you. I can't wait to hold you and kiss you."

At that moment I wanted to hold her in my arms more than I ever wanted anything in my life. I wanted to stroke her hair and hug her and make the pain go away. I repeated my message several times, hoping some of it would penetrate.

I know she wasn't awake or even aware of what was happening to her, but as her mother, I didn't want her to be afraid. I hated the thought of her being alone or confused, and I begged God to wrap His arms of love around her and comfort her in my absence. "Father, I know You can minister to her in ways we cannot. Please help Jen to know that You are with her and You will never leave her or forsake her. Please give her Your peace."

On Tuesday, two days after the accident, Josh was released from the hospital. Since Andy and I were still incapacitated and the grandparents were taking turns at the hospitals, he went home with the Clintons after stopping by to visit his father on the way out. I knew Tim and his family would take care of Josh like he was one of their own. Familiar faces, especially his good friend Zach, who had spent hours with him in the hospital, would be a comfort to Josh while he was separated from his family.

The next morning, November 8, Andy finally had his surgery. His sister, Jan, had flown in from Pittsburgh, so she was at the hospital that day, along with his brother and parents. Andy had been in severe pain ever since waking up in the van. In addition to a crushed pelvis, Andy's gluteus maximus muscles were torn completely away from the bone. He had a huge gash in his left leg as well as blood clots and damage to the sciatic nerve. He also had a broken collarbone and a broken thumb. It took surgeons more than four hours to put three plates and twelve screws in his hip and reattach the torn muscles. Though the operation was a success, it didn't ease any of his pain. It would be weeks before he was relieved even partially from that terrible burden.

After his surgery, Andy was transferred to the UVA hospital in Charlottesville to be near Jen and get the best therapy possible. From the moment he got there, all he could think about was seeing his little princess. Andy had always had a close relationship with his daughter, had always made time for her and given her his undivided attention whenever she wanted to be with him. As a little girl, she'd run into his arms with a squeal of delight when he came home from work. They would twirl and dance around the room acting out Disney movies, pretending she was the princess and he was the prince. She loved to jump off the couch and have him catch her too.

When Jen grew older and became involved in sports, Andy was his daughter's biggest fan. As much as he loved coaching Josh's sports teams, he never favored Josh over Jen. He came as often as he could to watch her cheer and play soccer. In fact, he often screamed so loud for her that she was embarrassed.

Andy took little time for himself, but one activity he regularly scheduled was playing competitive basketball two mornings a week before work. Since he left home at 6 a.m. on those days, he wasn't there to pray for Jen and Josh and read the Bible before breakfast as he usually did. So he started putting sticky notes beside their places at the breakfast table. He left short, simple messages like "I'm so proud of you"; "I'm praying for you today"; "I believe in you." To Jen he'd write, "You're beautiful" or "Daddy loves you very much." The kids looked forward to these messages so much that Andy started putting them in their lunch bags and other places where they'd be surprised by them. Jennifer didn't say much about them, but she carefully saved every one, arranged in bright clusters around the mirror in her room. She treasured them as signs that her dad loved her with all his heart and believed she was a beautiful and very special young lady.

Andy took his role as a father very seriously. Children are a gift from God, treasures given to us for a season to raise according to His Word. Andy and I invested countless hours in making sure our children were spiritually grounded. We often told them, "Mom and Dad love you so much, but hold on to Jesus. He is the only one who will never fail you or forsake you." Andy felt responsible to provide for his family and to protect them. He had always done whatever it took to fulfill that role. But now, disabled by his injuries and in constant pain, he felt helpless and frustrated.

As he waited to see Jen after he arrived at UVA, he was overwhelmed with sorrow and doubt. If only he could have protected her! If only he could have shielded her from the injury and spared her the pain! If only, if only, *if only*!

The nurses and doctors refused to allow Andy to see Jen right away. Maybe they thought he was still too weak or that the sight of her would be too much of a shock. That decision did not sit well with Andy. He hadn't seen her since the accident and was filled with a sense of urgency to see her and hold her hand in his.

When the nurses wouldn't take him to Jen's room, he decided to go by himself. He sat up and began to ease himself out of bed. As soon as he put weight on his legs they buckled. To try and steady himself, he grabbed the food tray for support, which started rolling away as he collapsed over it. The nurses heard the commotion and ran in to get him back in bed. They gave him a good scolding and put the side rails up on the bed so he couldn't try that again.

On November 15, ten days after the crash, Andy finally got to see his princess. A nurse wheeled him into the critical care room where she lay, still asleep. He called me a few minutes later, but he was crying so hard I couldn't understand him at first. He'd start a sentence then break down sobbing uncontrollably. Seeing her was such a relief. At the same time, looking at her was the hardest thing he'd ever done in his life.

"When I saw her lying there with a bolt in her head—"

"A *bolt* in her head?!" I interrupted, frantic.

Andy heard the fear in my voice and quickly changed course.

"It's just a little tube to monitor the pressure on her brain," he assured me. "She's okay. The doctors have everything under control. They're keeping her asleep to help her heal." I got the impression that Jen was going to be all right.

The next instant, Andy's rage at the drunk driver suddenly boiled over. "Linda, I feel such anger and rage inside. When I saw Jen, I literally wanted to kill the man who did this to my precious daughter. She is so innocent! She has done nothing wrong! Nothing! She loves God with her whole heart. She was singing praise songs to God one minute, and the next minute everything was taken from her: her health, her strength, her future, possibly even her life. All gone in a heartbeat! I would do anything in the world to trade places with her right now. And there's absolutely nothing I can do." He dissolved again into tears.

Andy was always the strong one in the family, the one who held the rest of us up in times of crisis. Seeing Jen in the hospital and feeling somehow responsible yet also so helpless was almost more than he could bear. In that moment on the phone, God gave me great faith and put the words in my mouth to comfort my husband.

"Andy, God loves Jen so much more than we do," I assured him. "He is holding her in His arms right now. He will take care of her."

A couple of my friends who were in the hallway outside my room wept as they heard my words of faith. They wept also because they knew that at the time I had no idea how serious Jen's condition was. I didn't know the true extent of her injuries and that her life was in danger, or that at the accident scene she'd had the same response level as a dead body. My friends and family were protecting me because of my own critical injuries, plus the high blood pressure and breathing problems due to the collapsed lung.

Ironically, Carl Johnson was down the hall from me in Lynchburg General, still in a coma. Several pastors from our church would make a point to pray for him outside of his room and visit with any company that he had. At this writing, five years after the accident, the driver who hit us remains in a vegetative state.

Andy's parents, my parents, and a host of friends kept us company in the hospital. My friends all knew how I hated to be alone. For five years I'd hosted a Tuesday morning Bible study at our house for twenty-five to thirty women. Now my spiritual investment in them paid rich dividends as they sprang into action, taking turns staying with me in the hospital around the clock. If I woke up in the middle of the night in pain, they would help me give my morphine pump a boost so I could get back to sleep.

The night my brother, Jonathan, and his new bride, Amanda, stayed with me was the most painful night of my life, and they were an incredible blessing. At first I had an epidural to help with the pain management, but when I got an infection a doctor had to take out the catheter without any warning. My body went from being numb to feeling as if every nerve ending were on fire. The pain was unbearable. I started panicking, unable to breathe, literally screaming in agony.

"I can't stand it!" I cried. "I would rather die than be in this pain!"

Jonathan and Amanda were so sweet to me, tenderly putting cool washcloths on my face and singing to me to keep me calm. Finally Amanda convinced a nurse to give me some drugs to sedate me. It was not the way I had in mind to welcome her to the family.

Whenever my pain would become too great, there was always a friend to say, "I'm going to make sure this pain gets under control." There were times when I thought I'd have to give up, that I couldn't go on another minute. In those lowest points God lifted me up and gave me the courage to say, "No! I will never give up. I will fight for the sake of my family."

Whenever I opened my eyes, someone was always there waiting to help me, usually reading the Bible or praying quietly. I never had time to brood, never had the chance for my mind to drift away into dark places, because friends gave me the priceless gift of nonstop encouragement. We believed God for miracles and prayed for a revival to start in our town. We prayed continually for our families, our church, our children's school, and that God would touch the hearts of people we didn't even know.

It was a very humbling experience to have someone bathe me, or help me go to the bathroom while I was hopping on one foot with tubes attached to me. Friends washed my hair, still picking glass out of it. A teacher from Liberty Christian Academy, somebody I didn't even know all that well, spent time patiently picking glass out of my backside—and let me tell you, that's humbling in the extreme! They ran household errands and did countless other jobs, all the time constantly asking God's blessing and healing for my family and me. One dear friend from Pennsylvania, Judy Ashley, left a precious note by my hospital bed. "I came to minister to you, and you ministered to me. I came to pray for you, and you prayed for me. I came to give you strength, and you are stronger than I. I came as your friend, and you treated me as family." This is not to my credit, but to God's, as His grace and peace covered me during such a traumatic time.

Everybody at LCA and Liberty University had been praying for us since the moment Dr. Falwell shared the news of our accident. The next Friday night, November 10, the LCA football team was playing for the state championship. All the players wore Jen's initials on their helmets. Each cheerleader on the squad had a wooden step stool called a cheer ladder that they painted and decorated to use year after year. The other cheerleaders put Jen's ladder where she would have stood on the sidelines and covered it with beautiful flowers. At halftime the cheerleaders formed a heart on the field and Jen's friend Jessica sang "It Is Well with My Soul." When she finished, the whole crowd was in tears. Thousands of spectators then prayed silently for a miracle.

Our good friends from Pennsylvania, Randy and Susan Seavers, created a web page to provide updates and prayer requests for our friends outside the Lynchburg community. They called Andy's dad for weekly updates and then posted status reports on our recovery through the spring of 2008.

Two weeks after the accident I was released from the hospital. It was such a weird feeling. Where was I going to go? I couldn't go home because I would have to climb a flight of stairs to get to my bedroom. Besides, who would take care of me? Andy and Jen were in Charlottesville, and Josh was living with the Clinton family. I was still in a wheelchair, and my left leg and arm hung limp and useless. I couldn't bathe or dress myself or cook a meal. Visionary thinkers that they were, Andy's parents, Al and Fran, had just moved into a house designed to be wheelchair accessible, planning ahead for the time when one or both of them would begin dealing with the limited mobility of advancing age. They invited me to live with them. When Andy got out of the hospital, we could both stay there until we could take care of ourselves in our own home. I gratefully accepted their offer.

My friends stayed with me around the clock at Al and Fran's just as they had in the hospital. The first thing I wanted to do after I was released was go see Andy and Jen, but I had to rest for a couple of days before I had enough strength to do so. Finally on November 21, sixteen days after I had seen them last, I traveled to UVA to visit my husband and daughter. Andy loved me in pink, so my sister, Christy, helped me get into a pink sweatsuit. I couldn't wear my regular clothes because of my broken ribs. Then Christy and her husband, Jeff, drove me to the hospital in Charlottesville. As Christy wheeled me down the corridor toward Andy's room, I felt butterflies in my stomach. I hadn't seen him in so long that it was almost like going on a first date. Andy's parents were with him when I arrived. They had scarcely left his room the whole time, but they excused themselves to give Andy and me some time alone.

I was shocked at the sight of him. Always strong and athletic, Andy had lost twenty pounds and was now frail and thin. He started crying when he saw me. I had missed him so desperately and wanted to hug him and kiss him, to have him hold me and tell me everything was going to be okay. The best we could do was maneuver our wheelchairs close enough to hold hands. It was a bittersweet moment. We had no answers for the future. Our hope was in God alone. We prayed together and cried together, assuring each other that with God's help we were going to get through this.

At last it was time for me to see Jennifer. Andy had not wanted me to see her without him being there. In a miraculous bit of timing, she was being moved that day from the pediatric ICU to the Kluge Children's Rehabilitation Center across town. Before her transfer, doctors removed the bolt from her head. They also took her off the ventilator, and amazingly she breathed on her own without a tracheotomy. It was God's providence that I never had to see Jen with all those tubes in her body and a bolt in her head.

Christy and Jeff loaded me and my wheelchair into their car, Al and Fran loaded their son and his chair into theirs, and the whole caravan made the short drive to Kluge.

We arrived just after Jen had been transferred by ambulance. We couldn't see Jen until the doctors at Kluge had examined her and the admission paperwork was completed. While we waited, I had a conversation with a lovely member of the housekeeping staff named Miss Christine. She told me she'd seen Jen for just a minute in the hallway earlier; then, much to my surprise, she declared, "God's in that girl! I just know it!" That was such a wonderful thing for me to hear. She didn't know Jen's story then or anything about her. How could she have known God was "in that girl"? It was soothing balm to a worried mother's heart. Miss Christine's words were the only encouragement I got all day, sent from God through a very unexpected messenger! She went on to say that she had prayed for Jen and that God told her Jen was going to be all right. It amazed me to think that although Jen was still in a coma and couldn't talk, Miss Christine somehow knew that God was in her.

From that high point of hope, my emotions were jarred a few minutes later when I met a nurse in the hall and asked for a report on Jen. At first I thought I'd misunderstood her answer, which sounded something like "skull fractures." Frantically, I replied, "Skull fractures! What do you mean she has skull fractures? When will Jen wake up and be better?" She had been kept heavily sedated until the transfer to Kluge, so to me it was no wonder she was still asleep. Now the doctors had weaned her off the heavy narcotics, which I thought meant she'd be her old self before long.

I had expected an upbeat report. Up to this time I had no idea how seriously Jen was injured. Friends and family had been protecting me from the truth, afraid of what effect it would have on me in light of my own pain and disabilities. The nurse brought me face-to-face with reality. She was obviously surprised at the question.

"Have you seen her CT scan?" she asked. "Her brain is injured in every area. It's a miracle she's even alive."

My heart felt like lead. I was beginning to sense the severity of Jen's injuries, but I was still in denial. I refused to accept the fact that she might never be the same. Impossible! My God was all-powerful, and He could do anything. God had already performed a miracle by saving her life, and I had faith He would heal her completely.

When they finally wheeled Andy and me into Jen's new room, she looked so peaceful. It was a small private room in the rehabilitation center, its compact space jammed with monitors and other machines that blinked and beeped and whirred softly. Jennifer lay perfectly still, breathing slowly and regularly like she was in a deep sleep. I felt tears welling up in my eyes as I watched her, then I broke down completely. I squeezed Andy's hand and looked over at him. He was crying too. We cried for our daughter. The fact that she'd been unconscious for so long was a bad sign from a medical standpoint, but not from God's standpoint. I still believed with all my heart that God would work another miracle. One day, according to His perfect plan, He was going to wake her up.

I wheeled over next to Jen to get as close as I could. How I wanted to crawl in bed beside her and hold her and never leave! I touched her hand for the first time in sixteen days, then stroked her arm. "I love you so much, Jen," I whispered. "I'm so proud of you. You are God's special girl. He is with you now, and He will never leave you." Even though she didn't move at all, I knew in my heart that she could hear me. "Don't give up, Jen. Never give up."

Through no fault of her own, my innocent daughter had to endure so much suffering, with a long and uncertain road to recovery still ahead. All I could do was trust that God would do His perfect will in her life. My faith and patience mingled with a desperate desire to shake her and wake her up. Surely God would heal her completely. Surely He had saved her from death as a testimony to His goodness and had great plans for her.

I was beyond exhausted and had raging pains in my injured arm and leg. As much as I wanted to stay with my girl, it was time to go back to Al and Fran's. Andy decided he was going home that afternoon too. His doctors reluctantly discharged him, as they still didn't have his pain under control and were concerned about the blood clots in his leg. He didn't care; he wanted to be at his parents' house with me.

We arrived back at Al and Fran's, and after what seemed like a lifetime, my sweetheart and I were back "home"—sort of. But the world I returned home to was nothing like the one I'd left behind sixteen days before.

CHAPTER 5

THE WAY WE WERE

Direct your children onto the right path, and when they are older, they will not leave it. PROVERBS 22:6

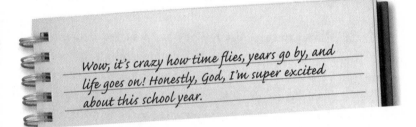

Wow, it's crazy how time flies, years go by, and life goes on! Honestly, God, I'm super excited about this school year.

Jen's journal, three months before the crash

I MET THE LOVE OF MY LIFE when I was a high school freshman at Liberty Christian Academy. I was fourteen and Andy was sixteen the year he transferred from Hershey, Pennsylvania, as a junior. He was a star basketball player, star baseball player, and also on the football team. I was the bubbly, smiley type of girl who said hi to everyone, but I had no idea he had noticed me or even knew who I was. I was a junior varsity cheerleader, so Andy would see me cheer when the varsity players watched the first half of the JV games. I concentrated on my flips and back handsprings, never imagining that Andy Barrick, Mr. Cool, was paying any attention.

The first time he spoke to me, I was with some other cheerleaders decorating the hallway outside the gym. Andy was practicing basketball, and a guy named Pete came up and put his arm around me.

"Hey, Andy!" he hollered, "Don't you think we make a good couple?"

Andy looked over at the two of us and said, "No, I think she'd look better with me."

I was shocked. I was only a lowly freshman, and he was a junior. Besides, he already had a girlfriend who was six feet tall and a basketball star in her own right. I could just imagine what she'd do if she suspected I was trying to steal her boyfriend!

Whatever it was he saw in me, Andy and I started dating after that. We dated for six years, even though his family still lived in Pennsylvania and he went home in the summers. He was very different from the local Lynchburg boys I'd known all my life. He was bold about his beliefs and didn't care what anyone else thought about him expressing them. I'll never forget one time when we were going to chapel and he asked where my Bible was. I said it was in my locker. "Why would you leave it there?" he asked. He'd been in public school until he came to Liberty Christian, so to him it was a privilege to be able to have your Bible at school and go to chapel. I had gone to Christian school all my life and took it for granted.

I like to figure people out, and Andy was the one person I couldn't quite figure out. There's a side of him that's very intense and never satisfied when it comes to sports or working. But when it came to me, he was always so kind and patient, treating me like a queen. I never met anyone else like him, never wanted to date anyone else. I believe our being apart in the summers actually helped our relationship. It gave us room to grow as individuals and also proved that we truly were meant for each other since our feelings survived those long separations.

Andy's parents drove to Lynchburg from Hershey almost every

weekend to watch him and his brother play sports. John Barrick was only a year older than Andy, so the two boys got to do a lot of things together. After college, Andy's brother followed in their father's footsteps and went to dental school. Their sister, Jan, went to law school. Though Andy developed an interest in the restaurant business, his career goal was professional baseball. He dreamed of having a chance to make it in the big leagues.

After a few years of college, I had no doubt that Andy would ask me to marry him one day and that I would say yes. Sure enough, we were engaged on Thanksgiving Day and set our wedding date for August 13, 1988. Then Andy got the fantastic news that he had been drafted by the Philadelphia Phillies! The invitations had already gone out, but we had to change our wedding date to October 1, 1988, after the regular baseball season had ended. I was so happy for Andy that he had earned this opportunity.

As Andy joined the world of professional baseball, his family bought a restaurant called Country Meadows in Elizabethtown, Pennsylvania, right outside Hershey. As soon as we were married, we began managing the restaurant. Andy was a success at everything he did because he worked so hard and had a real passion for excellence. He didn't know how to cook before we started, but his mother taught him and he soon became an expert. I, on the other hand, was not suited for life in the kitchen. After one disaster too many, they kicked me out of the kitchen and made me the hostess. That I could do. The same happy, bubbly personality that had helped me on the cheerleading squad enabled me to greet our customers and make them feel welcome and special.

We worked like dogs at the restaurant as we prepared to go to Florida for spring training. Then, only a short time before we were supposed to leave, Andy got a letter saying he'd been released. The Phillies had brought in a whole new coaching staff that made sweeping changes in the organization, one of which was releasing Andy from the roster. In retrospect, maybe Andy should have gone down to Florida and tried out for another team. He was at his physical prime and in top condition. He had the desire and also the ability. I feel sure he could have gotten a look from somebody else. But the restaurant business was all-consuming. At the time we didn't feel like it was God's plan for him to go. God had closed that door and would open another door at the right time. Even so, there have been moments since then when I think Andy wishes he'd tried out for a different team.

We bought a second restaurant, the Black Bear Inn, in a historical building that had been the second oldest home in Elizabethtown. Running two restaurants and catering weddings and banquets, we worked harder than ever. As busy as we were, though, we made time for a couples' Bible study in our home every Monday night. We knew that whatever success we might have in business would be founded on our faith. Our love for Christ had been part of our relationship from the beginning, and we weren't going to allow the pressures of the world to change that. The six couples who met at our house to study God's Word became some of our closest friends. Years later they would be some of the same couples who prayed so faithfully and helped us so selflessly in the wake of our accident.

Our daughter, Jennifer, was born in 1991, and Josh came along four years later. Jen started at Hershey Christian School, where I was the registrar and Andy was on the school board. Eventually I helped start a Moms In Touch prayer group at the school. I was also a group Bible study leader at the Hershey Evangelical Free Church. It was a fulfilling life—two young kids; many, many friends; and all these opportunities for serving the Lord.

On the other hand, running a restaurant is never-ending work. Sixteen-hour days were commonplace, and we never had weekends off because those were our busiest times. Looking back, I don't know how we survived. We were young and didn't know any better. Eventually we felt trapped, working around the clock to pay the bills and afraid to put a "for sale" sign out front because it might scare away customers and employees. It was simply too demanding, especially after we had children. Our family sold Country Meadows and the Black Bear Inn, and Andy quickly found success in the field of multilevel marketing. He was also a regional sales manager for a local phone company.

We had lived in Hershey for twelve years when Andy got a call from Vernon Brewer, a longtime family friend back in Lynchburg. In 1991 Vernon had founded World Help, a mission outreach to third world countries, and now he wanted Andy to come work alongside him. Andy felt that God wanted him to join the World Help team. He wanted his life to have a purpose and to use his God-given talents to serve people in need.

The thought of moving was scary to me. Even though I had grown up in Lynchburg, I loved my life in Hershey. I got a great sense of fulfillment from my Bible studies, I was happy with Hershey Christian School, and all of Jen's and Josh's friends were there. We had just finished building a beautiful home that I would be very sad to leave. Andy had a successful business and would be taking a huge pay cut. I would be leaving lifetime friends and solid financial security for an unknown future. At some level I knew God was working out the details, but I was unhappy and even a little nervous about the situation. We put up a "For Sale by Owner" sign in the yard one Sunday morning before church, and by that afternoon, our house had sold at full price. I felt it was God showing me that moving to Virginia was His plan for us. This was in the summer of 2000, after Jen's third grade year. Josh was only five and hadn't started school yet.

We had scarcely finished moving before I had the opportunity to start a Bible study in our new home. Andy's brother, John, had married Gina, one of my closest childhood friends, and they still lived in Lynchburg. Her friends immediately became my friends. One day she and another woman asked me if we could start a Bible study in my home.

"I'm not sure who will come," I said. "But I guess if it is only the three of us that will be fine." I started hosting a study every Tuesday morning that grew quickly to twenty-five or thirty women every week. Those women would become another essential source of strength, hope, prayer, and practical help after the accident. Several years later, I was also invited to cohost a TV show with my dad called *Lighting the Way*, which provides an in-depth look at the Bible and its relevance today. It was completely out of my comfort zone, but I said yes, and it was a wonderful new learning experience. I had to study God's Word for hours to prepare, and I quickly learned how to rely on God's strength instead of my own.

Though Andy's position with World Help was very meaningful and important to him, he later moved to a position as marketing director for Dr. Tim Clinton at the American Association of Christian Counselors. After five years there, Andy was given the incredible opportunity to build the endowment fund for Liberty University as the director of alumni affairs. We continued to grow and flourish as a family.

Jen started at Liberty Christian Academy in the fourth grade. Maybe it was the move or maybe it was her natural shyness, but she was a little backward socially. I volunteered to help in the lunchroom, where I spent part of my time cleaning tables and straightening chairs, and part of it watching Jen. She would concentrate so much on her food that she didn't pay much attention to the other girls. Okay, I admit it: I was one of those helicopter moms, always hovering around making sure everything was okay. I'd see her sitting by herself and go up to a girl nearby and say, "Hey, have you met Jennifer? She's really sweet. I bet you two would get along great. Do you like gymnastics? Jen likes gymnastics too." Then I'd go over and try to help Jen make conversation.

It crushed me to find her in the bathroom alone during recess. It evidently didn't bother her. I'd seen her on the playground sitting by herself or talking to the teacher and it would break my heart even though she seemed all right with it. I'm such a social person and thought everybody needed friends. The best way to make a friend is to be a friend. So I would role-play with Jen about how to meet other girls. In time she did make a few good friends. Still, she was quiet and reserved, tending to keep to herself.

Like most preteens, Jen struggled with insecurities and feeling invisible at times, trying to fit in. During this season in her life I think Jesus was her best friend. She had a close relationship with Him from a young age. I found that climbing in bed at night with Jen was a good way to get her to open up and talk to me about her day at school. Jen rarely talked about her feelings, and it often took awhile to find out what she was thinking. I would remind her that Jesus wanted to be her best friend and she could tell Him everything, that she was a priceless treasure and God had a very special plan for her, and that her security was in God alone.

Jen started a prayer journal to God during those preteen years. She would write the request and then leave room for the answer. Weeks later she would come back and fill in the ways God answered her prayers. She prayed diligently for her friends and family and had hundreds of entries in her journal.

Part of the reason Jen seemed so reserved may have been her

brother. She had been the sole focus of attention for four years, and then, all of a sudden, there was someone else to share the stage. Not only that, but Josh was always in the spotlight. Everybody loved him from the time he was a baby, just as they do now. He was fun, loud, silly, outgoing, and verbal. He had thick, blond, gorgeous curly hair. He got the star roles in all the school programs. He played comfortably with kids his own age, kids Jen's age, and everybody in between. He was that kid in the room whom everybody is attracted to. From an early age he excelled at sports and had a passion for them just like his dad. Josh never tried to hog attention or overshadow his sister; it was simply that he had a strong personality and was naturally outgoing, while she was naturally quiet and introspective.

Then, her freshman year in high school, Jen underwent a transformation. This shy girl was still very guarded about her private thoughts. But there was a newfound energy and—dare I say it?—a bubbliness that reminded me of myself at that age. She now had a great group of girlfriends, and they had silly, crazy fun together. Her closest friend was Kaelynn Queen, and they were inseparable.

I think it all started in her middle-school youth group, PowerSource, led by a youth pastor named Barry Rice. He taught the kids that Jesus was their power source and they had to plug into Him every day. Jen was on the gymnastics team sponsored by her youth group. Sometimes the gymnastics team would set up a trampoline in a parking lot and do wild flips and routines to gather a crowd. Pastor Barry, who was a huge, powerfully built guy, would step up and break bricks with his bare hands or rip telephone books in half. His power, he explained to the audience, came from Jesus, and they could plug into it too.

The summer after her seventh-grade year, Jen went on a ministry trip to Myrtle Beach, where the team did its routine and prayed with people on the beach. Something clicked in Jen's heart. God moved in her spirit to make her bolder and more outgoing about her faith.

The next summer she spent a week in Orlando, where Pastor Barry was starting a new church. She still struggled with confidence, but her desire to speak out became even stronger as she moved through her freshman year.

This new desire and determination was evident in everything she did. She went from being a good gymnast to being a great one. Not only did she make the varsity cheerleading squad as a freshman, she won second place in the individual competitions that year at nationals! It seemed like nothing could stop her. She made the varsity soccer team. She also developed a deep friendship with a junior football player she had known for a couple of years named Brandon Knight, who was fun, friendly, and absolutely respectful. I must admit this part of her emotional and spiritual growth all sounded wonderfully familiar: a freshman cheerleader and an upperclassman sports standout, both seemingly brought together in God's perfect timing.

Best of all, Jen had two opportunities to share her faith with large audiences. She still didn't reveal her innermost thoughts and feelings. But in a dramatic change, she was now eager to speak to a crowd about Christ and her personal commitment to Him. These presentations were carefully scripted in advance, not impromptu conversations with any sort of give-and-take. Even so, these were times when Jen poured herself into proclaiming the gospel of Jesus. All the energy and sparkle that for years had gone into gymnastics and cheering now went into her statements of faith as well.

She became convinced that God had special plans for her and assured Him she was ready to do anything He wanted.

At the local Junior Miss pageant her freshman year, Jen had an opportunity to speak of God's gift of forgiveness—through Christ—from all our sins. Though she was too young to be a contestant, she introduced her friend Jessica, a senior who performed a gymnastics routine to music from *The Passion of the Christ*. Jen confidently stepped up to the lectern in her beautiful fuchsia evening gown and set the scene by reminding the audience: "Two thousand years ago an event took place that fulfilled God's promise to a fallen world. For three days the sun refused to shine and the earth was silent as all creation mourned the death of its Creator. Then, bursting through the darkness, Jesus, the true light of the world, rose from the grave, conquered death once and for all. The penalty of sin had been paid."

The room rang with cheers at this proclamation of the Good News. It was something I know Jen had always believed, but before then I couldn't have imagined her standing up in front of a ballroom full of people and saying it.

Even more astonishing was her commentary at the Christian Cheer Nationals in March 2006, near the end of her freshman year. Her confidence and enthusiasm that day were incredible. Standing in her cheer outfit in front of a crowd, completely relaxed, she strolled onto the gym floor with a hand mike and I think, more than ever before in her life, spoke from the heart.

The way she expressed herself was a milestone in her young life. But her delivery style pales in comparison to the message she delivered:

About a month ago at a youth retreat, God spoke to my heart and I completely surrendered my life to Him. I realized that God alone is the only one that's worth living for. God has always been there for me and He is my confidence and strength when I am weak.

One of my favorite verses is 1 Corinthians 2:9. "No eye has seen, no ear has heard, no mind has conceived what God has prepared for those who love him." I know God has amazing plans for my life and I want to use all my talents and abilities to serve Him. In everything I do, I want to give God all the glory.

God has also given me a big burden for lost people, and I want to be a witness and testimony for Him. My prayer is that God would use me to make a difference for eternity.

Remembering these words after all that has happened in the years since gives me goose bumps. God was preparing Jen even then to serve Him in a way neither she nor anyone else could ever have imagined.

CHAPTER 6

REFUSING TO DOUBT

Faith is the confidence that what we hope for will actually happen;
it gives us assurance about things we cannot see.   HEBREWS 11:1

Father, even when I can't see where You're leading,
I am going to trust You through everything!

Jen's journal, three months before the crash

I HADN'T EXPECTED ANDY to join me at his parents' house so soon, but
it was a wonderful comfort to have him there. Al and Fran Barrick,
"Gramps" and "Nanny" to the kids and often to us as well, are people
of action who tackle challenges with everything they've got. Al is a
big-game hunter and has bagged everything from mountain lions to
polar bears. Fran is his unflinching supporter, an amazing cook, and
a tireless prayer warrior. Their family motto is "Whatever it takes!"
They did everything they could to make us comfortable, including
getting hospital beds for Andy and me. I still couldn't lie flat because
of my broken ribs; Andy tossed and turned all night trying to find
the least painful position so he could sleep.

Though Andy and I were under the same roof for the first time since the accident, we had very little time alone. The house was like Grand Central Station with a whole army of volunteers helping us, coming and going around the clock, and we cherished every one of them. My parents came to encourage us and pray with us. My dear friend Paula Egel, a petite, blue-eyed dynamo with a knack for organization, took on the huge job of recruiting and scheduling caretakers so that somebody was with me every day. Another volunteer was with Jen every night. For the next six months, Paula was the glue that held everything together.

Every morning the friend on duty would come to the house about 8:30 to help me get ready for the day. My lessons in humility continued as she bathed me, dressed me, and patiently fixed my hair. Then she loaded me and my wheelchair into her car and drove me the seventy miles to Charlottesville to see Jen. Meanwhile, Andy's parents would help him get up and out and take him for doctors' appointments to deal with his blood clots and other complications. He really should have gone back home after that to rest and keep his leg elevated. But most days, he had his parents take him to see Jen too. We rarely focused on our own injuries—we were consumed with thoughts of our daughter.

Once I arrived at Kluge, the overnight volunteer would tell me about anything that had happened during the evening. We kept a visitors' journal in Jen's room, where we invited the friends who stayed with her or came to visit to write down their thoughts, prayers, and messages. Eventually we had a stack of notebooks running to hundreds of pages that became treasured keepsakes, and some of the most powerful and moving documents in Jen's entire story. I always took time to read the latest entries in the journal as soon as possible after I got there.

Jen's room was so small that once Andy arrived later in the morning, we could barely get our two wheelchairs in, especially since we both needed to keep our left legs elevated. A friend, nurse, or therapist was always with us because I would have been unable to help Jen in case of an emergency. The exception was that sometimes when Andy and I were both there, everybody else left the room for a while to give us a little private time.

I was frustrated that I couldn't do anything to assist with Jen's care. I couldn't help bathe her or change her clothes or feed her because I had only one working arm and my wheelchair kept me from getting close enough to her bed. Grateful as I was for all the friends who stayed with Jen, I felt worthless as a mother as I watched them help the nurses take care of her. Andy and I sat in the room for hours at a time. I sat at the head of Jen's bed, praying for her, reading the Bible, reading journal entries (many of them written to Jen) out loud, and singing "Jesus Loves Me" over and over. I touched her hand and her face because that was all I could reach. Andy sat at the other end of the bed rubbing her feet, constantly telling her how much he loved her, how proud he was of her, and how beautiful she was. Hoping to penetrate her consciousness, we played CDs of praise songs.

Physical therapy at this stage consisted of therapists coming into Jen's room and trying to get her to sit up in bed or gently stretch out and move her arms and legs. She remained comatose most of the time, opening her eyes once in a while for a few seconds, making sounds, and moving her arms and legs. When she seemed to be coming to, whoever was with her tried to keep her awake as long as possible. Her periods of relative coherence lasted only a minute or two. She still couldn't follow a command such as "Raise your hand" or "Lift your leg."

At five o'clock every afternoon, Jen's evening caretaker arrived. Sometimes Andy would leave before then for a medical appointment. If he was still there, we'd both go over Jen's day with the friend. At 5:30 or so we'd leave for home, Andy in his parents' car and me riding with my friend for the day, since no one had a vehicle big enough for two wheelchairs and two elevated legs. We got back to Gramps and Nanny's about seven. Waiting for us on the porch would be dinner from At Home Gourmet in a thermal carrier. Businessmen Andy had played basketball with for years, men who respected him and wanted to reach out to us in some way, paid for those hot, healthy, balanced meals every weeknight for seven months. On weekends, church friends brought us a homemade dish.

Andy and I came in exhausted, swollen, and in pain from our day out and the long ride back and forth. Just getting through the day, eating dinner, and getting ready for bed each night zapped every ounce of our limited stamina. We took our morphine and had dinner, and then I went over the next day's schedule with Paula while a nurse friend came to administer Andy's blood thinner injections. In fact, three friends of ours who were nurses took turns giving him shots twice a day and caring for his wounds. (He was definitely high maintenance!) His mother would rub his feet, purple and swollen by blood clots.

I felt helpless as I watched Andy in so much pain, knowing there was nothing I could do. It was almost more than I could bear to hear him moaning in the bed across from me. This wonderful man who had been my best friend since I was fourteen, who had always been my provider and protector, lay there hurting and miserable. Everything ached. We both fidgeted through the night, adjusting our beds and rearranging pillows under our broken limbs to try to get comfortable, taking oxycodone every four hours. Andy's mom made sure he got his medication, which was practically a full-time job. Even after we were settled for the evening, Fran got up three times in the night to give Andy and me our medicine. I would lie awake worrying about Jen and wishing I could be with her. At times, the separation from her was almost overwhelming—*Lord Jesus, help me. Give me the faith to keep pressing on.*

Josh lived at the Clintons' house as long as Andy and I were in the hospital, then came to stay with us at Gramps and Nanny's. He would go to a friend's after school, and Nanny picked him up every evening after we got home from Charlottesville. It was so comforting to have my son with me again after all those days apart. He helped Nanny by bringing me a bottle of water at bedtime and putting my next round of pills in a plastic bag taped to the bed. That was one less time Nanny had to get up.

Josh, Gramps, and Nanny tucked Andy and me into bed every night, and we prayed together that God would heal Jen and our family.

I always begged Josh to stay in bed with me and hug me for a while. I hadn't realized until then how much I missed having the touch of a family member. Josh and I would fall asleep in each other's arms, then I'd wake up in pain about midnight and encourage Josh to go to his room to sleep because we were both getting uncomfortable. We did this for the next two months. The fact that Josh was only slightly hurt and had healed so well made me grateful for God's mercy toward him. I don't know how I could have survived the mental anguish if he'd been injured as severely as the rest of us.

One night Kevin Foster, Pam's husband, dropped by and said he had something special to give us. When he held out a stained, rumpled book, it took me a second to recognize what it was. Then a wave of recognition and emotion poured over me. It was Jen's Bible, covered in her blood. Kevin had been drying it out since the accident.

Taking it in my right hand and resting it on my lap, I opened it to the New Testament, scanning the pages covered with highlighting and underlines where Jen had marked her favorite passages. Every margin was covered with her precious thoughts and notes, and I noticed that the blood had spattered only on the New Testament. My fingers were drawn to the faith chapter in Hebrews 11, where the page had been ripped.

"Now faith is the assurance of things hoped for, the conviction of things not seen. . . .Without faith it is impossible to please Him, for he who comes to God must believe that He is and that He is a rewarder of those who seek Him" (Hebrews 11:1, 6, NASB).

After that comes a roll call of historical figures whose lives were transformed by faith: Noah, Abraham, Sarah, Joseph, Moses, and others.

Holding that Bible in my lap—having that physical connection with the old Jennifer—I missed her so much it was overwhelming. I cried all night. It wasn't that I didn't have faith in God; I did. I knew He could do anything. He spoke the whole world into existence. He is all powerful. He is *Jehovah Rapha*, the One who heals. I knew that the same power that raised Jesus from the dead lived within Jen. God could raise her up again. I just missed her desperately.

Every morning Andy and I woke up in pain but with great anticipation to see our little girl in Charlottesville. It was a daylong effort and always exhausting, but we wanted to be there when Jen came to. Every morning I thought: *Today could be the day Jen wakes up!*

By late November she had made a few sounds and slight body

movements but was still unconscious. I was determined to connect with Jen and help her wake up, reading to her, singing, and playing praise CDs, especially the recording of her choir concert the night of the accident:

> *Lord, You're holy! Lord, You're holy!*
> *And we lift You up and magnify Your name.*
> *As I look around and I see all the works Your hands have made,*
> *All the awesomeness of You and how Your love will never fade,*
> *Mere words cannot express what I feel inside.*
> *I can't describe your glory divine.*
> *But as a token of my love, this is what I'll do:*
> *I'll lift my hands and cry, "Lord, You're holy."*[2]

While I focused on reconnecting with Jen, Andy continued to struggle with guilt. His mind frequently raced back to the night of the accident. He wished that somehow he could return to that moment and protect her from the horror that followed. If only we hadn't stopped for chicken. If only we'd been on that road five minutes earlier, or even five seconds! He kept replaying the scene in his head, wondering if there was anything he could have done differently.

Along with everything else, Andy was under huge emotional and financial pressure. Because the drunk driver was uninsured and our accident was classified as a "catastrophic event," we had to battle our own auto and health insurance companies. The ongoing litigation created a psychological tension that few people understand unless they have been through it themselves.[3]

It was a nightmare of paperwork and stress—the last thing any of us needed. Taking his role as family provider very seriously, Andy shouldered most of this burden alone. He wanted to protect me from more worry, so I didn't know about any of this until much later.

Every day we continued our routine at Kluge. Andy rubbed Jen's feet, while I sat as close to her as I could and stroked her arm. I longed to know she heard me as I prayed to God for another miracle: that she would wake up and eventually be healed.

Along with the friends who took care of us at Gramps and Nanny's and Jen at the hospital, hundreds and hundreds of others at school continued to pray. Many students wrote to Jen, including some who didn't even know her, to say they loved her and were continuing to pray faithfully. Hundreds of letters came to the hospital, and I read them out loud to Jen, hoping she could hear and know how much people cared for her. I read through tears as I realized what an impact Jen had made in all these lives.

Hey Jen,

You are such an awesome girl and the best Christian example I know. We all love and miss you. Just remember the verse that you always kept telling me, "I can do all things through Christ who strengthens me." You can do anything with the power of God. Get well soon! I love you so much!

Brittany Gillispie

Jen,

Whether you know it or not, you are loved by so many, and your life example and reputation have changed so many lives, including mine. As a junior and you being a sophomore, I still look to your life as the living example that I want to be like. I love looking at you sing in choir because the love of Christ is radiating from your face and you truly look like you love and adore Christ.

Love always,
Melissa Glaze

Jen baby,

We met this morning at school and all of us cheerleaders prayed on our knees for your recovery. . . . The life you've lived so far has been an encouragement and one that shines the love of Jesus Christ to all you come in contact with. I couldn't help but think of the verse that you always share at your cheerleading competitions. "No eye has seen, no ear has heard, no mind can conceive the plans God has for those who love him" 1 Cor 2:9. Don't forget this, Jen, God is going to do an amazing thing through you and with your life, even more than He already has. I believe it and I believe in you.

Stay strong. I love you, Jen.

Courtney Vestal

Brandon Knight, Jen's boyfriend, was one of her most faithful visitors. There was no way then to know what their relationship would be like going forward. Even so, he remained dedicated to her and cared for her deeply, as an early entry in Jen's visitors' journal shows.

To my #1,

Hey babe, I can't put into words how I feel at this moment. I am totally heartbroken. I miss you so much. . . . Seeing you in the hospital has shown me how much I really do care for you and need you in my life. I just know that God is going to use this for good! He already has! Players on the football team are finally opening their eyes—it has already changed their lives! Jen, don't give up! Don't think God is letting this happen to you for no reason. . . . He has a plan! It's all worth it if people come back to Christ. I LOVE YOU SO MUCH!!!!!! and I'm praying for you nonstop. Here is a big Eskimo kiss for you!!!!

Brandon

Other friends and family added their heartfelt thoughts, prayers, and best wishes for her recovery.

Jen,

We just want you to know how much we love you and are praying for you. You are a testimony to us. I will not allow anyone to sit in your seat during 5th period math class. We just miss your presence so we decided (as a class) to have you with us in spirit.

Coach John Patterson

Hey Jen,

You mean the world to me, and you are one of my greatest friends. Every time I picture Sunday night in my mind, I think back to when we were singing, "Lord, You're holy" and the smile that reflected God's love so abundantly. I think about squeezing your hand and getting goose bumps as we sang to our Lord.

* I love you and am here for you always.*   *Megan Clinton*

Kaelynn Queen was Jen's best friend and another one of her most faithful visitors. She and Jen looked so much alike and spent so much time together that people thought they were sisters. Kae has long, curly brown hair and deep brown eyes. Like Jen, she's quiet around strangers, but once she gets to know you, she is warm, bubbly, and outgoing. I can't imagine any other fifteen-year-old showing the selfless love Kae showed Jen day after day.

Hey Chic-a-bee,

You are the best friend I could have ever asked for, and I cannot wait for you to open your beautiful eyes. I miss your smile and

*your laugh. Without you, who can finish my sentences or make
me laugh when I am sad? You have shown me what a true
Christian looks like. I just want to apologize for something
I thought this week about you. I was not sure if you would
still want to serve God with your whole life. I thought if you
knew that you would be in a coma you would not have been so
willing for God, but then it hit me that you would.*

Love you more each day,   *Kaelynn*

My brother and sister-in-law, Jon and Amanda, drove from
Atlanta for another visit. They were excited to see Jen sitting up,
even though she was slumped unconscious in a wheelchair with her
head hanging over to the right. She seemed much improved from
the last time they'd seen her in the ICU with tubes everywhere. Jen
was wearing her pink pajama pants with white flowers and a pink
T-shirt with red hearts. Her arms were rigidly crossed over a pillow
on her lap, and her fingers were stiff as a board. She looked peaceful but completely unconscious. Jon and Amanda stood next to her
wheelchair softly tickling her arm and singing to her. My brother
had always been a good singer—he sang in my wedding—and now
Amanda's voice harmonized beautifully with his. They sang ever so
sweetly to Jen, and before they left, Jon wrote in the journal next to
Jen's bed.

Jen—

*You look so beautiful and peaceful. Linda was reminding me
that you'll be 16 soon. You know, I was 16 when you were born.
I would sit with you on the couch for hours, just watching you
sleep. Now, you're all grown up, and here I am watching you
sleep peacefully. I can't wait to see what God has in store for you!*

To everyone who knows you, what an amazingly mature and godly person you are! You have already impacted so many people and so many lives at the age of 15. I was reading some of the notes that your friends at school wrote to you. You are so loved, so admired, and so respected for your faith and your walk with God. I'm already missing you, and we haven't even left yet.

All my love,
Uncle Jon Hindson

We took Josh to Kluge only a couple of times because we didn't want him to see the big sister he admired so much in a condition that might scare him. During his first visit at Thanksgiving, he told Jen she was the greatest sister in the whole wide world and gave her a kiss. He spent most of the visit playing basketball in the hospital courtyard with Brandon.

Faithfully and tenderly, Brandon sat at Jen's bedside every weekend, holding her hand, gently touching her face, and whispering to her. He would say, "Jen, you look good today!" even though she had knots in her hair and stains all over her pajamas from the feeding tube. He was just glad she was alive. Kaelynn also visited as much as she could during the week. She often stayed all night with Jen without sleeping because she was afraid of missing something. Brandon and Kae kept all Jen's other friends at school up to date on Jen's progress and what to pray for her.

Jen finally began to move on her own, which brought a whole new set of challenges. She started thrashing and rolling around uncontrollably—a symptom of her brain injury—and moaning more than ever in her sleep. Without warning, her arms and legs would begin flailing in every direction. The nurses put her in a bed with mesh sides that zipped up like a tent to keep her from falling out. It was hard to watch my beautiful, high-achieving fifteen-year-old daughter tossing around like an infant in a crib. What would the future be like for our family? I prayed, *Father, I refuse to doubt. I'm believing You! Things that are impossible with men are possible with God.*

One of the nurses at Kluge, Angie McWhorter, took a special interest in our family. Angie was a petite brunette with long hair pulled back in a ponytail and the face of an angel. Her sparkling eyes matched her personality—sweet, compassionate, and kind. She explained to Andy and me that, after experiencing a traumatic injury, the brain emerges slowly in varying stages of cognizance and recognition. There's no sudden, dramatic opening of the eyes and a miraculous awakening like you see in movies.

The therapists did everything they could to stimulate Jen and help her wake up. They used a mechanical lift to move her from her hospital bed into a wheelchair so she could sit upright. Angie wheeled Jen around and even took her outside hoping to get some kind of response. Once in a while Jen's eyes would open partway and she would react slightly to some sound or touch or movement.

I was encouraged to see her moving even a little, though I continued feeling frustration and helplessness building up inside day after day, hour after hour. The worst was when Jen got tangled up in her feeding tube, which seemed like every time they tried to feed her. She looked like a baby in the womb with a twisted umbilical cord. It took three people to keep her from pulling the feeding tube out of her stomach once it was wrapped three or four times around. She rolled around and constantly got turned upside down in the bed. Nothing they could do would calm her or stop her from moving. She had no control and was completely unaware of the danger. When the thrashing got especially bad the nurses tied her arms and legs to the bed rails with soft strips of cloth to keep her from hurting herself. The whole process was exhausting for me, even though all I did was watch.

Jen progressed to where she would open her eyes for up to a minute at a time. But there was nothing behind those eyes—no recognition of anybody, no sparkle, nothing but a blank stare. We did see signs that sometimes she understood what people were saying to her. When the nurses said they were going to give her a shower she would rub her head. She started making some sounds, though they were nothing like words, only moans and low, guttural sounds in her throat. Moving her head back and forth on the pillow twisted her hair into a huge knot. She was like a fifteen-year-old infant who was unaware of the world around her. She even had to have a neck brace to hold her head up in the wheelchair.

If only I could get a glimpse into what the future would hold for Jennifer and the rest of our family! Someone had put Beth Moore's book *Believing God* next to Jen's bed. I opened it at random, and a passage jumped right off the page. My eyes flooded with tears as I read, "God's specialty is raising dead things to life and making impossible things possible. You don't have the need that exceeds His power."[4]

I prayed, *Father, I refuse to doubt. I'm believing, God! With You all things are possible. You promise that in Matthew 19:26. Father, I know You left Jen on this earth for a reason. You have an amazing plan for her life. I have to believe that. Otherwise, You would have taken her home with You. God, I believe You are giving Jen a platform and positioning her for something huge! You are going to use this to shape Jen's destiny.*

By the beginning of December, Jen was still in the low-response category. Dr. Kenneth Norwood, a specialist in neurodevelopment disabilities in children, treated Jen and cared deeply for her. He was gentle and kind, but also honest and direct. He explained the dilemma with Jennifer's treatment. Jen's brain scans showed that almost every area of her brain had been injured, including deeper areas that controlled movement. She had shown signs of waking up, but remained incoherent and spent most of her time sleeping. She made erratic movements and tried sometimes to speak, but those flashes of awareness lasted only minutes, not hours.

In order for insurance to pay for her rehabilitation at Kluge, she had to be awake for at least three hours per day to undergo intense occupational, physical, and speech therapy. "We can hold the insurance company off for probably another week," Dr. Norwood said. "But after that, if she still is not awake, we'll have no choice but to send her home. I'd give anything if I had better news for you."

His words stunned me. I looked over at Andy with fear in my eyes. We were both in wheelchairs. How could we take care of Jen? We couldn't even take care of ourselves! *God*, I prayed silently, *why would You have brought her this far just to send her home from rehab like this? I know that can't be Your will for her.*

As we absorbed the news, Andy and I realized we needed people to pray—and fast!—crying out to God on Jen's behalf for a miracle. We were powerless, but God's power was limitless. Within an hour of that meeting the word went out, and thanks to the marvels of modern technology, thousands began praying specifically for the one miracle we needed most: that Jennifer Barrick would wake up.

CHAPTER 7

"YOU WON'T BELIEVE THIS . . ."

Give thanks to the LORD and proclaim his greatness. . . . Tell everyone
about his wonderful deeds.   I CHRONICLES 16:8-9

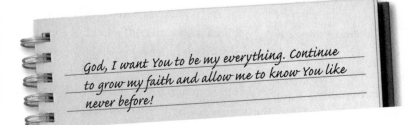

God, I want You to be my everything. Continue to grow my faith and allow me to know You like never before!

Jen's journal, four months before the crash

AFTER MY FITFUL NIGHTS OF SLEEP in the hospital bed at Gramps
and Nanny's house, I seldom felt rested. My side still hurt from the
broken ribs. My left leg was still in a cast, my left arm was in a sling,
my left hand hung lifeless beside me on the bed, and it was clear that
I would have a deep indentation and a bad scar above my left eye.
God had mercifully spared my sight. The eye that had been dislodged
from its socket during the accident was perfectly okay.

Every morning, whichever friend was on duty helped me through
the long, slow routine of getting dressed and to the hospital. I wanted
Jen to see a familiar face right away. Every day I thought, *This could
be the day she wakes up. This may be the day we've all prayed so hard*

for. I watched carefully for any sign that she was finally coming out of the coma. The hours were ticking away to the time when the insurance company would stop covering her care unless she could do three hours of therapy a day. That seemed like a long shot. Like so much else about the situation, when or whether Jen would wake up was out of my hands. Only God could make it happen. In 1 Thessalonians 5:17 the apostle Paul encourages us to pray without ceasing. Whenever I thought of it, day or night, I prayed that God would wake Jen up. Along with all my other aches, my heart ached to hold my daughter in my arms and comfort her. What if she woke up and didn't know I was there because she couldn't see me or touch me? I didn't even want to imagine that happening.

I didn't know if Jen could hear us or not, but the thought that she might be comforted inspired us to keep trying even though I couldn't detect any sort of reaction from her. One thing I noticed, though, was that sometimes she would smile in her sleep. Oh, if only I knew what she was thinking! *Where are you, Jen? What do you see? I'm right here beside you!*

The thrashing and moaning continued, and sometimes she'd open her eyes for a minute or so. She stayed zipped inside her protective "tent" on top of the bed, where she would start to flop around without warning, turn her head from side to side, and make guttural grunting noises. At the end of every day it was hard to say good-bye. What if she woke up while I was away? Or what if the Lord took her to be with Him that very night?

One morning I was sitting beside her, reading the Bible, praying, and chatting with three of my friends as she rolled around and grunted as usual. Then suddenly, breaking through my concentration on whatever I was reading and piercing the familiar background sounds of the hospital room—Jen's fidgeting, people coming and going down the hall, the beeps of electronic monitors and machinery—I heard a noise that sent chills through my body from head to toe. It started as a long, dull moan before slowly shaping itself into something else.

"M—O—M . . ."

She was calling for me! *Thank you, God! Jen is waking up! This is the miracle hundreds of people have been praying for!*

There are no words to describe the joy I felt. *She said my name!* How I had longed for and prayed for that moment, never knowing if I would ever hear her voice again! I wanted to climb into bed with her to make sure she knew I was there and heard her. Without waiting for my three friends to help me, I struggled out of the wheelchair and hopped to her bedside on one foot. My friends unzipped the net covering around her bed for me. As she lay on her back, I climbed in and leaned over her body, putting my face as close to hers as I could.

"I'm here!" I said. "Mommy is here, and I love you so much!" Overcome with relief and thanksgiving, I felt tears streaming down my face as I kissed her cheeks.

Jen was still moaning, and I wanted to calm her. The only thing I could think of was to sing. If she didn't know anything else, I wanted her to know that her Savior loved her and would never forsake her. In the overwhelming emotion of the moment, I started singing the first thing that popped into my head.

> *Jesus loves me! This I know,*
> *For the Bible tells me so.*
> *Little ones to Him belong;*
> *They are weak but He is strong. . . .*

Those simple words said it all. Jen was weak and helpless, but Jesus was strong. The Bible promised that Jesus would take care of her. The weaker and more dependent she was, the more He would be able to demonstrate His strength through her.

I was still absorbing the impact of the miracle before me when it was outshone by a second one even more incredible.

As I kept singing, leaning over her in the bed with my face inches from hers, I saw her start to respond. Her mouth began forming words. *She's singing along!* She joined in on every third word or so, not out loud but mouthing the words. She knew what I was saying!

It was the first time we had connected in any way since the accident. The soul and spirit that was Jen was still inside that broken body! My daughter was still in there! After only a minute the connection was broken. The effort had exhausted her, and she fell back into a deep and peaceful sleep. The miraculous moment was a brief one. But she had responded. *She was waking up!*

Angie McWhorter, the terrific nurse who'd taken a special interest in Jen and helped us so much, warned that the waking up process could be traumatic for our whole family. Brain injury patients are agitated, confused, and in pain. Often reviving patients are violent, lashing out with their arms and legs, fighting and swearing, using words you couldn't imagine the person even knew. "Even pastors and nuns respond that way," Angie assured us. She warned us to expect that during the next phase of recovery, our deeply committed Christian daughter could be cursing. For some parents this was a deeply distressing side effect. Filled with hope though we were, Andy and I took Angie's warning to heart. We had already seen many brain-injured children at Kluge screaming and throwing aggressive tantrums. We braced ourselves for the worst.

A few days after Jen first began to wake up, I was jolted awake by the telephone at 4 a.m. Since I couldn't reach over to pick up the phone on the nightstand, I kept my cell phone in bed with me. It was

Brandon's mom, Tammy, who spent every Saturday and Sunday night with Jennifer. My first thought was, *What's happened? What's wrong?* Tammy wouldn't call at such an hour unless it was a life-or-death crisis.

"Linda," Tammy said breathlessly, "you won't believe this, but Jen started praying out loud forty-five minutes ago and hasn't stopped since! She's speaking in a normal voice, and I can understand every word. She's thanking God for healing her, praising Him and saying over and over, 'Lord, You are good. Lord, You are so faithful.' It's the most amazing prayer I've ever heard!"

Tammy is a dynamic, take-charge kind of person who always seems to have the situation around her under control. I'd almost never seen her flustered. Now she was so excited she could hardly get the words out.

"Listen, Linda! Listen to Jen praying!"

Over the phone I could hear what sounded like a perfectly normal Jen Barrick, uninjured, unconfused, praying in complete sentences in the same tone of voice she'd had before the accident. I had never expected to hear that voice again.

Tammy came back on the line. "I was reading to her from Psalms," she said, "and she seemed so restless. I put the Bible down to rub her feet and see if that would calm her. She was moaning and grunting like she does sometimes.

"All of a sudden I realized that the sounds were words. I stopped talking and listened.

"'Lord, you are so glorious. How can we even fathom who You are?'

"She sounded perfectly healed, praising God over and over. I was afraid to move or do anything, but she's been at it now for forty-five minutes and I had to call you."

My mind was racing. I couldn't have gone back to sleep even if I'd wanted to. All I could think about was seeing Jen. God was giving us one miracle after another, and I couldn't wait to be there for them.

Pam Foster drove me to the hospital later that morning. Tammy was anxiously waiting for me to arrive. Jen had fallen back asleep for several hours but was now awake and talking to God again, and Tammy didn't want me to miss this incredible sight. As I wheeled into her room, Jen was flopping around in the bed. I moved as close to her bed as I could maneuver the chair, but she had no idea who I was.

My first impression was that nothing had changed. She looked and acted just like the last time I saw her—eyes closed, head tossing back and forth on the pillow, her hair a hopeless tangle of knots. Yet at the same time her body writhed around, I heard her voice. She was talking. No, she was praying. Praying to God in a normal voice as if He were standing in the room beside her.

"Father," she said, "You are so faithful. You are so good. You are magnificent!"

The words were perfectly clear. Everything Jen had said before this day had been barely intelligible—a few slurred words punctuated with grunts and groans. Here she sounded like her old self. She lay on her stomach as she spoke, almost as if she was lying prostrate in the presence of God Himself.

"There are no words to describe You," she went on. Then she stopped and seemed to be listening to something. "What will I tell them? You'll have to write it down for me because I can't explain it."

She listened again. I felt like I was hearing one side of a two-way conversation. Andy, Gramps, and Nanny squeezed into the room and watched in astonished silence with the rest of us. Jen had no idea we were there. The only thing she was aware of was her heavenly Father.

"Should I go, or should I stay?" Jen wanted to know. "What would You have me to do?" Another pause. "Yes, Lord, whatever You want me to do. . . . What will I say? . . . Okay." It seemed like the Lord was unfolding His plan for Jen's life to her and she was agreeing, saying she understood. At the same time, He was speaking through her to us.

God was with us in that room. He was absolutely real. We all felt that God was speaking to us; we felt His presence and an unexplainable peace. Jen's face was glowing with joy. I sensed that she had one foot in this world and one in the next, bridging earth and eternity as she and God discussed how and where she could serve Him best. As I sat there absolutely awestruck, my heart pounding, He was explaining to Jen His plans for her future. While her battered body lay in a Virginia hospital bed, her spirit stood in the throne room of the Almighty. Finally Jen finished her prayer and immediately fell into a deep, serene, relaxed sleep.

Pam and Tammy grabbed each other and fell to their knees beside the bed. Tammy started weeping because she thought God was going to take Jen to heaven right then. Whatever happened from now on, I knew that Jen was the Lord's and He had blessings to shower upon her along with great work to do in His name.

This was the turning point for me, the moment when hope met faith. I knew God had spared Jen's life and that He would lift her up according to His perfect plan.

For the week or so that she was emerging from the coma, Jen spent almost all of her awake time praying, reciting Bible passages, or singing hymns and Christian songs. Occasionally, we would get a glimpse of the uninjured Jen when she would pray in a normal, confident-sounding voice. After that, her speaking voice was still much clearer when she was praying than at any other time, although it sounded slurred and slow. But when she tried to answer a question or talk with one of us, she hesitated, garbled her words, and was often very hard to understand. She couldn't focus for more than a minute or two and still had long periods of uncontrolled movement and noise.

We kept waiting for the cursing and fighting Angie had warned us about, but they never came. Jennifer never stopped praising God. As she came out of her coma, she was raised to an entirely different level of consciousness: God consciousness. He was ministering to her in a way her family and friends could not. The Holy Spirit shone clear and brilliant in her and through her.

I can't help wondering what would be coming out of my mouth if I were in great pain and confused and had no control. Even the most upright Christian is liable to let loose a choice phrase or two when he pounds his thumb with a hammer or she hits her head on the garage door. Just for an instant, the pain takes control and all the filters we put in place to restrain ourselves are overwhelmed. In addition to pain, brain-injured patients must deal with overwhelming confusion about who they are and where they are, and their injuries often take away their inhibitions. It's no surprise then that so many respond by screaming and yelling ugly things.

Jen didn't do any of that. With all her inhibitions gone, the first thing that popped reflexively out of her mouth was a prayer of praise to her Creator. I remembered Jesus' words in Luke 6:45: "A good person produces good things from the treasury of a good heart, and an evil person produces evil things from the treasury of an evil heart. What you say flows from what is in your heart."

When you're shaken, whatever you're full of spills out.

What filled Jen's heart was thanksgiving to Jesus and a desire to draw close to Him. From the first moment she began her conversations with Him, the focus was not on what she needed or wanted, but on what she could do to serve and praise Him. Not "Oh, Lord, I'm in such pain and want to be healed," but "You are good. You are glorious. Yes, Lord, I will do whatever You want me to do."

Jen had been a shy Christian who hesitated to share her faith. She had prayed for boldness, for the courage to proclaim her faith out loud, to carry it off the pages of her journals and into the world and into the hearts of all who knew her. God had answered her prayer. God had made her bold.

One morning, when the speech therapist asked Jen why she was in the hospital, Jen answered, "To share my religion." That evening my cousin Heidi was reading the Bible to her to try to calm her. No matter what passage Heidi read from the Old or New Testament, when Jen heard the words she stopped thrashing in the bed and started quoting along from memory—long passages, not just a verse or two. Heidi was in awe and stopped reading. Jen, however, kept right on going, verse after verse, her voice clear and strong. It had to have been God speaking through her. When Jen finished, she fell into a calm and peaceful sleep.

The night after that, when Gina was in the room with her, Jen started praying at 4:30 in the morning and continued off and on for three and a half hours asking God for help, thanking Him for His presence and His goodness. It was as if she couldn't say enough in praise of Him.

As Jen continued to be more alert, many witnesses heard her praising the Lord in words and music. Sometimes the sound of a familiar CD would inspire her to sing. Other times somebody in the room would start a song or a Bible passage and Jen would join in. And there were days when she starting singing or quoting Scripture from some inspiration no one else could see. Everyone who saw her was amazed that a girl who didn't know she had been hurt, had no short-term memory, had no recollection of having a brother, and couldn't answer a yes-or-no question could utter such profound words. Most days she would be praying out loud in her room and praising God in a long, repetitious prayer, and then out of nowhere she would say something unbelievable.

I scribbled down many of her statements in the journal next to her bed:

"God, You alone know the burden I carry. Father, You alone know how long this journey will last."

"I'm here to share my testimony."

"Lord, where have You taken my memory?"

"Lord, thank You for all the people I have been able to influence."

"Lord, thank You for healing me and raising me up!"

After that one, I started to weep at her bedside because she couldn't even sit up and there she was praising God for healing her as if He had already done it. She was praying things she didn't know. The only explanation was that it was the power of the Holy Spirit praying through her.

One night as Jen was zipped up in her bed, she was moaning. My friend Susan Seavers was staying with her and asked Jen if she would pray to Jesus with her. Jen stated matter-of-factly, "He's right here; just talk to Him."

Susan's son, Luke, had made the trip from Hershey to Lynchburg with his mom and dad, and though he wasn't there that night, he had anticipated his family's visit to Jen for weeks. Since hearing about the accident, Luke had prayed for his childhood friend every day, even as he struggled to understand why God would allow this to happen to Jen. Just five months earlier, when his family had visited Lynchburg over Easter, he and Jen had spent an evening playing their guitars and singing praise songs together on our back porch. They had so much fun, they continued long after the sun had set.

Now Jen lay here at Kluge moaning in pain and Luke wanted to cheer her up. He brought his guitar into her room and sang softly to her. Jen grinned from ear to ear, while Luke was thrilled that Jen seemed to recognize him.

Now that Jen was more responsive, her daily routine was expanded to take advantage of every minute she was awake. At first, therapists came to see her in her room, and the tasks they had for her were very simple. Early on I often watched with a sinking feeling because my daughter was unable to follow their basic commands. At the same time, I wasn't completely surprised. So often the friend who had stayed with her overnight had been waiting eagerly for me to arrive so she could describe how Jen had been awake praying and praising God since well before dawn.

One morning her schoolteacher, Penni Crist, walked in to Jen's room. Penni, a high-energy redhead, always had a big smile on her face and the kind of positive personality that makes a great teacher. As she entered, Jen was talking out loud, saying, "Father" and "Daddy."

"Who are you talking to?" Penni asked Jen. "Your dad is not here today."

Jen replied, "I'm talking to my heavenly Father." Time and again we realized she saw things in her room that we could not.

As Jen drifted in and out of consciousness over the days and weeks that followed, the difference in her when she was talking to God and when she was talking to anybody else remained almost unbelievable. When Jen tried to communicate with me or Andy or someone else in the room, the best she could do was string two or three words together that were slurred and hard to understand. But when she spoke to Jesus it was as if He was standing in the room with us. Her voice was clear, her thoughts were logical and complete. She saw Jesus in the room and talked to Him for hours on end.

I believe that Jen was in the presence of God the whole time she was in a coma. She came out of it praising Him, reciting Bible verses and song lyrics perfectly, some of which she had never memorized before.

"There are no words to describe You," she said a hundred times. "How can I tell people what I see?" There's no way He would have her praying like she was unless He had very special plans for her. Every mental and physical ability she needed to do the work He had in mind was left intact. Everything else became secondary and fell away.

By the second week of December, Jen had the same rotation with therapists every day. She was scheduled for three sessions of therapy in both the mornings and afternoons, with lunch and a nap in between. As she progressed, Jen was wheeled to the therapy rooms and the school classroom each day for her sessions.

Each session was to last thirty minutes. The problem was that Jen still did not have enough energy to complete all her therapy sessions, and for her to qualify for continued insurance coverage, the therapists would have to show on paper that Jen had completed three hours of therapy each day.

Her first session was with Janis, the occupational therapist. They began with the simplest tasks: using a washcloth and toothbrush, putting her arm through the sleeve of a shirt. Jen didn't enjoy OT and wasn't very cooperative. She didn't want to try things, didn't want to follow Janis's instructions. Jen would shake her head and say, "I can't" or "This hurts."

After occupational therapy came speech therapy with Meredith. One of Meredith's first tasks was to teach Jen how to swallow again. They started with swallowing water, then graduated to Jell-O and solid food. Jen still had a feeding tube because she ate only a little by mouth.

Next came physical therapy with Chad and Scottie. They began by getting her to sit up in bed and to hold her head up while sitting in her wheelchair. After Jen's last therapy session of the morning, Penni arrived to tutor her. For her first lesson, Penni held up two index cards to see if Jen could point out the one with her name on it. She couldn't.

Following lunch and her afternoon therapy sessions, which were in the same order as in the morning, Jen took another nap and then had dinner. Around that time the volunteer who was spending the night with Jen would arrive, and we would go over the day's events. That person would have the strenuous task of getting Jen ready for bed, convincing her to brush her teeth, put on clean pajamas, and allow someone to brush at least some of the tangles out of her hair. Jen usually wanted to go back to sleep right after the evening meal. The volunteer tried to keep her awake until 9 p.m. with jokes and silly songs so she would sleep at night.

Even so, she was often awake before daylight, praising God in a strong and confident voice. No wonder, then, that she was exhausted by the time she was supposed to start her morning therapy.

One of the most reliable ways to get a positive response out of Jen was with music. I made sure the CD player in her room had her favorite praise songs going for hours on end. Whenever I played the CD from Jen's choir concert the night of the accident, she would sing along and raise her hands up to the Lord. She'd have a huge smile during the solo because she knew she wasn't supposed to sing then, but she sang it anyway and was so proud of herself. One song that she sang repeatedly was, "I sing because I'm happy, I sing because I'm free, For His eye is on the sparrow, And I know He watches me." This was so emotional for us to watch; even the nurses in her room would be crying. It was a reminder to us that if God could take care of the sparrow, surely He could take care of Jen. And she knew God was watching her—her face glowed with perfect peace and joy.

Although she was damaged and delicate from a physical stand-point, Jen's spiritual life had been enlarged and enriched to a mirac-ulous degree by all the events of the past five weeks. I could see

God moving in her heart. He had changed her forever, drawing her spirit closer to Himself. At the same time, the rest of her was broken and struggling. Sometimes she recognized friends and family and sometimes not. She prayed and sang as long as she was awake, but I couldn't have a conversation with her. A huge chasm had opened up between her spiritual life and everything else about her.

I continued to be amazed at how many Bible verses and song lyrics she knew from memory. That gave me precious hope. Yet at the same time, she didn't know her last name, or what year it was, or that two plus two equals four. She didn't recognize people she had known for years. She had a blank stare with a haze over her eyes. We were starting to realize that her vision was greatly impaired.

While I was in the room alone with her one afternoon, Jen looked directly at me and said, "I think about everything and wonder if God is going to be confident with you . . . if you will pass the test." I felt God speaking directly to me through Jen. *Test? What do you mean I'm in a test? This wasn't our fault. I'm not going to do very well, I can tell you that!*

I wasn't mad, I was *numb*. And heartbroken. I wasn't even processing all that had happened yet. I'd hardly had a moment to stop and think. Andy and I and our parents were just trying to help Jen, and I was struggling to survive through each day. The thought of God putting me through a *test* had never crossed my mind.

Jen's words caught me completely off guard. How can a child who is confused and doesn't know she's been severely injured tell me I'm in a test! *Where is God in all of this?* I had no idea what Jen was talking about. It was months before I finally understood.

CHAPTER 8

ROLLER-COASTER FAITH

Dear friends, don't be surprised at the fiery trials you are going through, as if something strange were happening to you. Instead, be very glad—for these trials make you partners with Christ in his suffering, so that you will have the wonderful joy of seeing his glory when it is revealed to all the world. I PETER 4:12-13

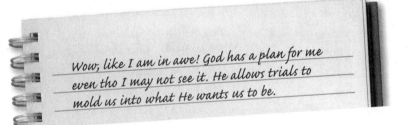

Wow, like I am in awe! God has a plan for me even tho I may not see it. He allows trials to mold us into what He wants us to be.

Jen's journal, three months before the crash

NOW THE ROLLER-COASTER RIDE BEGAN. My heart would soar when I heard Jennifer praising God and singing, reciting Bible verses, seeming to experience the Lord on a level we could only imagine. Then I'd plunge into despair when I saw this cheerleading champion slouched in a wheelchair, drooling, her head held up by a neck brace. Some days I felt like I had connected with her. Other times I'd roll my wheelchair into her room and say, "Jen, it's me. Do you know who I am?" and she would have no idea.

A dozen times a day I recalled the sound of Jen's voice at prayer during those early days of consciousness, so strong and confident. I saw such promise, felt so much hope. It was a shocking contrast to what the doctors and therapists reported during our weekly meetings with them at Kluge. Each member of the treatment team gave a report on Jen's progress. I felt like they were talking about someone else. "She can't follow a verbal command," one would say. "Jen is not responding as quickly as we would like." "She has a flat affect with no expression."

I sat there quietly taking notes, but on the inside I was screaming, *What are you talking about! Have you seen her sing complete praise songs from memory? Recite twenty verses of the Bible without a single mistake? When she prays her face shines with joy and fulfillment. Her progress is absolutely miraculous.*

How I wished her therapists could see and hear Jen praying in the middle of the night rather than only during the daylight hours when her energy was gone. Those who sensed Jen's spiritual side knew how far she had come. Yes, physically and mentally she was extremely limited. But spiritually she was completely intact.

December 18 was shaping up to be a crucial date. If Jen was awake long enough to handle three hours of therapy by then, her treatment at Kluge would continue. If she could not function that long, her insurance coverage would run out, and they would have no choice but to discharge her. The thought of it was more than I could handle. All I could do was turn it over to God.

One afternoon, Andy and I watched hopefully as a team of physical therapists came in and announced it was time to get Jen up on her feet. They lifted her onto a special platform with buckles like an amusement park ride. Then slowly they pivoted her into an upright position. It was the first time in months we had looked our daughter in the eye. As she moved upright she thanked the therapists over and over for their help.

Before dizziness and nausea took over, Jennifer started to slip sideways a little. "Help," she shouted, "I'm crooked!" Everyone in the room enjoyed a laugh as they slowly lowered Jen back to the horizontal position.

My sister-in-law Gina brought an armload of pictures from Jen's bedroom at home to put up around her room at Kluge. We wanted the nurses to know what Jen looked like and who she was before the accident. It also made her room more cheerful. There was a chance that the photos would somehow jog her memory as well.

Gina came to the hospital many times to visit Jen. She had a true servant's heart and made a special point of helping Jen with her personal needs. Sometimes Gina decided to take certain matters into her own hands. One day she declared to the nurses, "No niece of mine is going to have hairy armpits!" So she and one of the nurses took care of that little issue, laughing and joking the whole way through. Later, after Jen had gone off her blood thinner, Gina decided it was time to shave her legs. This was an even bigger chore because Jen still had uncontrollable leg movements. I told a silly story to divert Jen's attention while Gina and Angie climbed in Jen's bed and succeeded in shaving her legs, one at a time. What a mess we made! We also got Jen to cooperate by telling her Brandon was on his way to visit and she didn't want to be showing off her hairy legs.

One day the occupational therapist picked Jen up out of the wheelchair and sat her in a rocking chair. As the therapist rocked her back and forth, she screamed, "This hurts! This hurts!" The sight of it and of her screaming in pain was too much for me. I was crying so hard I rolled myself out into the hallway. *How could she do this to my baby?* But she felt she had to. The occupational therapist was trying to make Jen aware of her body's spatial movement. By rocking her, the therapist hoped she could feel her own limbs and know she had arms and legs. It was so hard to watch.

Further along in the recovery, Jen spent more time in the occupational therapy room, where there was a kitchen. Progress was so painful and so slow! When Janis tried to get her to stir a bowl of brownie batter, she held the wooden spoon in her hand and yelled, "This hurts! This hurts!" Hoping to connect with Jen's interest in jewelry making, Janis tried to get her to put a big wooden bead on a peg, but Jen could only cry and say, "This hurts! I can't!"

I sat outside in the hall, watching Jen through the doorway. As I watched her struggle, I prayed to the Lord in tears. "Please don't take her dexterity, too! Isn't it enough that she will never cheer again or play soccer again? Lord, You know how much Jen loves to make things with her hands. She loves making jewelry and quilts and crocheting. Please, God, heal her hands and eyes so she can do that again. She loves to be creative. It brings her so much joy. Are You going to take that from her too?" *O Lord, I believe. Help my unbelief.*

Since she still had no short-term memory, we had to remind Jen every day of her name, the date, and that she had been in a car accident. As hard as it was for Andy and me to leave the hospital at night, Jen never seemed to be sad or worried or even notice. She didn't know or care whether we were coming or going. Over and over we told her why she was in the hospital and what was happening.

The nurses let her help pick out her clothes in the morning. By this time, Jen had quite a collection of comfortable pajama pants, so she and Angie went through them and chose something for the day. Would it be the cupcake pants or the polka-dot pants? Monkey pants? Froggy prince pants? There were tops and socks to choose from too. Going through the process gave Jen at least a little say-so in what happened to her during the day, a small measure of control.

During her therapy sessions Jen would often cry in frustration and despair one moment and sing praise songs with joy and happiness in the very next instant. She thanked the nurses over and over again for their help, even when they gave her a shot. To me the fact that Jen could participate in therapy at all was a direct answer to prayer. Sometimes I caught a glimpse of the old Jen, but for now I had to be satisfied with the memory of who Jennifer once was and the hope of who she was to become.

The physical therapists, Chad and Scottie, helped her get out of bed and into a wheelchair under her own power. They would say, "Jen, it's dancing day! Stand up and put your arms around our necks." In that position they could maneuver her into a wheelchair without using a lift. They started teaching her to walk again using a wheeled support with a sort of shelf at elbow level on three sides that she could lean on. One of them always walked close behind her for safety. At first she took only one or two steps. Then she started walking in the hallway a few more steps every day. Not wanting to miss a minute of her recovery, I went ahead of her in my wheelchair, rolling backwards so I could watch her. I got to where I could move pretty fast in the wheelchair by pushing myself with my good foot. In fact, there were times when Angie, out of the corner of her eye, saw the top of my head fly by the nurse's station and thought a child was running in the hall. But that little running child was actually me zooming to the therapy room.

One day when I was watching Jen do her occupational therapy, she started putting her legs up on the table in front of her and pushing backwards in her wheelchair. The therapist was grabbing something across the room and didn't see Jen as she started leaning back farther and farther. My motherly instincts kicked in, and I jumped up to catch Jen's head as it fell, completely forgetting that I was also in a wheelchair and had a broken foot and arm. I landed sprawled out in a flying Superman position flat on my face. Jennifer, on the other hand, was completely fine because her wheelchair had a device on it to keep her from falling backwards. If only I had known! As soon as the therapist made sure I was okay, we all had a good laugh.

The roller-coaster ride was never ending. It was so exciting to see Jennifer praising God and singing songs to Jesus. Not only was her soul intact, it was more keenly attuned than ever before. But because it was so sharp and the rest of her was so injured, the contrast in everything was hard for me to take and at times almost unbelievable. Watching Jen sing and hearing her pray tempted me to think she was more physically healed than she was. But my dreams would be quickly shattered every time I followed her to therapy. Her mind and body were completely broken, yet her soul was uninjured. It was encouraging and devastating at the same time.

The whole time she remained at Kluge, Jen was never alone. Female friends stayed with her in shifts day and night for fear she might choke or hurt herself. Since initially she was almost blind, the visitor had to be someone Jen recognized from the sound of her voice. There was no bed for an overnight guest, so the volunteer slept in a reclining chair next to Jen. Brandon's mother brought a lawn chair from home to sleep in every Saturday and Sunday night because she said it was more comfortable than the hospital chair.

Because there was a rotating list of overnight volunteers, I taped a sheet of paper to the end of Jen's bed to remind them of their most essential jobs:

1. Comb hair
2. Wash face
3. Brush teeth
4. Sing praise music

5. Pray
6. Read the Bible

Jen was always on her best behavior when Brandon and Kae were there. Kae came to spend the night with Jen every Friday, sacrificing the start of her weekend to be with her friend. She would climb into bed with Jen, and they would laugh and giggle. Kae told Jen the same stories over and over to see if she remembered hearing them before.

As the weeks stretched into months, our faithful friends never wavered in their commitment to helping us. The visitors' journal grew as thick as a catalog, and still the inspiring messages kept coming. I read the new ones every day and never failed to be encouraged by them.

12/8/06

Chic-a-bee

Tonight was the first time I heard your beautiful voice. You said, "Kaelynn" and "I love you too!" That made me so happy! I love every moment I get to be by your side! We were up all night with you, and you were talking up a storm! We also had a burping contest—you won!

You're my hero, Jen! I'm always thinking about you and praying for you!

Kae Queen

12/10/06

Jen,

You poked fun at Uncle John Barrick and said he was rowdy and you were going to take him down! You reminded us how

*hilarious Brandon looked doing the Macarena dance at his
birthday surprise! You told Mr. Knight he had enough hugs from
you already, and then you burst out laughing.*

Mrs. Knight

The night of the accident was supposed to be the first time we had
Brandon's family over to our house. That seemed like a lifetime ago.
I didn't have any idea how Brandon's relationship with Jen would
develop now; that depended on the two of them and the nature of
Jen's recovery. Clearly for the foreseeable future she would not have
the emotional maturity or focus to have a boyfriend. Yet it was such
a blessing to have the Knight family's help and their heartfelt prayers.

On December 14 Jen took her first steps with a special walker.
And her wonderful sense of humor began flickering back to life: she
asked Chad and Scottie, who were both bald, if they'd like to borrow
her hair!

The bedside journal was filled with notes on that memorable day.
Jen's cheerleading coach, Kelly, arrived with three pieces of luggage
for her scheduled overnight stay. We jokingly asked if she planned to
stay for the entire week. On December 14 she wrote,

Jen's First Steps

*Jen, you took your first steps today in PT with a PT walker.
You didn't take just one step, you walked across the room! This
morning when you were confused and in pain you cried out,
"Lord, we need You," and within seconds you were calm!*

*In school Miss Penni asked for a word that starts with C . . .
and you said "Calvary." Penni asked you to spell your mom's
name, and it started with an L. You spelled L-O-V-E. How
sweet!*

That same day I wrote an entry in the journal. It was so clear to me how God was moving in the life of this brave young lady.

12/14/06

Jen, it's Mommy. I just wanted to tell you that I love being here with you every day and praying for you and singing to you (even though I can't sing very well)! You are such a precious treasure, and I am praising God for every blessing and miracle He does for you day by day. It is amazing, Jen, to see your sweet spirit and your love for God coming out and shining for all the doctors and nurses to see and hear. What a testimony you are—to Mommy, too! You are speaking out loud everything that is in your heart, and you are praying out loud for all to hear and be changed forever. I am so proud to be your mommy, and I am just truly blessed by being in your presence because you are continually in the presence of God.

I can't imagine the plans God has for your life. I believe God is using this time to prepare you for something big. I know God has an amazing plan to use you for His kingdom and to be His mouthpiece. God is definitely giving you the boldness you were praying for. I can't wait to see the ministries God has for you. For now, I will sit by your side and pray for you without ceasing, and I will praise God for each new step that you take and each new word that you say.

Two days later Jen sang along with the CD of the concert the night of the accident. In the visitors' journal that night my mom, who stayed with Jen every Tuesday and never lost her unwavering faith, wrote:

We couldn't hear your voice, but you mouthed every word and dramatized with hand gestures. You were so proud of yourself as you sang the solo part. You were singing, 'His eye is on the sparrow and I know He watches me.' I couldn't help but cry.

It wasn't the first time Jen had done something like that, but along with the other recent improvements it inspired my dad to add:

Your eyes are bright, your smile is big, and your spirit is glorious. You even quoted the names of all 66 books of the Bible. It is amazing to hear God speaking through you. Today you prayed, "You are good, Father. You allow things to happen. We love You because You are good." After forty-five minutes, Grammy Donna tried to say Amen so you would finish your prayer, but you didn't pay any attention to her. She was worried you would be too tired for therapy in the morning—and she was right.

As sure as Jen was of Jesus' presence in her life, she was still struggling to put her memories and experiences together in some order. Jen's dear friend Kae wrote about that challenge after a visit.

Everything is hard for you right now. You don't understand what is going on and why things are different. You don't wonder why you are missing school or why I am staying with you so often. Maybe God is protecting your heart and mind from the struggle that you will no doubt face when you realize what has happened. I know that when we tell you what has happened you don't understand and you soon forget. You have no emotions yet because of your injury so you never get sad. A laugh comes, but soon is replaced by nothing. It is like you go blank and forget what was funny. You inspire me to be strong and hold on. I know you are confused. I can see it on your face like when you said to me, "Kae, I can't . . . I just can't . . . I can't see anything.

*Not even you!" I just want to be able to have a full conversation
with you and for you to be able to understand and comprehend
what I am saying.*

Kae

One beautiful, sunny day just before Christmas, I thought it would
be good for all of us in Jen's room to get some fresh air. When I suggested we go outside, Jen shook her head no and began moaning
in protest. She didn't like going out into the bright light. Also she
was sometimes uncomfortable in the wheelchair because she couldn't
hold her head up and her chin would get stuck under the neck brace
if she moved her head from side to side. Knowing that going out
would still be good for her, I reminded Jen that she could do all
things through Christ who strengthens her. My friend Pam Foster
was there, and I convinced her to push Jen in her wheelchair. She
has a special gift of mercy and never wanted to upset Jen in any way.
I wheeled myself out close behind them for a "roll" in the hospital
courtyard. We went through the courtyard toward the gazebo.

Pam was feeling down that day. She had begged God for the
Rapture to come many times in the past few weeks because she didn't
want her dear friends to suffer anymore. She couldn't bear to see Jen
in pain. "Maybe we shouldn't have prayed for the Lord to save Jen's
life," she had said. "Maybe she would have been better off going to
heaven where there is no pain and no suffering."

Jen's legs started moving around uncontrollably. To calm her, Pam
knelt beside Jen's wheelchair and started rubbing her legs and feet,
and we started singing Christmas carols. At first, Jen didn't seem
interested and kept moaning with her eyes shut. We kept right on
singing and making a joyful noise. All of a sudden Jen opened her

eyes, but she wasn't looking at us. She didn't even know we were there. Her face had an ethereal look, and she was smiling. She started singing along, but she wasn't singing to us. It was as if she could see something that we couldn't. There was a joy coming from her face like I had never seen before. At the end of "Silent Night" she exclaimed "AMEN!" still beaming and looking at a spot next to her. I can't really explain what we felt. I wasn't sure what had happened.

"Jen," I asked, "do you see Jesus?"

"*Yes!*" she said, almost jumping out of her wheelchair. "Don't you see Him? He is standing right beside me!" She was almost giggling, and her face was like an angel's.

Pam and I started to weep. We had no doubt whatsoever that Jen could see Jesus. He had to be real because Jen wasn't capable of imagining that. We knew our lives would never be the same. There are no words to explain the sensation. We knew we were in the presence of Almighty God. Jen was filled to overflowing with joy and peace. This broken child who often didn't recognize her own mother could see Jesus standing right beside her. I felt an absolute assurance that no matter what the future held, Jesus was Jen's escort and He was never going to leave her.

I would have given anything to see God like Jen did! Pam and I cried the rest of the day because we felt God's presence in such a powerful way. God was so real to Jen. She couldn't do anything by herself. She couldn't eat, and she didn't have a memory. In one second her whole life had changed and everything had been taken from her. But none of that mattered to her now because Jesus was standing right beside her.

She had severe damage to her optic nerve and cortical blindness as well as the brain injury, which meant her eyes processed the light signals but her brain didn't know what they meant. She couldn't look at me and know I was her mother until she heard my voice. A more accurate description would be to say that Jen couldn't see things in the world the rest of us see. And yet God was revealing a miraculous world of His own to her day by day that she could see perfectly. She couldn't see me, but she could see Him!

This incredible experience took place on December 18, the do-or-die day that determined whether or not Jen could continue her rehab at Kluge. That day she stayed awake for three hours, the doctors declared her ready for full rehab, and she was officially approved to go forward. Once again God had piled one miracle on top of another.

On Christmas Day Jen and our extended family sang Christmas carols in the cafeteria while Grammy Donna played the piano. It was an awesome performance. The nurses even listened in on the intercom. Considering her injuries, nobody would have blamed Jen for being mad at God over what had happened to her. Instead she radiated joy and contentment and a sense of purpose. She was God's girl, completely content and at peace in His arms.

Josh sang along next to Jen's wheelchair, his eyes filled with hope and admiration. He was so proud of his sister. Even though she still showed no emotion toward other people and couldn't respond, he leaned over and tenderly kissed her cheek. On his Christmas card to me he wrote, "Dear Mom, I hope you have the best Christmas ever. I love you so much and am so glad you are alive. I believe with all my heart that God will heal Jen. So keep being strong! You are the best mom in all the world, and I want you to always remember that. Love, Josh."

A few days later, on December 29, I wrote a long journal entry while Jen was taking her nap. The words kept pouring out until it had grown into both a recap of all that had happened over the last three incredible months and a look ahead to whatever God in His mercy and wisdom had in store. Though I had no idea what to expect, I knew God had plans for us. My guess was that He'd already let Jen in on them.

All of the hours spent at cheerleading, soccer, and gymnastics. How we were running all the time! Jen's favorite thing to do was play her guitar in her room at night and sing praise songs to God. She loved sitting in her green chair and reading three chapters of the Bible every day. She longed for her quiet time in her room with the Lord. She loved journaling her thoughts and prayers to God. She wanted to be like Mary sitting at the feet of Jesus, and she made it a priority.

I think of her lying in that hospital bed for eight weeks, her little body thrashing and moaning in pain. We are all sad for Jen and for everything she will have to "give up"—sports, fun activities, etc. But Jen is singing praise songs to God and praying out loud continuously. When you ask her how she is, she says, "Wonderful" and "Fantastic." Her sweet spirit overflows to everyone who enters her room. The whole hospital is talking about her. Why?

She has been sitting in God's presence, sitting at the feet of Jesus for eight weeks. He has been communicating with her and filling her with His joy and peace. Instead of running from this activity to that activity, Jen has been sitting still while God has been using her testimony and her life beyond her wildest imagination. This was truly the prayer of Jen's heart. But none of us knew what that would mean. Jen hasn't done one thing except seek God with all of her heart. God has done it all! "He must increase . . . I must decrease" is one of Jen's new favorite verses.

Jen's life will never again be normal, and I must let go of my dreams for Jen and realize that God is preparing her for a ministry that is far greater. It is not a matter of what Jen will have to "give up," but rather it is a time for rejoicing because all that really matters is what we do for the Lord. That is the only thing that will outlive us and last for eternity!!!

I am confident that when Jen becomes fully aware of the accident and the coma and the months away from school and friends, she will be at total peace with it. God has already prepared her heart for such a time as this, and I believe she has seen Jesus with her own eyes and has been in His presence continuously. I pray that some day she will be able to write about it and tell us what she has seen and heard.

Just a few days later, on New Year's Eve, Jen herself shed some light on what she had been experiencing since the night of November 5. Tammy Knight was spending the night at Kluge with Jen, and in the journal we kept in our daughter's room, Tammy wrote about a conversation they had:

December 31, 2006

Hey Jen! It's New Year's Eve. It's 8 p.m., and we are both yawning already. LOL

I asked you if you felt scared or alone, and you replied, "He hasn't left me, not once. The journey has been good."

What journey, Jen? "With Him . . . there."

Were you in heaven? "No, not in heaven, but I was there. I was with Him."

Why did you come back, Jen? "He decided."

Who decided? "The Father. He is good to me. It was His decision. His plan."

Do you have things to do here? "Yes, I do. . . . Many things."

Then Jen said we needed to pray and thank God so we prayed.

CHAPTER 9

TREASURE UNDER THE BED

Your lives are a letter written in our hearts. . . . This "letter" is written not with pen and ink, but with the Spirit of the living God. It is carved not on tablets of stone, but on human hearts.

2 CORINTHIANS 3:2-3

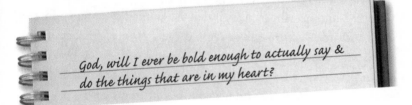

God, will I ever be bold enough to actually say & do the things that are in my heart?

Jen's journal, ten months before the crash

THE MOMENTOUS YEAR OF 2006 CAME TO AN END, and 2007 began with Jen continuing her slow progress at Kluge. I still held out hope that God would restore her completely and she'd go back to being the lively, active, quick-thinking young woman she once was. Though I wanted her to heal, I also hoped that as she recovered she'd hold on to her newfound outspokenness for the Lord. It was a gift she had always wanted, and it gave her such joy to talk about her faith so boldly.

While God clearly had a plan for her future, none of the doctors could tell us what would happen. Because the brain is so miraculously complex, the long-term effects of brain injuries are unpredictable. No two cases are alike, so doctors couldn't be sure what skills

Jen would recover, in what order they would come back, or how far she would progress. She would definitely have permanent damage, but they just didn't know how much; she might improve some more, but there was a chance she wouldn't progress beyond where she was now. The only thing doctors were sure of was that she would never be the person she was before the accident.

Judy Ashley, a close friend and my longtime prayer partner, was a nurse I'd known for years before we moved to Lynchburg. One day she called me and asked, "Linda, what is Jen's favorite color?"

"Lime green," I replied, thinking it was an odd question.

"And what's her favorite Scripture verse?"

After I told her, she explained that she wanted to order silicone wristbands for Jen's friends to remind them to pray for her. The wristbands would symbolize a special personal connection between Jen and everyone who wore one. And the money they raised from selling them would go toward her continued therapy costs.

Because she was a nurse, Judy could already sense what I didn't yet fully appreciate: the road ahead was long. Though Jen was now awake—one of many miracles we had already seen—she still had a long way to go.

Not long after our conversation, Judy began distributing the dazzling lime-green wristbands. One side read MIRACLE 4 JEN; the other side read 1 COR. 2:9, her favorite verse. Many of our friends in Pennsylvania began wearing them. Judy also sent one thousand wristbands to Jen's cheerleading squad, who began selling them every morning at the school's welcome center.

Andy and I greeted the new year still in wheelchairs, still sleeping in hospital beds at Al and Fran's. Andy remained in terrible pain, groaning through the night as he tossed around trying to get comfortable. He still had potentially dangerous blood clots in his leg and took medication for that problem as well as for the pain. His parents continued to take him to his own almost-daily treatments before driving him to Charlottesville to visit Jen.

My left leg and foot continued healing. In time, I was told, I should be able to walk again, although I might have a limp or chronic pain. Just as with Jen, only God knew my future. That included whether or not I would regain use of my left hand. Because of nerve and tendon damage, I still couldn't move it. Doctors were considering a tendon transplant after I became stronger. Meanwhile, it dangled at my side.

Along with praying for Jen's recovery, I sometimes prayed that I'd be able to move my hand and not have to have surgery. Lying in my bed at Andy's parents' one day, I realized my hand was raised up off the sheet. It was moving! This was the miracle I'd prayed for!

"Nanny!" I yelled. "My hand's working! My hand's working!" It took me a minute to realize I hadn't actually raised the hand after all. In my excitement I hadn't noticed that the upper part of my hospital bed was at an angle, which allowed my hand to stay in an upright position without falling forward. It had been a thrilling moment, though ultimately it was a false alarm. Maybe God would see to that miracle another time.

As the new year began, Paula Egel continued scheduling our faithful friends to be with me and Jen. Every morning someone came to help me get washed and dressed, then loaded me and my wheelchair into their car to go to Kluge. I could scarcely wait to see Jen. Sometimes I arrived after her therapy had already started. Those days I went flying down the hall in my wheelchair to her therapy room, anxious not to miss another minute. I was always eager to see God's plan for her life that day. That same volunteer stayed with me until it was time to drive me back to Al and Fran's house.

While I had help during daytime hours, Jen continued to have company through the night in her room at the rehab center. The entries these friends added to the visitors' journal became a powerful account of Jen's journey toward whatever God had in store for her. It was a shared diary of the whole community of devoted friends who came to visit, whether for the night or only for a few minutes.

One of the first entries for 2007 was from Dr. Jerry Falwell. Since the first hour after the accident, he had mobilized the Liberty University community, students and teachers at Liberty Christian Academy, and the people at Thomas Road Baptist Church to pray for us and lend a hand any way they could. On January 3 Dr. Falwell came to visit Jen and wrote, "Jennifer, you are a miracle! It is obvious to me that God has something very special for you to do. Jen, God is using you to bring spiritual awakening in LCA and TRBC. Thousands of persons you have never met pray for you daily." He signed his entry, "Jerry Falwell. James 5:16." The verse he referenced reads, "Pray for each other so that you may be healed. The earnest prayer of a righteous person has great power and produces wonderful results." Only four months later Dr. Falwell passed away, which made the message even more poignant.

The day Dr. Falwell came by was also the day Jen rode down the hall on a giant tricycle. I have an unforgettable image of her dressed in sweatpants and wearing a helmet, her expression one of intense concentration followed by a huge grin. I went ahead of her, pushing my wheelchair backward with one foot, because I didn't want to miss a thing.

Looking back at the journal entry for the next night, I see that Polly Wooldridge stayed with Jen, as she did every Thursday. Polly's daughter Kim is one of Jen's best friends. Though Kim was in school and usually unable to come with Polly, I do remember one day when she came with her mom and sang and danced to keep Jen awake long enough to get through her therapy. Jen's comment on Kim's performance was, "That's so sad," followed by her uproarious belly laugh that we all called the seal laugh. It was rambunctious enough that the nurses came in to find out what was so funny.

A few days later Brandon arrived for one of his regular visits and caught more of Jen's unbridled laughter—and then some. He was helping Jen eat, always a tough challenge for her because of her feeding tube, sensitivity, and continuing digestive problems. The two of them got the giggles to the point where Jen spewed red Kool-Aid all over Brandon, followed by spit-out oatmeal. Brandon pretended his feelings were hurt, as he wrote in the visitors' journal, "I worked so hard to make the oatmeal because you said it was nasty before! I love being up here and spending time with you," he added. "It is the highlight of my week." Another time, Brandon coaxed her out of bed to dance to praise music, and the two of them danced for twenty minutes. It was the longest Jen had stood up since the accident.

Even while dealing with his own serious injuries, Andy never wavered in the attention and constant encouragement he gave to Jen. The same day Brandon got his oatmeal shower, January 7, Andy wrote in the journal, "I have watched you blossom into a beautiful young lady who loves the Lord. . . . Your spiritual walk and testimony to others have inspired me. . . . I love you so much. No matter how big you get and no matter where you go, you will always be my little princess and angel."

In the midst of all of Jen's struggle and heartache, the journal documented countless funny moments and meaningful interactions that helped keep my spirits up and get me through the long hours at Kluge. Jen's uninhibited thoughts made for some hilarious situations. One day she insisted that Aunt Gina stand up and sing "I'm a Duck" in the cafeteria. Gina's daughter, Jen's cousin Amanda, wrote, "You are an awesome cousin. I pray for you every day. At night I read the devotional you gave me and I think of you."

When talking to us, Jen still acted like the severely brain-injured patient she was, whose halting, slurred words we could hardly understand. Yet talking to the Lord, she was always perfectly aware and spoke in clear, complete sentences. My sister, Christy, expressed the feelings of many others when on January 10 she wrote, "For generations we will tell the story of your miracle. Our children and grandchildren and great-grandchildren will know that God set you apart to do amazing things through your body, mind, and spirit." Christy also prayed Zechariah 4:6-7, claiming God's promise for Jen and asking Him to flatten every mountain Jen had before her.

Everyone who came in contact with Jen during this time sensed the two-in-one person she had become. Only vaguely aware of the world around her and marginally functional in it, Jen lived in the presence of the Lord, who gave her the power to communicate fully and clearly with Him. Time and again Jen's visitors recorded their thoughts using the same words: "amazing," "awesome," "miraculous."

Her best friend, Kae, wrote about one special visit during this time.

January 13, 2007

We prayed together, and you almost brought me to tears. It just amazes me that whenever you talk to God, you are never confused. It is like He is giving you an abundance of wisdom and understanding. Your prayer tonight was, "Dear heavenly Father, I come to You right now and just want to thank You for everything You've done. Thank You for everything You are doing in my life. I praise You for all the people I have been able to influence. I just pray that Your will be done. Let Your glory be done. And just let Your power be revealed in the next couple

of days. Thank You for everything. Amen." Tonight I asked
you what you wanted to do when you grow up, and you said,
"I want to impact others." I know you will because you have
already impacted me in a way I will never forget.

Love, Kae

My good friend Michele Krick and her daughter Jill came from Pennsylvania to give our Lynchburg friends a break. Of all the things about Jen that Michele appreciated, including her incredible laugh and a smile that "lights up the room," what she loved most of all, she wrote, was "the way your face lights up at the mention of Jesus. The Holy Spirit fills every part of you. As I sit in the room with you while you sleep, I am drawn closer to the Lord. I feel His presence."

Jill and Jen had been friends since they were five years old. When Jill tried to feed Jen a sandwich, Jen took it in her hands and asked, "What is it?"

"It's a turkey and cheese sandwich," Jill explained.

Jen kept staring at the food with a confused look. "What do I do with it?" she asked.

"Pop it into your mouth and eat it," Jill explained.

In the journal Jill wrote that the day she heard about the accident, she was completely devastated. "I love you so much, no words can describe it! You are the reason I am more faithful with my devotions. It is hard to see you in this state, but I know God will do great and amazing things in your life." Of her first day with Jen in the hospital she said, "This has been one of the hardest and best days of my life."

As Jill had discovered, mealtime remained a challenge. Though Jen still had her feeding tube, doctors were trying to get her used to eating normally again. At first it looked like it would be easy. For two weeks she eagerly ate everything, even hospital cafeteria food. Every day she ordered a grilled turkey and cheese sandwich. Her favorite meal was a cheeseburger from Five Guys, and when anybody brought her one she devoured it on the spot.

Then suddenly she began refusing to eat any solid food at all. I think chewing was painful, and food always upset her stomach. Once she made the connection between eating and being uncomfortable, no amount of encouragement or cajoling would induce her to take a bite. We tried to bribe her with Five Guys burgers and her favorite chocolate desserts, but nothing worked. She'd say, "You eat it," or "I'll eat it later," then put it aside and forget about it.

This was a huge setback for us because we'd been so excited when she started to eat, and now she was regressing. We thought we'd overcome this challenge but we hadn't; we thought something was healed but it wasn't. This, we eventually learned, was how everything happened with Jen: three steps forward and two steps back. Or sometimes three steps forward and four steps back. Her friends challenged her to milkshake contests, seeing who could finish their shake first. Once in a while that did the trick, and we added nutritional supplements or protein powder to her serving, trying to get nourishment into her. Brandon and Kae were better than anyone else at convincing her to eat. The nurses were always glad to see them because it meant Jen would eat at least some solid food.

Since Jen couldn't stand up in the shower, she sat in a special wheelchair that the nurses wheeled into the shower room to bathe her. Whatever friend of ours was on duty went into the shower room to help the nurses—and always got her clothes soaked. Jen's skin was supersensitive so that the slightest touch made her cry in pain. Jen begged the nurses to turn off the water as soon as it started hitting her. Her screams pierced the quiet hallway, even though the nurses covered her body with towels to minimize the sensation of water spraying on her skin.

"You're hurting me! Don't you understand?" she would cry. Later when she could express herself better, Jen described the droplets of water as feeling like a thousand needles piercing her skin.

When her shower was done, I could hear Jen quietly thanking the nurses over and over for turning off the water. "Thank you. Thank you so much. Thank you." Fortunately for her, she forgot about the experience as soon as it was over. By the time she got back to her room she was praying and singing again. One day when Nanny was with her, Jen was being wheeled to her room after screaming in the shower and started singing, "Glory to God in the Highest." Nanny wondered if at that moment Jen could see angels.

Brushing her teeth was excruciating for the same reason that the shower was such torture—the slightest touch was painful. When my cousin Heidi tried to use the toothbrush on her, Jen clamped her mouth shut so tight Heidi was afraid that as she pried Jen's mouth open, she'd either hurt Jen or Jen would bite Heidi's finger. Every two hours, whoever was helping Jen that day put on a rubber glove and lightly stroked Jen's gums in hopes of desensitizing her mouth so she'd be more comfortable eating.

Jennifer had to endure so many terrible stages as her body started the long road to recovery. Every touch, every movement, and every sound was being overprocessed by Jen's struggling brain. Seeing the effects of her continuing hypersensitivity was extremely tough on Andy and me. Janis, the brilliant occupational therapist, trained the volunteers who stayed with Jen each day on how to complete the Wilbarger Deep Pressure and Proprioceptive Technique (DPPT). After learning the method, the volunteers would brush Jen's arms, legs, hands, and feet every two hours. They used a special brush with plastic bristles designed to help with sensory desensitization. This was also when Jen's helper worked on desensitizing her gums.

During one of Jen's therapy sessions, a therapist handed her a shoe and asked, "What is this?" When Jen said she didn't know, I could feel the hot tears streaking down my face. She didn't know how old she was. She didn't know if she had a brother or a sister. She couldn't write her name. When she first tried to write, all she could do was make a long horizontal squiggle on the page before breaking down in tears and shouting, "I can't! It hurts!" Her teacher, Penni, asked her what flew, a bird or an elephant? She just stared. The only time Jen wasn't confused was when she was talking to God.

Up until now, I'd been focused on nothing more than getting through the day. I hadn't thought about the future. Now I found myself wondering what we had in store over the horizon. Gina and Paula convinced me to go to a surprise birthday party for a friend of ours at a restaurant. When I arrived in a wheelchair, the restaurant had to clear a path to the table. They handled it well, but I was embarrassed at all the attention I attracted as Gina wheeled me through the room. I couldn't cut my food with one hand and had to have someone else do it for me. Another time I'm sure I would have enjoyed the conversation with my dear friends, but that day everything they talked about seemed so trivial and unimportant.

Was this what the rest of my life would be like? Would I ever be able to walk normally or use my left hand? And what about the others? Would Jen ever eat again? Would she someday enjoy a meal around the dinner table or an outing at a restaurant? Would she ever remember the life she had before the accident? Would she retain any of the knowledge or memories of those years? Would Andy recover fully? Would the pain ever go away? Would he ever play basketball again?

Even though Jen was in God's presence, praying and singing praise songs, I still couldn't have a real, coherent conversation with her. She still didn't know she was hurt. She didn't know she was in the hospital. She wasn't in reality. She had no emotions. I wanted to hug and cry with her, but she wasn't sad. If only I could connect with her again heart-to-heart! If only she could tell me what she was thinking!

I remembered how Jen used to love journaling. I knew she had journals hidden all over her room. She was such a private person that she didn't express her innermost feelings very often. The only time Jen really showed her feelings and emotions was in her journals. They were my window into the real Jennifer.

I had to see them! I had to read those journals that would reconnect me with my precious daughter.

Though it was almost three months since the accident, I hadn't been back to our house because I couldn't climb the stairs and couldn't maneuver around inside with my wheelchair. If only I could see Jen's room again! I believed it would take me back to the carefree days before the accident when Jen and Josh would come flying through the kitchen on the way to the car because we were late for school. The times we all cheered as a family for Josh at his baseball games. The times we took vacations together or had dinner out or went to a movie. Would we ever be able to do any of those things again?

I finally convinced my dad to take me to the house so I could go to Jen's room. We pulled into our driveway, and as my dad unloaded my wheelchair and helped me into it, I felt the cold January wind blow across my face. He eased me through the door, then pushed me to the foot of the staircase in the hall before going into the living room to wait. This was something I needed to do by myself.

I crawled out of the wheelchair and sat down on the first step. It would be a long haul to Jen's room at the top, but I didn't care. All I could think about was reconnecting with the daughter I knew. Steadying myself with my right hand, I pushed myself with my right foot, scooting up one step at a time until I got to the top. As I moved, I remembered the wonderful conversations I used to have with Jen, lying in bed with her at night and asking about her day. We would laugh and talk in bed for hours. Those evenings seemed an awfully long way off now.

I scooted to her door and pushed it open. Except for the dust, her room looked like she'd left it an hour ago. It was as though she'd walked out that morning and would be back any minute. Her bed was made, her brushes and hair accessories were lined up neatly on the dresser, and her favorite green chair in the corner was piled with her stuffed animals. How many hours had she sat in that chair playing the guitar and singing praise songs? How many hours reading the Bible or writing faithfully in her journals? I could almost see her there and hear her voice. *Oh, Jennifer! Oh, my precious daughter. Who on earth could have imagined what was in store for you the last time you walked through this door?*

From my vantage point on the floor I noticed an old Victorian-looking box under her bed. I fished it out and opened it. Inside was a stack of journals! As I picked up the worn, tattered notebook on top, stuffed with notes and pictures and little keepsake treasures, I felt as if I were holding Jen's heart in my hand.

I lifted the cover. Hopeful as I was, I was not prepared for the first entry, written the summer after her freshman year in high school. As I read, the old Jen sprang to life in my mind and heart. Waves of love and gratitude washed over me.

Hey God,

Wow, have I told You lately how amazing You are? Father, why do You continue to bless me? God, as I was just thinking about this past year I've realized that I can honestly say that this has been the very best year of my entire life!

Like no joke! Like I am speechless! I've been able to be on varsity cheerleading, winning States and taking second at Nationals. I was in the Junior Miss pageant and was homecoming representative for the 9th grade class. I made varsity soccer as a freshman which is hard to do! I was able to go to the junior-senior banquet with Brandon Knight and have had an absolutely wonderful year getting to know him. I also got highest honors in academics.

So, God, now do You understand what I mean? Like I could go on and on! Wow, You have been so good to me and I want to thank You for that. I feel like I really don't deserve all the blessings but I am so thankful for them!

God, I'm beginning to wonder how I will ever be able to top this year. Nothing bad has happened and I HAVE NO REGRETS. I pray that this upcoming year as a sophomore will blow my freshman year out of the water. God, use me in ways I never imagined in the years to come.

I could scarcely catch my breath. All I wanted to do was weep. Jen loved the Lord with all her heart. She didn't deserve to be struggling in a rehab clinic. I cried out loud, "Lord, why?" I secretly wondered if she would ever be able to do these things again. As I flipped through the pages, my eye caught an entry written just before the beginning of her sophomore year, less than three months before the accident.

August 21, 2006

Dear Heavenly Father,

So here I am with my summer drawing to a close and with the upcoming school year fast approaching! Wow, it's crazy how time flies and years go by and how life goes on! Honestly, God, I'm super excited about this school year. I am mainly excited about having an impact on everyone around me! About being a witness, a light in the darkness, showing God's unconditional love. I want not only for God to be recognized but for Him to be worshiped, adored, and lifted up! God, I can't stand the lifestyle of the world! It is repulsive. Why would anyone desire to become like the world? It just doesn't make sense!

Lord, I am not going to blend in because I know I was born to stand out! To stand alone? Maybe (if that's what it takes). Lord, this life that I now live is not mine, but Yours. It is Yours to do with it as You please. I have died to self! My desires, dreams, and hopes for the future don't matter. So God, pretty much I'm begging You to use me.

Father, I know You take the foolish ones, the weak ones, the lowly people, and use them to shame the strong and wise, God, so that means You can take me just as I am (1 Cor. 1:26-29). You can take me, a nobody, and turn me into a somebody. God, I know with You all things are possible (Matthew 19:26). Take this year and my life and allow Your glory to shine! Take it and use it to its fullest potential!

Your faithful servant, Jen

I fell on my face, sobbing uncontrollably, fighting for air. For the first time I understood that before the accident God in His sovereignty had prepared my daughter's heart for all that happened, and she was completely surrendered to Him. She had begged God to take her life and do the impossible. Of course, God knew exactly what was going to happen. With God there are no accidents. And I took comfort in the fact that God could still restore her to be exactly as she was, only better, with this intense and wonderful outspokenness. Surely that was why He'd spared her life and put her through so much.

August 28, 2006

Dear God,

I realize that I am not perfect and I fail You every day. Lord, if I could focus on improving one thing this year, I want it to be BOLDNESS! I realize that is what I need in order to really make a difference.

God, I have prayed constantly about You doing great things in my life. I realize that in order to actually follow through I will need the boldness and courage it requires. I want to lead many people to Christ. I pray that You will use my life to be a testimony to others.

God, please bless this year and use me to accomplish the impossible. I am open and ready to be used by You and for Your glory. I pray that You will give me the faith of a mustard seed. Lord, I want to move mountains.

My eyes devoured the pages like a starving beggar at a banquet. Jen had prayed constantly for boldness and courage to proclaim Christ, no matter what the cost.

As her sophomore year started, Jen was on fire for the Lord with an intensity and dedication that showed no signs of slacking off.

September 2006

Go Anywhere . . . Do Anything!

Clayton King spoke at our Wednesday night service, and I was completely moved. It was so clear to me that God was calling me to missions. I am not really sure what that will mean! Lord, I want You to know that I am willing. . . . I am willing to go anywhere and do anything.

I'll admit, I have no idea where You are leading my life and honestly, when I think about it, I become very excited, but at the same time, scared!

I just pray, God, that You will direct my life and allow me to completely trust You. I know You will reveal Your plan for my life in the right timing, so there is no need for me to become anxious! Lord, I just feel like You are calling me in this direction and I want You to know that I am Your obedient servant! I am pressing forward toward the goal to win the prize that You have in store for me! (Phil. 3:14)

Amen!

October 10, 2006

A Day to Remember

I don't really know how to put this into words. My testimony is that I was saved when I was four and was baptized at age seven. This is what I have always said when people ask me when I was saved. But it hit me recently with the reality that I don't know the time, place, or day. I don't even know if I meant it, I was so young!

Today, Father, I put an end to my doubt. Satan can no longer rob me of my joy! He no longer can put any doubt in my mind because today, October 10, 2006, around 10:30 a.m. in chapel, I got rid of all doubt forever!

Adrian Depres was the speaker in chapel and during the invitation, I went forward and fell on my knees. Tears just streamed down my face as I rededicated my life to the Lord. How could I be satisfied where I was at? I wanted more!

I surrender all to You, Lord!

Every year, Jen's school had a See You at the Pole rally, a day when students gather around the flagpole for voluntary prayer (which even public schools have to allow!). Jen wrote about how Josh impressed her with his prayer, and how she longed for her little brother's boldness.

October 2006

Lord,

As many people began to gather and pray and share their hearts, suddenly I heard this sweet little voice that was all too familiar to me. It was my little brother praying out loud and I about had a heart attack anticipating what he would say. His prayer was short, sweet, but definitely to the point. At that moment I have never been prouder of him in all my life!

Lord, if he is already bold enough to stand out for You in the 5th grade, then I can't even begin to fathom what You are going to do in his life. There is no doubt that You have made him to be a leader. I pray that in the years to come he will continue to draw closer to You.

God, I don't think Josh will ever realize the impact he made on my life that day. Even though I had been praying in my heart, I wasn't as bold as Josh to pray out loud. I know You heard my silent prayers but I want Josh's boldness in my life. I am practically jealous of it!!

Reading Jen's journal entry written three days before the accident gave me goose bumps. She wanted to be different. She wanted a challenge. God heard her heart.

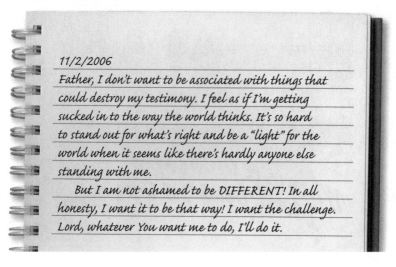

> *11/2/2006*
>
> *Father, I don't want to be associated with things that could destroy my testimony. I feel as if I'm getting sucked in to the way the world thinks. It's so hard to stand out for what's right and be a "light" for the world when it seems like there's hardly anyone else standing with me.*
>
> *But I am not ashamed to be DIFFERENT! In all honesty, I want it to be that way! I want the challenge. Lord, whatever You want me to do, I'll do it.*

As I read, I realized that God had a much bigger plan for Jen than we did. She had begged Him to take her life and do the impossible with it. Jen prayed for boldness, and now she had it. She was completely uninhibited and didn't care what people thought of her. This reserved child who once could not say her thoughts out loud was now wearing her heart on the outside for everyone to see. She gave voice to every thought she had without hesitation, and it was all about the Lord!

I couldn't explain it at the time, but finding those treasures under the bed gave me a great hope that God was going to bring thousands to His Kingdom through Jen's words. I tore out some of the pages and carried them with me everywhere I went from then on, as an encouragement and a reminder. I have them with me to this day.

CHAPTER 10

STARTING FROM ZERO

God is our refuge and strength, always ready to help in times
of trouble.   PSALM 46:1

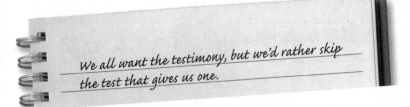

*We all want the testimony, but we'd rather skip
the test that gives us one.*

Written on Jen's homework pad, four days before the crash

ANDY, JOSH, AND I MOVED BACK HOME ON FEBRUARY 1, 2007, almost
three months after the wreck. Jen would be released from Kluge in
little more than a week, and we had to figure out how to take care of
her without hospital staff on call 24/7. We had hoped Jen could stay
longer at the rehab center because she was receiving such fantastic
therapy on a level we could never duplicate at home. Her doctors
tried to convince our insurance company to allow Jen to stay at
Kluge for ten more weeks, but they only agreed to seven more days.
Jen wasn't ready to leave the world-class facilities at Kluge, but we
had no choice. Now that she was medically stable and walking with
guided assistance, the insurance company wouldn't pay for any more

treatment. She met their physical requirements for release, and they knew her brain would take years to heal—if it ever did.

Faithful friends who had already spent weeks or months with Jen in rehab and with me in the hospital or at Gramps and Nanny's made plans to help us around the clock—as though they hadn't already poured themselves into our lives and sacrificed so much for us! It amazed me that they seemed as fresh and enthusiastic as the day they started. Lisa Bryant, our nurse friend, agreed to come to the house every weekday as a paid attendant for Jen and me so Andy could go back to work part time. During those first several weeks, he remained on crutches and had to elevate his leg while at work. My childhood friend LeeAnn Miller, who had rushed to my side in those first days of crisis, left her family in Ohio again to help encourage all of us with the transition home.

Our weekly meetings with Jen's treatment team at Kluge began to focus on how to continue her rehab at home. The doctors reminded us again that Jen's recovery would continue for years, and they had no idea how much she would ultimately recover. One of the hardest things to hear was that, after all we had been through, this was only the beginning of Jen's long road back. Dr. Peter Patrick, a brilliant psychologist and director of psychology/neuropsychology at Kluge, had more than thirty years of experience treating patients like Jen. "You're in a marathon," he told us, "and the race is just beginning. What you've been through so far is the easy part. The hard part lies ahead." Those were chilling words to someone whose physical, spiritual, and mental resources were already absolutely exhausted.

Before our final meeting, we had to go on a family outing with only a driver from the hospital along to help us. This was one of the tasks required in order for Jen to be released. They gave us a list of destinations to choose from. My heart sank as I read down the page, eliminating each choice one by one and becoming more depressed by the minute. Jen still could hardly see anything, so she couldn't enjoy a shopping mall or clothing store. Getting her to eat solid food was a daily battle due to her stomach pain and nausea, so a restaurant was out of the question. The January weather was far too gloomy and cold for a trip to the park. Finally we settled on a visit to a nearby pet store.

It was a dry but dreary, bone-chilling day. To accommodate two wheelchairs plus Andy's crutches, we had to travel in a cargo van. Our friend Lisa Bryant and Jen's cheerleading coach, Kelly Neighbors, who'd both been trained to help with Jen's home care, came to lend a hand. Just getting us all bundled into our winter coats and gloves and then loaded and buckled in was a major ordeal. I was worn out and demoralized even before we left the parking lot. As the van began to move, Jennifer immediately started feeling dizzy and queasy. We loudly sang praise songs trying to give her something to focus on besides the nausea. By the time we finished the ten-minute drive to the pet store, Jen had already erupted into tears of pain and frustration.

Getting everybody out of the van and Jen and me into our wheelchairs was another hassle. When we were all finally ready our wagon train was wheeled inside, where a friendly clerk pulled a soft, white rabbit from a cage and set it on Jen's lap. Stroking its long, soft fur seemed to calm her down. Though she still didn't register any emotion, it looked like she enjoyed holding the bunny. A few minutes later Jen was wheeled over to the fish tank where brightly colored tropical fish flashed and darted among the gently swaying underwater plants. Within seconds, watching the fish brought on another wave of nausea. Jen started crying and saying she was dizzy and sick. We packed up and headed back to Kluge.

The trip was a devastating experience. Being with Jen in the outside world underscored to me how seriously affected she was by her brain injury. It was one thing to be with her in the hospital and in therapy sessions, surrounded by professionals and other patients with similar disabilities. The fact that Jen was nearly blind, couldn't walk, and had the brain function of a four-year-old was nothing out of the ordinary within the protective environment of Kluge. But in a public place, it was a disaster both for Jen and for us. Even if Andy and I were perfectly healthy, how could we ever handle Jennifer at one of Josh's ball games or on a trip to the grocery store?

How would we ever function again as a normal family?

The doctors still gave us no hope for any type of "normal" future for Jen. "What we do know," one of them said, "is that every brain injury is different and each person heals in their own way. You'll have to be patient. Jen has already astounded us by surviving the accident and coming as far as she has. But we simply have no answers for what the future may hold for her."

Even after three months, I was still getting my head and my heart around the truth of what Jen's future would be like. She would never be able to play sports again. No soccer, gymnastics, roller coasters, bicycling, ice-skating, trampolines, or anything else that would shake her brain. Everything, *everything* was going to be different. All I could do was pray that the Lord would show me what to do and give me the strength to do it somehow.

Back at our house, I got a sense of how different life would be every time I went into Jen's bedroom. Being there was such a reminder of who she had been before the accident. Her door was completely covered front and back with fun pictures of cheerleading and friends and gymnastics, along with Jen's favorite verses and quotes typed out and placed diagonally and strategically throughout the pictures. Using her creativity and love of color, she'd produced a montage masterpiece. She'd even painted purple and lime-green circles and taped them to her bedroom walls one day when I wasn't home (because she knew I'd object). She had cheerleading and soccer trophies everywhere, along with a triathlete award for playing three seasons of varsity sports as a ninth grader.

Above her bedroom light switch she had taped words from John 3:30: "He must become greater, I must become less," so she would see it every time she entered her room. Next to her bed on her nightstand was a piece of hot-pink posterboard where she had boldly printed a paraphrase of Philippians 4:6-7: "Do not be anxious about anything, but in everything by PRAYER and petition with thanksgiving, present your requests to God. And the PEACE of God which passes all understanding will guard your hearts and your minds in Christ Jesus." It was amazing to me that a fifteen-year-old child would choose that verse to be by her bed. It was exactly what I needed to hear.

There in the corner sat her lime-green oversize chair. She loved to sit in it every day and have her quiet time with the Lord, journaling her prayers to God and reading her Bible. I remember getting upset at her one day because she had been setting her alarm and getting up at 6 a.m., which I thought was way too early. But I felt guilty when I learned she was spending that time with God before she got ready for school. That's an example of how private she was—she never told me why she was getting up early. Beside the chair was a wooden table with devotionals and prayer journals. There were also notes I'd written to encourage her; she had saved every one.

I kept drawing hope and assurance from Jen's journals. After we moved back home, I found about ten more journals in her room that I hadn't discovered during my January visit. There were journals on the nightstand, journals on her dresser, journals hidden in closets and drawers all over her room. My once-quiet daughter, who seemed to keep every deep thought inside, had poured her heart into one notebook after another.

On the first page of one journal she'd written:

> *This book contains my hidden feelings and emotions that most people don't normally see. If anyone ever reads this then maybe they will get a small glimpse of what really goes on in Jennifer Nicole's head. My hope is that this journal will be a written account of how I am growing closer to the Lord everyday!*
>
> *My main goal and focus is God Alone! Only the things you do for eternity will last and I want to make the most of my life here on earth. God, make me and mold me into the person I was meant to be....*
>
> *God, I believe that together we can be an unstoppable team!*

Two journals were filled with prayer requests for her friends and family, nearly four hundred entries in all. Then she'd gone back and written how God had answered each prayer. Sometimes it wasn't the answer she prayed for. For example, she prayed for her great-grandpa Don to be healed from his cancer, and the answer she recorded was, "God took him to heaven!"

In another journal she wrote a whole page about me, thoughts she'd never shared with me before:

> My mom is totally awesome! She sacrifices everything, from her free time to giving us the biggest piece of cake. She is a hard worker and she never slacks! She is always busy and puts others above herself. I am so thankful for a godly mom who loves me with all her heart, I know she will always be there for me and support me 100%.
>
> My mom is very different from other moms because she is very pretty and I always keep her in style. Some people think we are sisters (LOL). She goes with me on all my missions trips and is my gymnastics coach. She supports me in cheerleading by leading the devotions weekly.
>
> She can be very embarrassing, but super FUN! All of my friends love and adore her. I bet they wish they had a mom as cool as her!! :)

Besides prayer journals, there were books full of sermon notes and personal diaries with impressions and thoughts about her friends, her life, and her goals. Some were stuffed with loose notes and clippings. One of the most awesome and moving journals was full of messages and prayers for her future husband. She didn't even know who it would be or when she would meet him, but she was already praying for God's blessing on him and on their life together.

I sat on the floor in her room reading page after page for hours at a time, feeling lifted up and encouraged but also confused and unsettled and devastated. I sobbed uncontrollably, the huge, unrestrained sobs of a frightened child. There are no words to describe the emotion I was feeling. I was so proud of my daughter, so amazed at her spiritual depth, but I was so torn.

How could God let this happen to Jen of all people? She had such a pure heart! She loved Him so completely!

Yet at the same time I knew on some level that I believed in God with all my heart and soul. I believed God would heal her completely. I refused to let myself doubt Him and His purposes.

We had one last administrative hurdle to clear before Jen's discharge. Two people had to take care of her at Kluge for twenty-four hours on two separate days with no help from the staff. Because of our injuries, Andy and I couldn't possibly do it, so Lisa Bryant and Kelly Neighbors tackled that challenge on our behalf. They handled everything flawlessly—keeping track of a long list of medications; feeding Jen through her feeding tube; helping her to the bathroom and back dozens of times; encouraging her in her physical, occupational, and speech therapy; getting her to brush her teeth and wash her face; singing praise songs, reading the Bible, and praying together. They responded professionally and selflessly to every need.

February 9, 2007, dawned gray, cold, and windy. This was the big day. Jen was coming home. The fact filled me with equal parts joy and apprehension. It was an essential step in her healing, though I still had no idea how we could manage taking care of her in the long term. Only God could see the future; only He had the answers.

The discharge report, which summarized Jen's current condition, was not encouraging. The first page was from the speech therapist. I opened the file and started to read: "Jen is in the Confused,

Daddy and his little princess at Jen's second birthday party

GROWING UP

RIGHT ▶

Jen (seven) and Josh (three) clowning around. Josh looked up to Jen and wanted to be just like her, and she always took care of him.

ABOVE ▲

This is the first photo ever taken of Andy (sixteen) and me (fourteen). I was afraid to smile because I didn't want my braces to show!

Jen, Brandon, Megan, and Kae on the field after a Liberty Christian Academy football game, just a few weeks before the crash

As a freshman, Jen competed at the 2006 Christian Cheer Nationals—and placed second!

SPECIAL MOMENTS

Jen and me before her first formal banquet. I was nervous about letting her go since she was only fourteen, but she had a wonderful time . . . and now I'm so glad she had that experience.

Our van, after the accident, with the roof removed. You can see why I believe it's a miracle any of us survived this crash.

EVERYTHING CHANGES

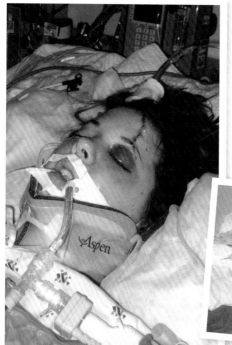

◄ LEFT

Jen in a coma and fighting for her life in the ICU

BELOW ▼

Finally reunited with Jen, sixteen days after the accident. I'm reading from a notebook full of letters written to her by friends and family.

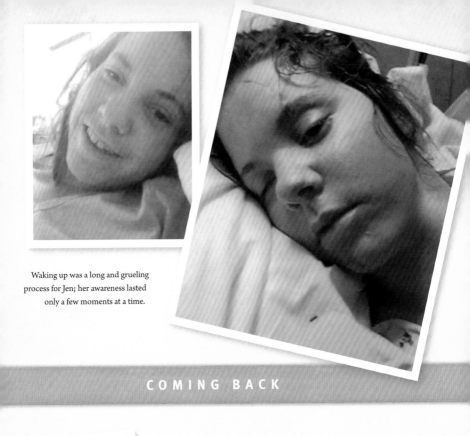

Waking up was a long and grueling process for Jen; her awareness lasted only a few moments at a time.

COMING BACK

◄ LEFT

Jen taking her first steps for the second time in her life

BELOW ▼

Jen with my father ("Papa Ed") on Christmas Day 2006 at the Kluge Children's Rehabilitation Center

ABOVE ▲

Josh kissing his beloved big sister

◄ LEFT

Jen's vision was so impaired that I had to get very close in order for her to see me.

SURROUNDED BY LOVE

Bringing Jen home on February 9, 2007! We kept the celebration small and simple so she wouldn't be overwhelmed: (left to right) Kae, Megan, Brandon, Zach, and Josh.

WE COME HOME!

8/21/06

Anything is Possible w/You!
Dear Heavenly Father,
    So here I am w/my summer drawing to a close & with the upcoming school year fastly approaching! Wow, its crazy how time flies, years go by, & how life goes on! Honestly, God im super excited about this school year. I am mainly excited about having an impact on everyone around me! About being a witness, a light in the darkness, showing God's unconditional love. I want not only for God to be recognized by for Him to be worshiped,

adored, & lifted up! God, I can't stand the lifestyle of the world! It is repulsive! Why would anyone desire to become like the world? It just doesn't make sense! Lord, I am not going to blend in b/c I know I was born to stand out! To stand alone? – Maybe (if that's what it takes). Lord, this life that I now live is not mine, but yours! It is yours to do w/it as you please. I have died to self! My desires, dreams & hopes for the future Don't matter. So God, pretty much I'm begging you to

The pages I found in Jen's journal begging God to use her life (continued below)

ANSWERED PRAYERS

use me. Father, I know you take the foolish ones, the weak ones, the lowly people & use them to shame the strong & wise God, so that means you can take me just as I am. (1 Cor. 1:26-29) You can take me, a nobody & turn me into a somebody. God, I know w/ you all things are possible. (Matthew 19:26) Take this year & my life & allow your glory to shine! Take it & use it to its fullest potential!
            Your Faithful Servant,
                        Jen

ABOVE ▲

Jen and me sharing her story together.
I love to watch Jen speak on stage,
boldly living out her dream to make
an impact for Christ.

In 2009, we were so happy and amazed when Jen was able to walk with her high school class and graduate on time. She even won a special leadership award!

ALL FOR HIM

Jen singing "Lord, You're Holy" with her friends Kae (left) and Megan (right), in front of four thousand people at the service of thanksgiving our church held one year after the accident. She was so excited to be praising the Lord and didn't even realize what she had lost.

Visiting one of our heroes, Joni Eareckson Tada, at the Joni and Friends International Disability Center in California in 2010

"I don't want to limit You
and what You want to do through me . . .
use me just as I am.
Lord, I know I can't do anything
without You being by my side."

JEN'S JOURNAL

◄ LEFT

Jen singing praises to God right before
addressing hundreds of college students

THANKFUL

Our family today . . . confident in God's love
and His plan for our lives

Inappropriate Behaviors Stage. A delay greater than two minutes requires repetition of task instructions. New memories are NOT being formed. Jen . . . is not oriented to place, date, or situation. She refuses to hold a pen. . . ." That was all I could bear to look at. When I closed the file my hands were shaking.

Jen had one last round of rehab that day. Brandon came to visit and went with her to physical therapy. Afterward, Jen walked slowly back to her room, leaning heavily on Brandon to steady herself. She showed me a Polaroid photo of the two of them dancing during PT.

After admiring the picture I asked, "Jen, did you know today was your last day at the hospital?"

"No, I didn't," she answered matter-of-factly, without emotion.

"This is your last day, and you're going home today."

"I know that, Mom!" she declared, reversing her previous comment with a hint of impatience.

"I love you, Jen." I said that a hundred times a day but couldn't say it enough. After all, she only remembered it for a minute. "Everyone loves you."

"I know," she answered shyly. This was her standard reply to anyone who said something like "I love you." She didn't feel love yet, and had no idea even what it was.

My friend LeeAnn arrived at the hospital wearing a red knit winter hat and bright red lipstick. She was there on a mission to videotape all of the doctors, nurses, and therapists. LeeAnn wanted to get words of encouragement for Jen that she knew she would cherish in the years to come. Since Jen still didn't have short-term memory, LeeAnn and I both knew it would be important for her to see the faces of the people who had helped care for her on her journey and to hear the impact she had made in their lives. As we waited for the paperwork to be completed, the nurses and staff came into Jen's hospital room one by one to say good-bye as LeeAnn captured their words on camera.

Clearly this young patient's life and testimony had made a powerful impression. Many of the well-wishers gave her wonderful words of encouragement and wept openly when their turn came.

One of her nurses said, "It's great to see how far you have come. Even when you were frustrated with me you said 'thank you' to me over and over." With tears in her eyes she added, "It touched my heart that no one ever left you alone. You always had a friend or family member right there with you."

Christine Vaughn was the custodian who had told me early on, "God's in that girl!" During all the weeks since, if Jen was singing when she came in to empty the wastebaskets, Miss Christine would join in, singing up a storm and clapping on the offbeats. "This journey is nothing but God," she said to LeeAnn. "First time I saw Jen I did not know her, but some way God connected our spirits. God told me He would never leave her nor forsake her. She is a living testimony! She can tell the world what my God has done! He never fails! Jen, keep on doing God's work! Keep on living! Keep on sharing that God is good!"

Another nurse was overflowing with emotion. "Jen, you stole my heart when you first came. Look at me! I'm crying and I have goose bumps just thinking about it! Be patient. You will get there. You are a miracle! God brought you through this for a reason. Don't give up. You could go to Jen's room and she would be singing to her music. She prayed out loud when she couldn't talk to us. Her prayers were so real, so beautiful, so miraculous! That little girl is going to be His forever!"

Jen's schoolteacher at Kluge, Penni Crist, said, "What has impacted me most about Jen is how she shares her faith. God has been glorified. The faith of a child—how it can bring you through the worst tragedies!"

Of all the wonderful nurses and therapists at Kluge, I always had a special place in my heart for Angie McWhorter. She was in tears as she spoke. "You are one of the most special patients I have ever met or will probably ever meet. I pray for you every night. I go home and hug my children harder because I met you and your wonderful family. I know God's miracles will come true for you."

These people were like part of our family. They had saved Jen's life and put her on the road to recovery. Now it was up to us to continue the marathon at home.

On her way to the door, Jen was wheeled through a corridor lined with hospital staff waving a final good-bye. Leaving was a bittersweet moment, wonderful for the progress it indicated but sad because we would be leaving people who had become such an important part of our lives.

The doctors prescribed a strong dose of Phenergan to help Jen sleep through the ninety-minute drive home. I had hoped she would have her feeding tube removed before she came home, but she seemed to need it more than ever. Because food continued to upset her super-sensitive stomach, she had quit eating by mouth almost completely and had to get all her nourishment through the feeding tube. On top of everything else, once Jen was home we'd have to use the tube, which often made a mess when she squirmed around. Furthermore, the tube had to be kept clean, firmly in place, and protected from being yanked or damaged. Jen would often pull at the feeding tube. She would even offer it to people and say, "Do you want this? You can have it."

Thanks to our army of volunteers, Jen would be sleeping in her bed again at last. We hoped being in her own room would jog her memory and help the recovery process. One of the points the doctors made that really stuck with me was that most of Jen's improvement would come in the first year. I decided I would do everything in my power to help her move ahead as much as possible during that year. A big part of that was getting her back into familiar surroundings. But how could we possibly do this on our own? We couldn't. Quietly but fervently I prayed, "Please, Lord, come to our rescue. In our own strength this is impossible. Only You can lift us over the obstacles ahead and through this experience. I know You saved Jen's life for a reason, Lord. Help us to follow You and trust You and seek Your will."

I felt such joy to be back home with Jen at last! But very shortly that joy dissolved into frustration and despair. This was going to be a marathon all right, with no end in sight. The excitement of coming home gave way to stark reality. I couldn't get around on crutches because my left hand and arm were still limp. About all I could do for Jen was say how much I loved her, read the Bible to her, and sing her favorite songs.

My day began with the sound of Andy clomping up the stairs on crutches to bring me a cup of coffee every morning since he was worried that I would injure myself scooting up and down the steps. Of course, by the time Andy got to the bedroom, he had more like a half cup of coffee since it was tricky holding a hot beverage in one hand while negotiating the stairs on his crutches. I'm sure those steps still have coffee stains on them as a testament to Andy's love and devotion. Our family would never have survived without Andy's leadership and his steadfast faith. His perspective was, "I know God has chosen our family for this, and we are going to honor Him every step of the way." He never complained or focused on himself but found his greatest joy in serving his family. Andy is the most selfless man I know.

Since Andy and I were so limited in what we could do, Josh had to step up and assume some of the responsibilities of taking care of himself and maintaining the household. It was hard for him to see his sister struggling and in pain every day. He said many times that he wished he'd had the brain injury instead of her. He was always so kind and sweet, but I could see the sadness in his eyes as he helped me feed Jen and take care of her. In God's providence their roles were switched, with the younger brother taking care of the older sister he had always looked up to and admired.

Josh took on more of the routine housework, too, making his own lunches and even doing laundry. I never heard him utter one word of complaint, only praise and encouragement for his sister and offers to do anything he could for Andy and me.

As we established our routine at home, Lisa Bryant began her daily visits. Lisa is a ball of perpetual energy—athletic, feisty, and full of fun. She was perfect for Jen because she never got tired, never got impatient, and invested 110 percent in everything she did. Also, she was a woman who always spoke her mind, which fit beautifully with Jen's unfiltered personality. At home or at one of the countless doctor's appointments they went to, Lisa sang and danced to praise music on Jen's iPod right along with her. When Jen got tickled at something and broke into uproarious laughter, Lisa roared right along with her. Jen didn't care what anybody else thought of her, and neither did Lisa.

Impromptu dancing was one of the only ways we could get Jen to exercise. She couldn't do much except walk, which she didn't like. Only Lisa could talk her into it, and then only if they took the iPod. Music was the first stimulus Jen had responded to when coming out of her coma, and it remained one of the few things she would always react to. The first motor skill she'd learned when she got home was how to turn on the CD player. So music helped lure her outside every day. The three of us were a sight to behold going through the neighborhood, with Jen and Lisa boogying to iTunes like their lives depended on it and me bringing up the rear in my wheelchair.

God knew Lisa was the perfect person to help us because I still didn't get it. I remained completely focused on getting Jen back to normal, back to the old scholar and star athlete she had been. Lisa already knew the long journey that was ahead of us. She clearly saw the marathon route long before I did. I wasn't ready to accept the fact that Jennifer Barrick would never be the same. I was waiting for God to answer my fervent prayer to heal Jen completely and restore her, changing her back to the way she'd been.

Instead, God was changing me.

In the meantime, every minute at home with Jennifer was exhausting. She remembered isolated details around the house, like where the silverware drawer was, but most of what she saw was either unfamiliar or didn't register at all. She couldn't remember the answer to a question for more than a few minutes and so asked the same questions over and over. Nothing seemed to stick. As Lisa and I helped her relearn personal care and hygiene, her lack of memory and lack of balance became big challenges. She didn't know how to brush her teeth, had no concept of bathing, and needed help getting dressed.

The hypersensitivity that had made showers such torture for her at Kluge was still an issue, and it affected not only what she felt on her skin but what she felt internally. Because her stomach was so prone to pain, she didn't want to eat. We tried feeding her in front of the TV, in bed, anything to distract her, but it was a constant battle.

Even though her stomach was never full, hypersensitivity made Jen feel as if her bladder were full all the time. And with no short-term memory, she wouldn't remember going to the bathroom and so had to be helped in and out of the bathroom literally a hundred times a day. She'd scarcely be through the door when she'd say, "I have to go to the bathroom! I've been holding it all day!" There was more confusion when she would sit and nothing happened. Lisa would ask, "Do you have to go?" By "go" Jen thought she meant leave, so she'd stand up. It's funny now, but it wasn't funny then.

A couple of weeks after Jen came home, I asked her if she'd like to go to a Sunday evening praise concert at church. She said yes. It would be her first time back to Thomas Road Baptist since the accident. To avoid confusing or frightening her with the big scene her arrival would cause, we sneaked her inside backstage. With Brandon's help she walked in and sat in the front row. When Dr. Falwell announced that Jen was there, she got a huge standing ovation. I don't know if Jen knew why they were clapping, but she grinned from ear to ear. Jen couldn't see her face on the huge TV screens flanking the stage, but I could; she made me so proud as she sat there beaming. To my amazement, she stayed put for a whole hour and thoroughly enjoyed the music. I think this was the longest she'd gone without having to visit the bathroom since coming home. We left the way we came in, through the backstage area, so people wouldn't touch her. Her hypersensitivity made well-meaning hugs or even touches very uncomfortable.

"Jen," I said, "you were amazing!"

She looked at me with a confused expression. "What do you mean? I'm here every Sunday."

CHAPTER 11

ROCK BOTTOM

Always be joyful. Never stop praying. Be thankful in all circumstances,
for this is God's will for you who belong to Christ Jesus.

I THESSALONIANS 5:16-18

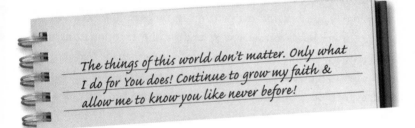

The things of this world don't matter. Only what I do for You does! Continue to grow my faith & allow me to know you like never before!

Jen's journal, two days before the crash

IF THIS WERE A NOVEL OR A MOVIE, now would be the moment when
something wonderful happens and everything turns out okay. A faithful family touched by tragedy is somehow restored to health and
wholeness, and lives happily ever after.

It didn't work out that way. Every day was a battle. Every day was
hard. I was in constant pain, still unable to walk or take care of myself,
much less care for Jen. I had a wheelchair upstairs and another one
downstairs, but I hopped around on one foot a lot because it was so hard
to get the wheelchair through a doorway. Andy was even more broken
physically and his pain more intense than mine. Though he was at work
every day, he still had severe nerve damage and walked with a limp.

My excitement over Jen's return to Thomas Road led me to hope she would continue to improve, moving faster at last along the road to recovery now that she was home. That sense of hope made it all the harder when, just a week later, Jen suddenly became so anxious that she couldn't be around people at all. That first night back at church when she had seemed to enjoy the attention so much had been replaced with a wall of anxiety. She couldn't go to church or even sit in the waiting room at the doctor's office without panicking, which hadn't been a problem before. She now had to sit in the car until the doctor was ready for her.

Everyday life became overwhelming for Jen. The least bit of activity or stimulus caused severe anxiety and emotional distress. Strangers, any sort of noise, even a ride in the car made her so upset she'd start shaking. As her brain struggled to adapt and reprogram itself, every input from the outside world confused her. She was walking more but still unsteady on her feet.

The headaches that started during Jen's last few days at Kluge now became a daily problem (and in fact still plague her today). We tried every type of over-the-counter pain reliever we could, along with natural supplements, prescription medications, chiropractic treatments, and massage therapy. Nothing seemed to help! Doctors still don't know what is causing the pain, though they think it could be because of pressure in her head, nerve pain due to the damage and skull fractures she incurred during the accident, or her poor vision.

Her eyes were severely impaired, with permanent damage to the optic nerve and a right visual field cut, which meant she would never be able to see at all to the right and therefore could never drive a car. She also had cortical vision impairment, which is an injury in the brain. One doctor said that for her it was like looking at the world through holes in Swiss cheese. She often ran into walls or doors as she struggled to keep her balance, identify things in front of her, and gain a sense of depth perception. She couldn't get up and down the stairs to her room without help. When she was tired, her vision was even worse.

Since she could see only part of her surroundings, she would knock over things right in front of her because she didn't know they were there. Her ocular tracking was off, which is why she got so dizzy in the car or when she looked down and tried to read something. Any movement in front of her face, even the waving of a hand, made her dizzy.

We took her to world-renowned eye doctors at Duke University Medical Center and UVA. When Jen couldn't read the huge E at the top of the eye chart, I broke down in tears. The doctors said surgery wouldn't help. All we could do was wait and hope she would improve.

In the meantime, I thought it was important for her to sleep in her own bed because the familiar surroundings might help her start remembering things. Unlike at the hospital, there was no protective zip-up tent to keep her from tumbling out of bed or from getting up at night and falling down the stairs. We got bed rails for her, but that wasn't enough to make sure she stayed safe at night. Once again faithful friends gave sacrificially of their time and love. Kae spent four nights a week on a cot in Jen's room to keep an eye on her. Kim Wooldridge, the close friend who had sung and danced for Jen at Kluge so she'd stay awake for therapy, stayed one night a week. Brandon's mother, Tammy, who had already spent so many weekends at Kluge, now spent her weekends watching Jen at our home.

Having these temporary roommates led to a funny moment. One morning I was wheeling down the hallway when I was shocked to see Jen standing at the top of the stairs. I yelled, "Jen, what are you doing? You're about to fall down the stairs!"

"Mom," she said, "there's some lady in my room with brown hair.

I don't know who she is, so I pretended to be asleep until she got up and left the room."

"That's Mrs. Knight," I explained. "She has been in your room here or at the hospital every weekend for four months. She's been staying with you in case you need help in the middle of the night."

I was pleased that Jen, confused as she was, had finally noticed someone else in the room after all this time. It was a rare lighthearted moment in a life that seemed to be getting darker every day.

Despite the difficulties she faced, Jen herself was a source of encouragement. Her unfiltered, uninhibited prayers were full of thankfulness, humility, and a desire to serve. Now her lack of inhibition brought on instances of uncontrollable laughter. I loved seeing and hearing her. The deep, joyful sound that we called the "seal laugh" was one of the best things about those days. It was a gift from God we could enjoy even as we felt more and more defeated by the enormity of the job ahead of us.

At the end of Jen's first month at home, she and I sat in our favorite oversize "chair-and-a-half." I was scheduled to undergo another round of surgery on my left foot and arm later in March, and I wanted to explain to Jen in the simplest terms I could about my injuries and the upcoming operations.

Jen looked closely at my face, seeming to notice the large scar above my left eye for the first time. She reached up and touched it, then rubbed it gently with her finger.

"That's not normal," she observed solemnly. "Oh, Mom, that worries me! I wish I was hurt instead of you!"

Tears started rolling down my cheek. My precious girl was so hurt that she didn't even realize she was hurt.

"I love you so much, Jen," I said, through the tears. "I'm the one who worries about you."

"Don't worry about me," Jen said brightly. "Anything that happens to me is in God's hands."

A few weeks later, doctors removed two plates from my left foot and transferred three tendons within my left forearm and hand in hopes of restoring use of my hand. The surgery was considered a success, though I had to go through a long series of physical therapy sessions on my left hand before I could use it. Even now I don't have full range of motion in that hand; for instance, when typing, I can use only one left finger.

Five months after the accident, Jen was finally eating enough that her feeding tube could be removed. The doctor said the simplest and least risky way to remove it would be to simply pull it out. To have that done, we had to drive to the hospital in Charlottesville, and we took Kae with us to help with Jen. The doctor there told Jen to say when she was ready and he would just pull it out. Well, Jen was never ready. We waited and waited. We prayed over her and tried to calm her. Finally, realizing she was never going to be "ready," the doctor just yanked it out without warning. This was very traumatic for Jen. Though this procedure causes most people only a little pain, her hypersensitivity multiplied the pain and discomfort a hundred times over. It was so traumatic that it became her first new memory after the accident, one that she would relive over and over every day, talking about it repeatedly and becoming upset all over again.

This experience made me realize what a blessing it had been that Jen didn't have short-term memory in the hospital. As much as I wanted God to heal her, I now understood how much God had been protecting her. She didn't remember having a bolt placed in her head or being zipped up in a bed or getting two shots a day or screaming in the shower. She didn't remember the hospital at all. She had been spared all of those scary, painful memories. And now I was starting to see what Jen had seen all along—that God really was good.

That spring, the household settled into a routine of visitors and care-takers streaming in and out around the clock, long days taking Jen to doctor and therapy appointments, joy at her unbridled praise for the Lord, and frustration and crushing disappointment at her continuing struggles with daily living.

Jen's nose dripped all day long. On one fifteen-minute trip to the grocery store, I counted thirty-two times that she blew her nose. It got so bad that the doctors were afraid she was leaking brain fluid. So we added yet another round of CT scans and visits to neurosurgeons to our routine. It turned out that the continuous runny nose (which lasted more than a year) was a result of damage to her sinus cavity. On top of that, she continued to battle chronic stomach pain, poor vision, trips to the bathroom every five minutes, and all her other problems, requiring visits to the gastroenterologist, urologist, radi-ologist, and seemingly every other "-ologist" in the world.

Twice a week we drove Jen across town to continue the physical, occupational, and speech therapies she'd started at Kluge. Jen was very wary about going anywhere. She didn't understand what was happening. Her stomach hurt; riding made her nauseous; she asked the same questions over and over.

The first time we went, Andy and I were both crying before we even made it to therapy because we were so sad for Jen. Our hearts ached for her and all she had to go through. It seemed so unfair!

We cranked the music up really loud because we knew that when Jen concentrated on the songs, she'd forget she was in a car and was less likely to get sick. Sitting in back with Lisa, Jen was soon oblivious to anything except the praise music blasting from the CD player as she sang along at the top of her lungs.

"I can't help it," Jen explained to Lisa. "I am so full of joy!" Focusing on music may have lifted Jen's spirits, but Andy and I returned home that afternoon completely drained, literally collapsing from fatigue.

Just getting Jen's clothes and shoes on exhausted her and made her want to take a nap. She had to consciously think about doing things most people do involuntarily, like swallowing. One day I asked her to stir some cake batter, and while she was concentrating on stirring, she started drooling. I realized she could focus on only one thing at a time. Thinking about the batter made her forget to swallow.

Jen never felt good. Many days she didn't want to get out of bed, and I'd say, "God has told me it is going to be a great day! You've got to get up!" She would just sit there and not know what to do unless we directed her, though once she was up and moving she could do more than you'd expect. She had huge mood swings, from laughing and being silly one minute to being totally overwhelmed and frustrated the next. On one hand she was hilarious because she said everything she was thinking out loud, yet on the other hand she was high mainte- nance. Lisa and I would have the "best" and "worst" day all rolled into one. We used to joke that we were going to have T-shirts made saying "I survived Jen!" We meant it all in good fun; we were just worn out.

Lisa and I made a big poster-sized list of basic tasks and put it up in Jen's bathroom so she could check off washing her face, brushing her teeth, and all the rest. It didn't work. She couldn't read it, didn't remember what it was for, and refused to look at it. *Lord Jesus, how in the world will this girl ever be able to take care of herself?* She couldn't remember if she'd taken her pills or not. She'd wake up from a nap and think it was the next day.

With the feeding tube out, eating was obviously more important than ever. I hoped she'd be more cooperative. Not so, at least not at first. When I handed her something to eat, she'd hand it back and say, "I'll eat it later." Polite, but stubborn. Then when she did start to eat, she went to the other extreme, wanting to eat every hour as if her body were starving for nutrition. She'd have lunch three times because she didn't remember she'd already eaten. She would insist she hadn't had dessert and eat five servings. She started hoarding candy, hiding it like a preschooler. I found it everywhere: in the piano, in the freezer, in her bed.

As her eating habits improved, one of the first things she enjoyed was broccoli cheddar soup from Panera. I think she liked the smooth, warm feeling of it in her mouth, and since she didn't have to chew it, it didn't hurt. She became obsessed with this soup, having it for lunch at eleven o'clock, again at noon, and a third bowl an hour later. For weeks, we sent friends out to buy it by the quart. One day when my sister's husband, Jeff, came back from Panera with a container of soup, he shared a heartwarming story.

"I told the people at Panera that this soup is saving Jen's life because it's the only thing she will eat. When they heard her story, they said from now on she can have all the broccoli cheddar soup she wants for free. Whoever picks it up just has to say that it's for Jen Barrick."

I poured a serving into a bowl and set it in front of Jen. Rather than digging in as she always had, she looked up at me with a troubled expression like I was crazy. "Mom, I am so sick of this soup! You've been feeding it to me four times a day!" We all got a much-needed laugh out of that. *It took you long enough to figure that out, girl. But you did! Your memory is coming back!*

Reading, however, was still almost impossible. Jen couldn't even look down at a book without getting dizzy. One day in the early spring the doorbell rang. I limped slowly to the door to answer it, and there on the porch, unannounced and unexpected, stood my dear childhood friend Missy Davis.

"Hi, Linda! I've come to teach Jen how to read and write."

I was dumbfounded.

"God put a burden on my heart to do it," she explained. "I know if I don't, God will send somebody else. But I don't want to miss the blessing."

Believe me, the blessing was ours as Missy went to work. Missy is a dark-haired, five-foot-two dynamo with a big, blustery laugh and outsize tenacity. From the first minute, she made it clear that whatever needed doing, Jen was going to do it. There was love in Missy's every word, every gesture. "No" was simply not a word in her vocabulary. She gave Jen a pen and asked her to write her name.

Jen held the pen for a moment, scribbled a few marks on the page, then said, "I can't do it." Again, louder and more agitated, "I can't do it. This hurts. It hurts!"

Missy just laughed and kept on encouraging her. "You can do it, Jen. I know you can. See, you've already got it started." Missy never gave up and wouldn't let Jen give up. When Jen wasn't interested in reading or writing, Missy would pray aloud with Jen, asking God to help her. Gradually Jen started to improve.

Before long Missy had Jen focused on reading and writing, really working at it and concentrating like never before. Missy came to our house to teach Jen three days a week. After only a few sessions, Jen completely focused on Missy for two solid hours. Lisa and I were so grateful to have a break. We watched in amazement as Jen obeyed Missy's every instruction. Why couldn't Jen listen to us that way? We couldn't get her to do anything! We joked about getting black wigs and a tape of Missy's voice so Jen would mind us as well.

Missy started helping Jen do oversize ten-piece puzzles made for toddlers. Jen would hover over the puzzle and put her face right up to it to see it, unable to do it without help. Missy spent hours teaching Jen her ABCs and numbers. They would write them down and use flashcards over and over again. Gradually they worked up to "C is for cat" and "D is for dog." Once that clicked, it was like a lightbulb went on in Jen's brain, and her language skills started to come back. Jen was like a small child growing up all over again. For instance, when Andy came home from work, she would squeal in delight at the door and wait to hug him like a three-year-old.

Reading the simplest words remained a stumbling block. Jen couldn't even read a one-word caption for a picture: "house," "bird," "flower." One day Missy had her color a picture of a horse. When she scribbled only on the left-hand side of the page, we realized again how severe her vision loss was. Though eye problems kept her from reading, Missy discovered she could write. The biggest motivator in getting her to practice was to have her write verses of Scripture or prayers to the Lord. The words were a spidery jumble that ran off the page, sometimes with words scrawled on top of each other.

One of her first sentences was, "Thank You for giving me the brain injury." Though by that time I cried at practically anything, these words opened the floodgates wide again. She had no idea—no memory—of all the things her injury had robbed her of. All she knew was that she had a hardwired connection with the Lord, lived in His presence, and trusted Him absolutely to use her in whatever way would best glorify Him.

Surprising things she said out loud gave me a hint of how deep her spiritual waters were flowing, even though she expressed herself very simply. "Mom," she declared, "your problem is that your brain gets in the way. You think too much! You have to just trust God."

Jen's speech remained very hard to understand. Her lazy tongue made her slur her words, and sometimes she would stop in the middle of a sentence. She did better when she was singing along with her praise CDs and better still when she was praying. Even at her best, though, she was nothing like she'd been during those early days in the hospital when she was coming out of her coma. That had been absolutely supernatural—her voice had been perfectly clear and sounded like the old Jennifer. I remained convinced that those first prayers at Kluge were the Holy Spirit praying out loud through her. She and God were having a conversation, and she was answering His questions. It was like she was on holy ground, in a spiritual realm not of this world. I believe God allowed us to hear Him then so we would have hope. God was giving us hope out loud through Jen.

I needed a big dose of hope every day. Yet as much as I worried about Jen, she never worried about herself. At the time, I figured that was obviously because she had no idea what was going on. But now I think it was that Jen could see something from her perspective that I never could. "If God doesn't heal me completely," she said, "it's because He has something far greater in store for me." When I wondered if I sounded ungrateful to God because I kept praying for Jen to be completely healed, Jen said, "God already knows your thoughts, so you might as well tell him how you feel!" I hadn't discussed these things with her, yet she sensed them anyway. I believe God was speaking to me through Jen, reassuring me, reminding me to rest in Him the way she did.

Lisa, Missy, and I welcomed another tireless helper in the spring. Kim Cherry, a Jefferson Forest High School teacher to homebound students, started coming to the house to help Jennifer and continued teaching her all summer. Jefferson Forest, the public school near our neighborhood, had special ed resources to help Jen that were not available at Liberty Christian Academy. At first I couldn't imagine Jen doing even the simplest arithmetic or retaining basic facts, much less handling assignments for a high school sophomore.

Kim charged confidently in, learning where Jen was in every subject and modifying her teaching techniques to allow for Jen's disabilities. She wrote multiplication tables in huge numbers with a black marker on big, brightly colored construction paper. She was infinitely patient and encouraging, taking advantage of every minute Jen was plugged into her lessons, yet never getting frustrated when her mind wandered. Jen responded beautifully to Kim's bubbly personality and positive approach, and the two developed a special connection. Jen loved getting her off topic by asking her about her jewelry or her family—anything but schoolwork.

It became clear after a while that Jen knew more than she could tell us. On a multiple-choice test she could almost always "guess" the right answer even when she kept saying, "I don't know." One day she was having trouble with a simple math concept, although Mrs. Cherry had hoped to go on to a much harder one that seemed impossible to explain under the circumstances. Something like "four to the third power." To my amazement, Jen grabbed the paper with the harder problem and said, "Oh, that's easy. I know how to do that."

To encourage her to read, Mrs. Cherry copied pages from Jen's favorite book, *His Princess: Love Letters from Your King* by Sheri Rose Shepherd, enlarging the type to half an inch high. Other than the Bible, it was the only book Jen read willingly, even though it was a struggle. She could get through only a couple of sentences before she was completely exhausted.

She could remember how to work with exponential notation in math, but she could not recall the names of everyday items. Sometimes in a conversation she knew what she wanted to say but couldn't find the right word. She said "up" when she meant "down," and "ketchup" instead of "mustard." She called windshield wipers "propellers." Her recovering memory was so inconsistent and random. One morning

I told Jen we were having pancakes for breakfast, and she asked, "What's a pancake?"

Lisa and I spent hours telling her stories from her past, hoping she would remember them. Trying to jog her memory another way, I started reading the journals from her room aloud to her. One day I asked her if I could share one of the entries with some of my friends. At first, she gave me a very surprised look and said, "My heart is in those journals!" Then after a few minutes, she told me it was okay to read her words aloud to them. Much to my amazement, she added, "I believe God wants me to share my journals with the world."

Missy kept up her regular visits through the summer. She and Jen played memory games with cards, wrote prayers to God, colored pictures, and even planted flowers together. On the weekends Kae and Brandon came over to visit. Jen's favorite activity with them was watching a movie. She loved seeing scenes she remembered, which meant watching the same movie day after day, sometimes several times a day. Her favorite was *A Walk to Remember*, which Kae and Brandon must have sat through at least thirty times.

Another favorite pastime for Jen was playing Uno. Like eating and watching movies, playing Uno would become compulsive. She would want to play game after game. Anytime she lost she would get frustrated and upset, so we always let her win. Whatever she was doing, she seemed to constantly be in motion: fidgeting in her chair, getting stuck on a phrase—"FYI, for your information," for example—and repeating it a hundred times. Missy and Mrs. Cherry could get her to focus for a while, but these were rare moments of calm in otherwise endless days and nights of questions, resistance, singing and laughing, frustration and confusion.

Experiencing the two sides of Jen as she recovered kept me on the spiritual roller coaster I'd been riding for so long. As she became more aware of herself and the world around her, Jen started to sense her limitations. For all her bravado over math problems, she still had a devastating brain injury. She couldn't dress herself. She got lost walking through the house. Nearly everything about her was damaged and broken. But her faith and spirit seemed completely unaffected. The contrast was wonderful and heartbreaking at the same time.

There was a time when I thought we would never have the celebration we enjoyed on May 17, 2007: Jennifer's sixteenth birthday. By God's grace, she had made it to that milestone, and now it was time to party!

It was a perfect spring night. We celebrated on the back deck at John and Gina's house with both sets of grandparents. Nanny decorated the tables with white tablecloths, fresh flowers, and candles on glass pedestals and made a chocolate birthday cake. Uncle John made Jen's favorite meal on the grill—big, juicy steaks. Andy and I gave Jen a gold-and-silver ring adorned with little diamonds to remind her that she was a miracle. Andy cried tears of joy as he handed it to her. Josh wrote the sweetest card, telling Jen she was a "beautiful angel from heaven." He made sure to write large enough so that she could read it herself. It was a joyful evening of praise to God for His faithfulness, goodness, and miracles to us.

Later in the week, on another perfect spring night, Jen had a Sweet Sixteen celebration with her girlfriends at the Clintons' pool. There was lots of karaoke and dancing and acting goofy. Jen didn't want to swim—she said it sounded like "too much work"—so the girls cooked up the idea of surprising their friend Parker Spencer, who was away at a track meet. Parker was infamous for toilet-papering the girls' yards and had even toilet-papered one of their dogs. It was time for revenge: the girls called Parker's mom and got permission to paper his bedroom!

Off we went to the dollar store for toilet paper, streamers, confetti,

Silly String, lipstick for the mirror, stickers for the tub in the adjoining bathroom, and the crowning touch, a gigantic bra. The girls did a magnificent job, captured the scene with photos and videos, then went back to the Clintons' for cake, ice cream, and presents. The biggest surprise came an hour later when Parker waltzed into the party wearing his new mammoth-size bra over his T-shirt! It was an unforgettable night, especially the souvenir photo of Jen and Parker, with him in his distinctive party attire.

Earlier that month Jen had started keeping a journal again. Although the handwriting was barely more than a scribble, the thoughts behind her words were clear and confident. On May 7, 2007, she wrote, "I want to come as close to God as I possibly can. Lord, please use my life for Your glory! I love you so much! Amen."

The journals that had been a private part of her life were now front and center. Her entries that month were one of the things that helped me hold on when I didn't think I could last another minute. I was exhausted, in pain, still limping, hoping Josh didn't feel ignored, worried about Andy who was still fighting with our insurance company, and feeling completely used up after long days with Jen. Then I read entries in Jen's journals like these:

> *May 9*
> *Lord, I just want to thank You for all the amazing things You are doing in my life. Lord, I pray that You will completely heal my brain injury. Give me the strength that I need.*
>
> *May 14*
> *I so believe in You and I know that You will stay right by my side no matter what. Thank You!*

May 16
Lord, I just want to thank You for everything You are doing in my life. I pray that You will help me be a witness and testimony in everything I say and do.

May 23
Lord, I love You so much but I really need Your help to get through all the problems I am facing. I know I can always count on You. I put all my trust in You. Amen.

May 31
Never give up! If we are really burdened and feel down, we need to give it all to the Lord. He is the one that will help us through it. Never stop praying! Always believe!

That broken body held such a faithful heart! I prayed for my faith to be like hers. I prayed that God would keep lifting her up. On my knees I cried out to the Lord. *God, for all she has suffered, how can we be bitter as parents about our precious daughter when she is continually praising You? This is not a plan any mother would choose for her daughter. God, it is awful to watch. Don't allow Jen to be discouraged or depressed. Continue to fill Jen with your joy, Lord.*

There were times when I wished we'd all gone to heaven that November night. Our serene, content life as a family seemed pretty much over. *We'll never know peace again, never know contentment, never know relief from pain and misery and worry.*

Then a smile from Jen, or a word, or her laugh would bring me out of the darkness for a moment. One day she was dancing around the room as she sang praises to the Lord.

"Jen, what do you think about when you're praising the Lord?"
I asked.

She gazed at me with a far-off look and said, "When I praise God,
I feel His presence. I feel so close to Him. I raise my hands and I want to
touch the hem of Jesus' garment just like the woman in the Bible. I long
for the day when Jesus will look at me and say, 'My child, your faith has
healed you.' That's what I'm thinking about when I'm singing."

I, on the other hand, felt *nothing*! I knew I was a Christian. I knew
I loved the Lord. But something was wrong with me. I felt completely
dead inside.

Later that day Jen was taking a nap. Andy wasn't home from work
yet, and Lisa was away. It was the first time I could remember being
by myself since before the accident. Overcome with emotion, I shut
the door to Jen's room and collapsed on the floor at the top of the
stairs. I got on my face and confessed my thoughts to the Lord. I
didn't know what else to do. As I lay there, I didn't hear an audible
voice in the room, but I heard God speaking to my heart.

Linda, do you love Me as much as you love Jen?

Lord, You know I do!

In that instant I realized that at the root of our greatest fear is often
something we love more than God. I didn't want to love Jen more than
I loved God. I didn't mean to do it, but my priorities said otherwise.

*Then you have to stop being consumed with trying to fix Jen. I don't
want you to be consumed with anything else but Me. I want to be your
number one obsession.*

Jen is mine. You have to let go and trust Me.

My heart was so worn and raw. I tried to express my thoughts in
my journal, crying out to the Lord for help and direction:

*The only way to survive is one day at a time. When I rely on my
own strength, I am a basket case, a mental and emotional mess,*

and I haven't even begun to process what has happened to our
family. It is a nightmare that never ends. Nothing is normal.
My whole life is consumed with wanting Jen back to the life she
had. My only hope is in God alone. I have to believe God loves
her so much more than I do and that He is going to heal her
exactly the way He wants. And she will be better than before
in His eyes.

God knows my pain. He alone understands my struggle. He
is not overwhelmed by my feelings. Lord, I'm right where You
want me and there's no way out. I don't want to miss one thing
that You want to teach me. Lord, help me to recognize Satan
and rebuke him. I am just going through the motions. I am
numb. My heart is broken for Jen that she would have to go
through this. My heart is aching for normalcy. I refuse to believe
his lies any more. Lord, give me Your heart and re-wallpaper
my mind with the truth of Your Word.

Sometimes I am in a dream. I can't allow my heart to feel.
I can hardly sing praises any more. I want to run and hide and
wake up when it is over. I am obsessed with laundry because
it is the only normal thing I can do with one hand. Forgive
me for focusing on Jen instead of You. Satan accuses me daily
and makes me feel inadequate, like I have failed in helping
Jen. I didn't do all I could have to help her brain heal quicker.
Satan wanted to destroy me but he could not keep me down.
To God be the glory!

Father, I admit I have never wanted to pray for faith. I have
never wanted to go through bad times. This is worse than my
wildest nightmare. I can't fathom Your ways. I can only say,
"I surrender all." I have no feelings, only paralyzing anxiety
and Satan's lies of condemning thoughts. I torture myself with
second guessing. Have I done everything right today? I should

*have done this differently! I should have, I could have, I didn't.
Obsessing about "I" is going to lead to my emotional and
spiritual destruction.*

*Andy is constantly reminding me that God is going to heal
Jen exactly as HE wants her to be. We have to wait on the Lord.*

As I finished this long entry, I still struggled with the question of
whether or not God would disappoint me. I was still pondering that
thought an hour later as I was fixing Jen a snack in the kitchen. Jen,
not knowing what I was thinking or what I'd written, walked up to
me and said, out of the blue, "God is never going to leave you. Even
if He disappoints you and you think He has let you down, it's only
because He isn't finished with you. His plan will exceed your wildest dreams." It was as though she could read my mind. Her words
absolutely blew me away.

For many years my father, Dr. Ed Hindson, has hosted *The King
Is Coming*, a TV program on the TBN network. I cohosted more
than one hundred broadcasts of a local TV show called *Lighting the
Way* with him as well. We even did a series on how to handle life's
toughest problems. I was always the one saying God would help us
through our darkest trials. I taught a Bible study in our home for
years, led moms' prayer groups, facilitated Bible studies for teenage
girls, and just a few weeks before I had spoken at Thomas Road to
hundreds of women on the power of prayer. I told all these people
to put their hope in the Lord. That their faith would carry them
through and God would make everything right.

Would He? Did I believe that? Had God been good to my family?

Everything I ever taught or believed was being put to the test.
Either God's Word was true or it was a lie. It was time to claim His
promises or reject them. The choice was between God and—what?
What other hope was there? Nothing! My *only* hope was in the Lord

and His work in Jen's life. She was in perfect peace, and when she prayed it was as if God Himself spoke out loud through her. She prayed about things she couldn't possibly know. She praised God for healing her and raising her up before she could even sit up in bed. Through her, God was teaching us to praise Him in advance.

God, I am Yours. Lift me up. There is no other way.

CHAPTER 12

IN GOD'S HANDS

Jesus said, "Come to me, all of you who are weary and carry heavy burdens, and I will give you rest." MATTHEW 11:28

You can't talk enough about God, even if you are repeating yourself!

Jen's journal, nine months after the crash

To HELP ME SURVIVE THE LONG, hard days I began telling myself over and over that this life on earth is only a dot on the timeline of history, leading to God's eternity where we will experience unparalleled joy. Off and on, I'd repeat that truth out loud, so Jen nicknamed me Polka Dot, evidence of one of her first short-term memory triumphs. Every time she called me Polka Dot, it reminded all of us that this difficult and challenging life is a moment in time anticipating life in heaven, with no pain or sorrow, just ahead.

Tucking Jen in bed at night became a family ritual. Andy sat on the antique trunk at the end of her bed and rubbed her feet to help her relax. Josh and I knelt on either side of her bed and prayed mostly for God to heal Jen and take away her pain. I often prayed, "Lord, please connect a new pathway in Jen's brain tonight."

When it was Jen's turn to pray, she was always full of thanksgiving and praise. One night, she astounded us all when she prayed, "Lord, did I meet all of Your expectations today? Did I fulfill all that You had for me to do?"

Wow! It had never crossed my mind to pray a prayer like that. I'd been so busy begging God for healing and help that I had forgotten that this life is not about me or my family's comfort; it is about God and His plan. Jen had a completely different perspective from the rest of us. She knew God had left her on this earth for a reason. He had things for her to do!

"I just want to proclaim Christ to a lost and dying world," she would say. "I want to tell them the good news that no sin is too great to be forgiven. No matter how hard we try, if the Lord's not in it, we won't succeed." Almost every day she repeated a favorite phrase with confidence: "Every day God is healing me and making me stronger." Such sincere, childlike faith reminded me of what we all could have if we would only dare to rely totally on Him instead of getting bogged down in our own human emotions and frailties. Jen never worried about the future. "God is never going to leave you where you are," she said confidently. "God's plan is perfect. I would never doubt my Creator, my Lord, and my Savior."

One day I made the comment that God was healing Jen every day. She turned to me quickly, looked me in the eye, and said, "Even if God doesn't heal me, He still deserves my honor, glory, and praise. I would be willing to die if just one person got saved. Even if I didn't know them, I would meet them in heaven."

Again Jen's simple, absolute faith had pierced my heart. I prayed, "Father, forgive me. I want Your blessings, but I don't want to share in Your sufferings. Forgive me for being so self-centered. Forgive me for being earthly minded instead of heavenly minded. Forgive me for caring more about my comfort than lost souls. Lord Jesus, give me Your heart and Your mind and Your perspective. Today I am trading in my ugly, selfish heart for Yours."

By now Jen was occasionally going to the youth group's worship service on Sunday morning. She sat with a friend so Andy and I could go to our Sunday school class. Most of the times we tried it, I would no sooner get to my class than my phone would vibrate with a text message saying Jen felt sick and wanted to go home. She couldn't sit for more than a few minutes in the worship service. We couldn't let her go out into the lobby by herself because she would get lost, so one of us went out with her and walked her up and down the hallway until the service was over.

Considering how uncomfortable Jen was in crowds and how she didn't like being hugged or even touched without being asked, I was surprised when she said she was willing to come as a guest speaker to the afterschool Bible study for sixth grade girls that her aunt Gina was leading. Gina asked Jen's opinion about friends, and Jen answered, "Jesus is Your best friend. He is the only one who will never let you down." The girls hung on Jen's every word as she told them about her prayer journal and how it was her "hiding place" where she could tell God everything. Afterward, five of the girls thanked her and said it was the "best Bible study ever."

Several of the girls wore the lime-green MIRACLE 4 JEN bracelets Jen's cheer squad had sold at school. Jen wore one too (and still wears it today as a statement of her faith). These sixth graders had been wearing them for almost a year and praying for God to heal Jen. It was a miracle for them to see her walking around and talking. Jen was so excited that she could share what God had put on her heart even though later she couldn't remember what she had said. She left with a new feeling of purpose as she realized that God could still work through her.

The girls' Bible study was the first time I saw Jen transformed from a confused, brain-injured teenager with limited function to a speaker totally in command. As soon as her presentation was over, she would revert to her confused state of mind. The same thing happened in front of eighty women at a church function. These two events prepared the way for an experience that gave me new proof that the Lord had anointed Jen for a very special mission in the world.

It all began with a sports tournament. As soon as we came home from the hospital in February, Andy had started going to Josh's basketball games again. He even coached the team while still on crutches. When baseball season came around, Andy worked out every day to strengthen his muscles so he could coach the baseball team too. I got frustrated with Andy sometimes because I knew how much he hurt, how hard any sort of movement was for him. However, no pain was going to stop him from coaching—or from pitching at batting practice! Their team, the Mustangs, had a great season and won a berth at the AAU Grand National Baseball Championship at the Disney Wide World of Sports Complex (now the ESPN Wide World of Sports Complex) in Orlando. Eager for a break, our whole family made the trip to cheer Josh on, including both sets of grandparents. It was too hot for Jen to go to the games, and she didn't have much energy. But God wanted her there for another reason.

One of the biggest milestones in Jen's spiritual walk before the accident was the PowerSource youth group she attended during middle school led by Pastor Barry Rice. Barry was the bodybuilder who used demonstrations of strength, like breaking cement bricks with his bare hands, to get kids' attention, then told them about the Creator who is the source of all strength. Pastor Barry had planted a church in Florida called Greater Orlando (GO) Church, and he invited Jen to share her testimony the Sunday we were in town for the baseball tournament.

Sunday, July 22, was the day Jen made her first presentation as a featured speaker. It was a typical cloudless, scorching Florida summer morning. The temperature was already nearly ninety as we pulled up to the church. The congregation didn't have a worship center of its own yet and met in the auditorium of a local high school. After asking Jen if it was okay, Barry greeted her with a big "sweaty" bear hug. Jen was so excited to see him. She knew exactly who he was and remembered the awesome youth group program with him. She was tentative and nervous at first, asking lots of questions about where she would stand, which steps she would go up, and other little details. Then she'd forget she had asked the question and ask it again, nervously flicking her wrists back and forth. Barry told her not to worry; God had given her a powerful story to share.

Barry introduced us, I gave Jen's hand a squeeze, and the two of us walked onstage together. Barry stood on the other side of her the whole time she spoke to help her stay calm. There were about 150 people at the service, and within moments all of them were spellbound. I asked Jen questions to lead her through her story. I asked about the accident's impact on her spiritual life. In simple, heartfelt terms, she explained what had happened to her and how her life had changed, how now every day she was living for Christ alone. She spoke slowly but with a clear, confident voice that filled the room. She looked over at me often, and once in a while I nodded encouragement and prompted her with the next word or two. Her eyes sparkled in the lights as she shared her testimony and invited everyone present to surrender themselves to the Lord. One person came forward, inspired by God through Jen's story, and gave his life to Christ. Jen flashed a smile that reminded me of the old Jen's beaming expression when she cheered. Only this smile had a radiance and power no cheerleading smile could ever match.

Later in the week Jen recorded her impressions of that amazing morning in her journal.

July 27, 2007

Dear Lord,

Well, here I am in Florida. So Sunday I got to speak at
Barry Rice's church. It was awesome! Thank You Lord for
speaking through me. I gave my testimony and someone
got saved forever! Wow, Your plan is perfect! Through the
car wreck you would think that would be hard for me to
say but since lives have been changed, I know that it was
worth it. For goodness sake, I have been changed! Thank
You Lord for making Yourself so real to me during this
hard time. The car wreck has made me love You so much
more! In Your name, Amen!

Despite Jen's limited emotional capacity, she understood exactly what God was doing through her. The Bible teaches us that the weaker and more broken we are when the Lord does His will through us, the clearer it is to a watching world that it's the Lord's work and not our own. I had seen a miraculous transformation in Jen's life from the first moment she came out of her coma, through her recovery at Kluge, and continuing now at home. Her speech at GO Church made me realize for the first time what a powerful witness she could be to a bigger, broader audience.

Later that summer Jen shared her testimony at a Wednesday night youth group service. She stood on stage in front of over three hundred of her high school peers, yet it didn't seem to affect her at all. She was still nervous beforehand. Once again, I led her through her story with questions, and her words deeply stirred the hearts of everyone in the room. Because of her impaired brain function she couldn't plan her presentation in advance; a few minutes after it was over, she didn't remember anything she had said. But while she was in the spotlight she was sure of herself, clear in her expression, and a living testament to God's presence and power.

I knew in my heart that when Jen prayed or spoke about her faith, her words came directly from the Lord. This was true even when it was just the two of us in a room together. I felt I had to preserve them! I'd grab whatever I could get my hands on quickly—a napkin, the back of a sales receipt, a sticky note—and try to jot down her words even if what she said didn't make sense to me at the moment. It would be important to have them later, I thought, as a record of her miraculous spiritual journey.

Here are some of my favorites from around this time:

I have never had so much joy in my life. When I'm singing and praising my Savior, nothing else matters.

God keeps speaking to me and revealing things to me in new ways. Things I couldn't have known. I don't have any negative thoughts, only positive.

If He doesn't heal me completely it's because He has something far greater for me to do.

Lord, how was Your day today? It must be hard having to deal with so many people and all their problems.

Don't give up on God. He never gives up on us.

You can pray while you sing.

When we don't ask, we don't expect God to show up!

If you are praying and believing that God can do more, then why would He hold back?

Mom, if you need joy, just ask Him to fill you.

As I read back over these notes, the message is so clear to me: *God's plan is better than ours. We just can't see it from where we are.* While I would never have wished for what happened to our family, God rewarded us all, and Jen most of all, with a spiritual richness and clarity we couldn't have experienced with all the distractions of the "normal" world.

During Jen's naps, which lasted several hours a day, I reread these statements of hers and her new journal entries. I watched her sleep, read the Bible, pored over her journals, and prayed for her.

As Jen continued to heal, she became more aware of her limitations and disabilities. She couldn't do most of what her peers were doing. Getting a driver's license was out of the question because of her coordination and vision problems. Even if those two things were corrected, she wouldn't have remembered how to operate a car or where she was going when she got behind the wheel. She should have been starting her junior year at LCA. Instead Mrs. Cherry came to our home a few hours a week to help Jen recover the years of past education that had been erased. She couldn't sit still and focus in a classroom at school, couldn't remember how to get from one class to another. She couldn't go to concerts or parties because she couldn't stand loud noises or crowds. She was tired all the time. She was exhausted even as her soul seemed to be at peace. Everyone else was moving on, and Jen couldn't keep up.

After nearly a year, the time had come when Brandon, Jen's ever-faithful boyfriend, had to face the reality that their future together would be different from whatever it might have been before the accident. Now God was closing old doors and opening new ones. Brandon had been Jen's constant companion in the hospital; his mother had spent every weekend there with her and continued to do so after she went home. Brandon was one of the few people who could get through to Jen in those first months of recovery, who turned physical therapy into dancing lessons and nutrition into a milkshake-chugging contest.

Brandon had loved Jen sacrificially for ten months, putting her needs above his own. It was painfully obvious that Jen was not emotionally capable of having a romantic relationship. It was time for him to move on. As a young man with so much kindness and integrity, it was a hard step for Brandon. He had to be direct and clear to make sure Jen understood, but he agonized over the possibility of hurting her feelings and making her think he had abandoned her because she was somehow not good enough.

Brandon repeated what he would say to her over and over in his head, praying for the right words, knowing that the truth would hurt no matter how careful he was. He never wanted to hurt Jen. He talked to Andy and me about it, wondering if it was best for her, wondering if he should wait a while longer to see what might happen since her medical future was so unpredictable. We reassured him that it was the right decision for him and for Jen.

After he explained the situation to Jen as tenderly as he could, she asked, "Will we still be friends?"

"Yes, Jen," he said with a broad smile. "We will be friends forever!"

Jen put on a brave face during Brandon's visit, though after he left she began crying and wondering aloud what she'd done wrong. I hugged her tightly, wrote down her questions, and invited Brandon over the next night so they could talk through them. Brandon reassured her that she had done nothing wrong and that he just needed to figure out God's plan for his life. He reemphasized that he would always be her friend. This second talk seemed to bring her peace about the breakup, and she laughed and joked with Brandon over pizza afterward.

As parents, Andy and I knew that God had brought Brandon into Jen's life specifically to help her through this hard time. We were so grateful for everything Brandon did for Jen and how kindly and respectfully he always treated her. The Knight family has stayed very close to us. Brandon's parents still take Jen out to eat and remain a great blessing in her life.

Fortunately, Jen's short-term memory was slowly improving. The gradual return of brain function continued to be a two-edged sword. On the one hand, it was so exciting to see her writing and speaking more clearly, becoming more independent around the house and better able to take care of herself. She continued getting better at her schoolwork as well. On the other hand, it was hard for her to face the enormity of the changes in her life as they came into focus for her.

As a way of encouraging Jen, I wrote a letter that I often read to her before nap time.

Dear Jen,

You are going to have an amazing ministry one day to help others. You will have learned so much from this journey. God never wastes a trial. He promises to use it for good. The only thing in this world that matters is whether our lives bring glory to God. Yours—my precious daughter—has already impacted thousands of people young and old. I have to believe this is only the beginning!

I LOVE YOU with ALL my HEART, *Mom*

As Jen became aware of her severe memory loss, she realized that she had lost everything she had studied so hard at in school for so many years. "I wasted all those hours!" she exclaimed with a note of despair. "I can't remember *anything*! Imagine being at the top of everything and now you're at the bottom and have no confidence." She would get down on herself and say, "This brain injury is horrible. There are some days I don't think I'm going to make it."

I would remind her, "Honey, it's not your fault."

Jen would reply, "I know, the car accident—but I am left to deal with all of the consequences!" including the raging headaches that continued every day.

Sometimes the questions would rush out in torrents: "Will I ever feel normal again? Will I ever eat without getting a stomachache? Will I ever finish college? Will I ever be able to drive a car? Will my vision ever completely heal? Will I ever get married? Will anyone ever love me again?"

And one of my favorite Jen-isms: "It would be great if your whole life were a book. You could just skip a couple of chapters and find out why."

She could switch back and forth in a heartbeat between doubting her ability and having unquestioning faith in the Lord. "Who could ever want to put up with somebody who has a brain injury?" she'd ask. "I don't even want to put up with myself!"

Then in the next breath she would smile her radiant smile and declare, "God is speaking to my heart. After the storm has passed, the sunshine comes and everything is way more beautiful than before."

CHAPTER 13

WHISPER HOPE IN MY EAR

I tell you, you can pray for anything, and if you believe that you've received it, it will be yours. MARK 11:24

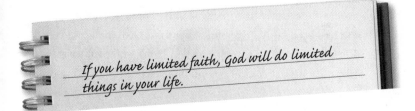

If you have limited faith, God will do limited things in your life.

Jen's journal, eleven months after the crash

SOON OUR FAMILY WOULD BE MARKING ANOTHER MILESTONE. As the one-year anniversary of the accident approached, it was a natural time to consider where the Lord had brought us since then and to look forward to what the future might hold. Josh had just started another school year. God had been so merciful to him in that he had no permanent injuries. He had always loved sports and was able to go on playing football, baseball, and basketball like nothing had happened. He had shouldered extra responsibilities around the house without a word of complaint. Most important, he still loved his big sister with all his heart, protected her, encouraged her, looked up to her, and was inspired by her unflinching faith.

Andy walked now without crutches, though he still had a limp and was in extreme pain day and night. He was back at work full-time and also coaching Josh's sports teams. Because of the damage to his pelvis, he hadn't been able to resume the early morning pickup basketball games he'd always loved so much. His teammates continued to rally around him and had paid to have hot meals delivered to our home every weeknight all summer.

I had also been able to put away the wheelchair. My left leg and foot worked reasonably well since the two steel plates had been removed, though they will probably be somewhat stiff. The tendon surgery on my left arm had been fairly successful. After months of therapy, I could finally lift my wrist, make a fist with my left hand, and pick up things that weren't too heavy. I could do some housework now, taking over for my cousin Heidi and her friends who had been coming every week to clean. All year long, Heidi had anticipated my every need and had selflessly stepped in many times to do whatever was necessary. My grip remained weak, and I couldn't type with my left hand or do anything that required fine motor skills. I have a scar on the inside of my arm from wrist to elbow from the surgery, and another scar on the back of my arm from elbow to shoulder where a permanent rod was implanted. There is also a deep scar above my left eye from the impact of the collision.

Though we'd sat in opposite corners of the van that night, Jen and I had scars on our faces in almost the same place. The trauma to her brain had somewhat altered her expression too. Yet for all the changes, her bright smile remained undimmed and her shining eyes were full of warmth, sincerity, and a desire to serve the Lord. I still worried about the prospect of her not being healed completely. Eventually I would realize that the Lord had prepared her for that. He had made her—made us all—into the people whom He knew could serve Him best . . . people completely dependent on Him to make it through the day.

If there was one word to describe Jen in the fall of 2007, it would be "unpredictable." Sometimes she felt good; often she was tired, nauseous, anxious, and had terrible headaches. She didn't remember what happened from one day to the next, but once in a while she would unexpectedly recover some nugget of a thought. Some days she was very agreeable and cooperative; others she was grumpy, irritable, sneaky, and frustrating.

Jen loved her brother dearly, but she often had very little tolerance and grace for him. She could be singing loudly or watching TV with the sound turned way up, but whenever Josh ran through the house or made an unexpected noise, she was quick to get upset at him and remind him how badly her head hurt.

Being the older sister, she was always trying to mother him. She tried to control how much junk food he ate and reminded him to chew with his mouth closed. She would tell him not to go outside alone because he might get hurt.

One night Andy and I went out to dinner for a much needed date while Josh stayed home to keep an eye on Jen. At 8 p.m. I got a text from my son: "Mom, please come home soon. I am confined to my room because Jen wanted to go to bed and she thought I needed to go to bed too."

I chuckled and texted back, "Just sneak out of your room." But Josh refused to do that because he was so afraid to upset Jen.

However, the day finally came when even he had had enough. Exasperated, he told me, "Mom, I don't know any twelve-year-old boy who is quiet all the time, chews with his mouth closed, and doesn't eat junk food. It's completely impossible."

I said, "I agree, Josh," and we both had a good laugh. At times we all felt like we were going crazy. It wasn't fun to argue with Jen and get her upset. It usually wasn't worth it anyway because her memory was so bad she wouldn't remember to change her behavior the next time.

Eventually, Andy and I realized we did need to tell her when she was being too hard on Josh or irrational about a situation, even when it offended her. No matter how careful we tried to be, her usual response was to run to her room in tears. It was so sad for all of us—especially for Josh, who would beg us never to make her upset again. But inevitably a wonderful transformation took place. After a little while, Jen would come out of her room and apologize. This was a major sign of recovery, since brain-injured people have difficulty seeing things from another person's perspective. It was proof that God was healing her a little more.

Caring for her as a mother was all-consuming, even as she preached to me every minute of the day in both word and deed. She had the mental capacity of a child, the body of a teenager, and the spiritual wisdom of a great theologian.

Some of Jen's higher brain functions had been restored, and some were still missing. They might always be missing. The best way a therapist explained it to me was that the brain is like a filing cabinet, and Jen's brain has been through an earthquake. Some of her files are scattered on the floor and all mixed up. Some are locked in drawers that are jammed and can't be opened. Some are gone altogether.

Whatever drawer in her brain had held the definition of a pancake was topsy-turvy, while the drawers of spiritual discernment were in perfect order. Her journal entries proved this anew to me every day.

August 1, 2007

Lord, I want to live my life like You lived Yours. Jesus, help me to be a replica of You. I want You to be in my life every second of every day! Help me become more like You. Place in me love like You had and help me be able to show that love to the world just like You did. Amen.

September 24, 2007

Lord, I could not live a single day without You. I just feel like talking to You! You know, doing the one thing that matters! I love the quote, "When the whole world walks out, You walk in." I need You 24/7. Thank You for accepting me as I am. I have to fight to get better every day.

We were sitting together in our favorite chair-and-a-half one day when Jen reached up and gently traced her finger over the scar on my face and then the one on her own. She had done this several times since she first discovered it. That was the day she said that she wished she'd been hurt instead of me. This time we started talking about scars.

"Does the place still hurt?" she asked.

"No," I said. "It doesn't hurt anymore."

"But the scar will always be there?"

"Yes, Jen, it will."

"Does it bother you?"

"Sometimes," I admitted. "I wish I didn't have it, but I'm getting used to it."

"I have scars too," she observed. Jen has a scar on her stomach from the feeding tube and another on her hand. We sat quietly for a moment.

"Even though I don't like them," I said, "I try not to think of them as scars. They're beauty marks. My scars are a sign that I've been specially chosen by God to serve Him." Jen nodded thoughtfully.

Since that day, our scars have gone. We have beauty marks instead.

Not long after that conversation, Jen was having an especially tough day. She had a raging headache, had absolutely no energy, and kept asking over and over what day it was, only to forget as soon as I told her. It wasn't even lunchtime, and I was already frazzled. I came around the corner and saw her sitting in our chair with her eyes closed, praying out loud with an urgent edge to her voice: "Lord, I *need* you. Whisper 'hope' in my ear. Lord, whisper 'hope' in my ear."

I tiptoed over, leaned down quietly, and put my mouth next to her ear. In a stage whisper I said, "H-o-o-o-p-e," drawing it out. It was something that was on my heart every minute of the day but something I didn't give voice to nearly often enough: Hope out loud.

Jen's eyes flew open with surprise. She looked at me and then grinned from ear to ear. "Mom!" she exclaimed, "I wasn't talking to you!"

"Hope!" I said again, smiling back.

"You are *not* the Lord, and that is *not* what I meant," she said, trying to be stern but unable to suppress a giggle.

"I know, Jen." I gave her a hug.

"I love that the Lord always knows what we need to hear," she went on. "I was asking the Lord to tell me that I was beautiful, I was smart, I could do it, I could make the finish line, and that He believed in me."

Jen had no reservations about having a conversation with God out loud. To this day she continues to put a voice behind her faith. Often she'll say aloud to herself, "Jen, you love your life!" or "Jen, you're smart!" She says out loud the way she wants to feel. She prays out loud to the Lord all day long, and He whispers in her ear the things she needs to hear.

Hope out loud. You have to keep saying it.

The one-year mark after the accident was about the time I finally understood what God was doing in Jen's life. It wasn't a revelation that hit me all of a sudden, like a light coming on. It was more of a gradual unfolding of His plan in my mind and heart. I believe everything in the world happens for a reason, for the Lord to work out His perfect will in us. From our point of view it may not look good at all. It may look horrible. How can anything good come out of a near-fatal car accident that permanently altered the lives of four innocent people, one of them profoundly?

I'd already seen how the Lord was working in and through Jen to transform people's lives. He had drawn her close to Him, taking away everything about her that interfered with her spiritual walk, removing every distraction to her experiencing and proclaiming His love. He had made this once-shy teenager a bold voice for His Word, as if He had set her apart for Himself, releasing her from all the cares of this world that the majority of us have.

That was all great, but in the meantime I'd spent a year waiting for Him to bring her back to normal. Knowing that the first year was the most critical for recovering brain function, I'd thrown myself into reading to her, taking her to therapy and doctors, and observing what the therapists did so I could help her at home. I lived every day with a very high-maintenance teenager who was a divine inspiration one minute and a petulant child the next. I was ready for the Lord to fix everything.

I must admit I struggled desperately with this. I knew Jen's situation was God's plan for our family, but I wasn't ready to accept it. Why would God want to change a teenage girl who already loved Him so much? Why would God allow her to go through so much pain? As I healed physically, I started to struggle more emotionally with letting go and trusting God. It's easy to say but so hard to do, especially when it is your precious child who is suffering.

But just by watching Jen, I realized she had such *peace*. She was absolutely content with where God had her. She had already accepted the fact that God might not heal her completely. She was praising Him and thanking Him continually. She knew this world was not her home and she was just passing through. She had been in God's presence and had seen a glimpse of His glory. Every time she talked about the Lord, her face was radiant. It made me realize that by worrying so much about Jen's future, I was missing the blessings of today.

One day at church my friend Paula Egel, who is usually very positive and encouraging, pulled me aside and said very directly, "Linda, it's time for you to stop mourning and start celebrating." At first I was caught off guard, thinking, *She has no idea what I'm going through. How dare she say that!* But I knew Paula had my best interest at heart. She had been my faithful friend every day of this long journey.

Later that same day as I was reading my Bible, I came to Isaiah 43:18-19. The words jumped off the pages like never before: "But forget all that—it is nothing compared to what I am going to do. For I am about to do something new. See, I have already begun! Do you not see it?" I knew God was speaking to me. I had been mourning all of Jen's losses and all of the things about our family that would never be the same again. All that was out of my control. It was time for me to stop grieving and mourning for the "old Jen" and start celebrating the "new Jen." God had *new* things for her to do. She was never going to be "normal"; she was going to be *better* than that. God had set her apart to be extraordinary and to shine for Him. As I looked down at my Bible, I read in the very next sentence, "I am making a way in the wilderness and streams in the wasteland." In other words, God was telling me, "I can do the impossible! Have faith like Jen. Let go and trust Me!"

Then I came to a huge, life-changing realization: God *had* fixed everything. He had changed Jen's destiny. God had answered the months and years of prayer Jen had poured into her journals before the accident in a way no one could have imagined. She wanted to shout out the gospel. She wanted God to use her for His glory. She wanted boldness to be a witness. God had answered every prayer. She was on fire for the Lord, living for Him alone every minute of every day. God answered her by taking her life and doing the impossible with it. Through Jen's incredible ministry, He would bring glory to Himself.

On November 4, 2007, we joined a packed crowd at Thomas Road Baptist Church for an unforgettable celebration. Almost exactly a year ago that night, I'd sat with Andy and Josh in the same worship center, watching and listening as Jen and the rest of her school choir performed a roof-raising concert, including Jen's favorite song, "Lord, You're Holy." Then I heard my father preach an inspired sermon on prophecy. An hour later I had woken up in the crushed wreckage of the family minivan to see Andy and Jen bleeding and unconscious, their lives hanging by a thread.

The fact that we were even alive a year later was a miracle. But that paled in comparison to the miraculous journey God had led me on since then. It was a year when I, a pastor's kid, prayed more often and more fervently than I'd ever prayed in my life. A year when my prayers were faithfully answered not according to my will, but God's.

Thomas Road was celebrating that first anniversary with a huge thanksgiving service in our honor. Jen's high school choir was planning to sing "Lord, You're Holy." Jordan Davis, the soloist who had sung on the night of the accident, even came back from college to repeat her performance. The week before the service, I took Jen to school to practice with the choir. She was too anxious to walk into the choir room, where over a hundred students waited to rehearse with her. Instead, she sang along with the choir behind closed doors in the choir director's office. As the music played, Jen sang her heart out, lifting her hands up to the Lord where no one could see her.

That Sunday night four thousand people packed the auditorium as the walls reverberated with praise and music. Literally everybody in the room had prayed for Jen and the rest of our family. They were excited to see the miracle they'd prayed for. It was our way and the church's way of declaring loud and proud, "Satan, you're not going to win! We're going to keep praising God and proclaiming His name! You've already lost! We've read the Book, and we know how this story ends!"

Jerry Falwell, who had led TRBC since its founding in 1956 and had been such a faithful friend to us, had died on May 15, only four months after he visited Jen at Kluge the last time. His son Jonathan, Andy's high school friend, had succeeded him as senior pastor and led the celebration that night.

At the last minute, Jonathan asked our family to say a few words to the thousands who had come to share the moment. Jen became anxious, quickly turning to me and saying, "Mom, don't ask me any questions!" I didn't want Jen to get upset, yet I suspected that once she got onstage she would be fine, just as had happened at GO Church in Orlando. So I leaned over and whispered to Andy, "You'll have to be the one asking Jen questions."

Spontaneously, our family stepped into the spotlight and shared from our hearts. Andy thanked everyone for praying for us. I shared some of the miracle stories about Jen in the hospital when she praised God, talking to Him for hours and quoting Scripture out loud before she could even communicate with us.

Then it was Jen's turn. She expressed no emotion, though she was fidgeting on the stage. Andy turned gently to her.

"Jen, I want to ask you a question." Jennifer nodded her head and stopped moving around. "Has it ever crossed your mind to doubt God?"

Jen looked shocked, as if she hadn't expected anyone to ask her that question. It took a few seconds for her to process. Then she smiled broadly and said with confidence, "I would never doubt my Lord and my Savior. He is the one healing me daily!"

What a testimony! My heart was so full of joy I thought it would explode. When Jen finished, four thousand people expressed their own feelings of joy and appreciation with a standing ovation.

After we finished, the LCA choir came onstage to perform "Lord, You're Holy." Because of Jen's huge anxiety problems, we had no idea if she could actually stay onstage with the choir. Jen stood on the floor in the front row between her best friend, Kae Queen, and her other good friend Megan Clinton. Jen didn't have the balance or coordination to stand on the risers, so her two friends stood on the floor with her and supported her on each side.

Jen sang her heart out, her face glowing with joy. She raised her hands to the heavens as she worshiped her Lord and Savior with music. She was smiling and laughing, having the time of her life. At the end of the song Megan started to cry. She leaned her head on Jen's shoulder and said, "I love you, Jen." Megan was surely thinking about that night a year ago when the two of them had stood side by side singing the same song and Jen had squeezed Megan's hand as they got to her favorite part. Who could have imagined what would happen later that night?

After the choir finished, my dad began to preach on Revelation, just as he'd done the year before. Megan and Kae quickly escorted Jen offstage, and I met them in the hallway. Kae, who had been completely composed up until then, burst into uncontrollable tears when she saw me. We hugged and wept and hugged some more. Jen hugged us both and said, "I want to cry too, but the tears just won't come. I'm so full of joy!"

Afterward we had a big reception in the fellowship hall with a cake and a chocolate fondue fountain to thank all the people who had helped us and cared for us. It had taken an army of God's people to keep us going, a beautiful example of the body of Christ coming together and using their different gifts and talents to meet our every need. Only God could have orchestrated all that. We could never have survived on our own.

We had sent out invitations to the reception, and more than a hundred friends from church came, plus four faithful families from Pennsylvania. We showed a video of pictures from the year, beginning with Jen in the emergency room. Many of the people in the room that night were in the pictures because there had been someone with Jen and with me almost every minute around the clock for four months. Though it was a very emotional night, it was also amazing to see how far all the members of our family had come in a year. We couldn't think of a better way to celebrate and honor our friends than to praise God together for His faithfulness.

Brandon was the last guest to leave, bringing a gift for Jen. She took the little box from him and opened it. Inside was a silver charm bracelet with two charms, a girl praying and a boy praying. Brandon told Jen this was to remind her that he would always be praying for her. They shared a meaningful hug, and to this day they are still close friends.

At the end of the evening I was so grateful that God had given Jen the energy to enjoy it all. She was happy and content all night and went peacefully to bed. I have no doubt that as she slept, God was whispering in her ear the things she needed to hear.

A lesson I learned from Jen is that even if it isn't what I *want* to hear, God always tells me what I *need* to hear. That changes everything.

CHAPTER 14

THE COMEBACK KID

I have spared you for a purpose—to show you my power and to spread my fame throughout the earth.   EXODUS 9:16

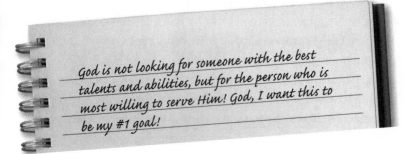

God is not looking for someone with the best talents and abilities, but for the person who is most willing to serve Him! God, I want this to be my #1 goal!

Jen's journal, a year and four months after the crash

THE FIRST ANNIVERSARY CELEBRATION at TRBC marked a turning point for Jen. Before that night she was mostly focused on survival and rehab, though she had been ministering to people around her since before she was even fully conscious. After the event at Thomas Road on November 4, 2007, she became more centered on speaking and sharing her testimony, even as her rehab continued. God began sharing with the rest of the world the miracle only a few of us had seen up until then.

My father invited our whole family to be guests on his Thanksgiving 2007 broadcast of *The King Is Coming* to talk about Jen's recovery and the amazing journey the Lord had taken us on. Under any other circumstances Jen would probably have been nervous and uncomfortable on the air. Fortunately, in her mind, the host of the show was not a renowned biblical scholar with five graduate degrees and a part in the writing or editing of more than forty books. He was just her grandfather—Papa Ed! And so at the moment she faced the biggest audience of her life to that point, Jen was probably the most relaxed she had ever been when speaking outside her own home.

The four of us sat on a long couch in the middle of a living room–style set with Dad in a chair at one end and Mom in her chair at the other. Seasoned interviewer that he is, Dad made sure to include everyone in the conversation, asked penetrating questions, then got out of the way to give each of us plenty of time to talk.

I explained that with God there are no accidents and that what had happened to us was all part of God's plan for our lives. That gave us a choice to make. We could focus every day on the tragedy, or we could focus on the miracle. We chose the miracle. God created us, so how could we ever doubt Him?

One very important point I wanted to make sure people understood was that just because we accepted God's plan didn't mean it was easy. Our lives were hard. They still are. Every day, every minute, is filled with pain and limitations. Every day I have to fight to stay positive. Every day I have to struggle to remember that this is God's plan and that He knows better than I do. Every day I have to make the decision all over again not to be angry or bitter. Every day I'm tired. Every day I'm concerned about Jen's safety and happiness and recovery. Every day I have scars on my body and a hand that doesn't work nearly as well as it once did. But God's grace is sufficient. In 2 Corinthians 12:9, God promises, "My grace is all you need. My power works best in weakness." I claim that grace every day.

I told our viewers, "Jennifer has ministered to all of us through her brain injury because she is so joyful and she praises the Lord."

Then I turned to Jen beside me on the couch and asked, "Are you ever tempted to doubt God or question why?"

Jen thought for a moment, then smiled and said, "Not one bit, because I have constantly reminded myself that the Lord's plan is perfect. And that He will help me through it. And He's been my stronghold every step of the way."

She also shared one of her favorite Bible verses, Nahum 1:7. I gave her the first four words, then she paraphrased the rest from memory: "The Lord is good. He is a stronghold in the day of trouble. He knows them who trust in him." She added, "The Lord has been my stronghold through it all. Before I could even talk to you I could pray for hours."

Jen loves that word *stronghold* as a description for the Lord. I think that's one reason she likes the song "Lord, You're Holy" so much, because it describes Him that way.

I told the story of Jen singing carols at Christmas. She couldn't see, couldn't eat, couldn't walk, but she sang carols of praise to her Lord and always ended each one with a hearty "Amen!"

Jen was such a lesson and inspiration to me, as I tried to explain. "I think people are hurting today. So many are hurting and going through struggles." Yet Jesus stands right beside believers, I added. He never leaves them. We can't all see Him the way Jen does, but we can have faith that He is there and will always carry us.

When my dad asked my mom about her experiences with Jen at the hospital, she reinforced that thought. "I went to help Jen in the hospital and I came away so blessed," Mom said. "She taught me what worship was. I had always played the organ and piano at church as a way to worship God, but my prayers were mostly asking God to help me with my requests. When Jen prayed, she never asked for one thing for herself. Her prayers were all worship and praise. One day she even prayed, 'Thank you for putting me into this place so I can spread Your Word.'"

When my dad asked Josh what he was learning as a result of the accident, Josh said, "God is teaching me that we aren't guaranteed tomorrow and that the most important thing in life is to go out and proclaim His name. I want to trust God with my whole life, and I know He will guide me and protect me."

Andy shared one of his favorite verses, Psalm 27:14 (NKJV), quoting: "Wait on the LORD; Be of good courage, and He shall strengthen your heart." Andy explained, "I take the second part of that verse to mean don't give up. Be of good courage. Never give up. Never reject God, because where else are we going to turn?" The things with which we fill our lives do not last, he said. "Only Christ lasts."

I tried to share more about my daily struggles with all the challenges around me. I explained that we are in a battle with Satan for our minds, and he wants to discourage and destroy us and keep us down. "So we're in a battle for our minds every day," I said, "and this battle has been long. It's been a year now. You have to re-wallpaper your mind with the truth of God's Word." I talked about how I had written Scripture verses on sticky notes and placed them around my bathroom mirror, in my purse, in the car, and scattered everywhere to remind me of God's promises. Satan is always looking for a weak place in our faith, trying to twist things and get us to doubt the truth. I need to be reminded that God's power and presence are always with me.

Andy spoke the prayer on all our hearts when he closed the interview by saying, "We're only here a brief time. This is not our home. Our home is in heaven, and we're going to spend all of eternity with our Lord and Savior, Jesus Christ. We just ask that Christ is glorified through this whole experience and that people would come to know Him as Savior."

A few weeks after our TV appearance, the director of women's ministries at TRBC, Lisa Harrington Bryant (no relation to Lisa Bryant, our nurse), asked me to lead the women's Bible study at church. I had led a group in my home since we lived in Pennsylvania, and I had been planning to start a study at church before the accident, which put those plans on hold along with everything else in my life. Now, a year later, Lisa reminded me that the need and the opportunity were still there. Would I take charge?

Lisa was perceptive enough to know it was time for me to get out of the house and pour myself into other women instead of focusing on my own problems. In my heart I knew God wanted me to follow through on my commitment even though I felt completely inadequate to the task. Still I hesitated. It took all my mental and physical energy just to get through the day with Jen and with my own physical challenges. I wasn't sure I could do the Bible study now. Besides, I couldn't leave Jen at home, and she couldn't sit still in the classroom during my lesson.

I decided that if God would give me the strength, I would serve Him any way I could. Starting in January 2008, I began leading an ongoing Bible study called Mountain Blend at Thomas Road Baptist Church. The first Tuesday morning I was there, we had about two hundred women. Someone came to the house to keep Jen company every week so I could go. Even with that help, I could barely make it to church most weeks.

Yet it didn't take me long to realize that teaching those women did far more for me than it did for them. It forced me in a new way to rely on God instead of on my own strength. It was as if God was asking me to live my life and struggles out loud in front of these women. Some days it was all I could do to keep from weeping in front of them. I knew I had to be real and honest. Life was hard for all of us, and every precious woman in that room had a story. If I had just quoted a few verses and acted like life was easy, I would have been lying. These women had not been hit by drunk drivers and their daughters didn't have brain injuries, but they had been broken and crushed by other things. I also knew that God was faithful and His mercies were new every morning. Just as He had carried me one day at a time, God wanted to help them too.

I knew from my own experience that there was incredible power in prayer. I had a burning desire to teach women to pray out loud in small groups around their tables—just short sentence prayers. I taught them to start by praising God for who He is and what He means to them, getting their focus on God instead of on the sadness, fear, or misery of their circumstances. I showed them how they could pray their requests instead of talk about them. *There's no power in talking, only in praying.* I wanted these women to experience the power of prayer the way I had, confident that once they did, their lives would never be the same.

Leading the Mountain Blend Bible study at that time is one of the hardest things I've ever done, but it was also one of the most rewarding. Today our women's ministry at TRBC welcomes over 550 women on Tuesday mornings, meeting around small group tables, plus the same number at a nighttime study under another leader. These women are now doing outreach ministries all over our local community. Look what God and the power of prayer can do. It is all about God! I am so thankful for Lisa Harrington Bryant and her vision for our women's ministry. Thankful, too, that she encouraged and prodded me at the beginning when it all seemed so impossible.

As the Bible study got underway at TRBC, Jen went back to school for a few hours a day for choir and Bible class, always accompanied by a friend to watch out for her safety and keep her from getting lost. While she never gave up hope, there were plenty of days when Jen felt depressed with her life. She turned to Scripture and her own journaling for comfort.

On January 13, 2008, she wrote, "I feel like the beggar who cried out to Jesus to be healed. Lord, honestly right now it is so hard. That is why I am crying out to You. Waiting patiently, Amen." If I thought I had a hard time overcoming the desire to stay in bed and dealing with my pain every day, Jen's obstacles were vastly greater. She inspired me by doing everything she could, every day she could, to fulfill God's plan for her life.

Jen had dreamed of working one day for Christian Cheerleaders of America. CCA had cheer camps all summer, and Jen wanted to have an influence on the girls who participated. She thought those dreams of being part of CCA were gone forever, but God decided otherwise. On March 7, 2008, Jen was invited to speak to more than a thousand girls at the CCA Nationals banquet. She couldn't believe it. This was better than her dream!

As Jen stepped onstage in her long, beautiful bronze-colored dress that shimmered with sequins, she absolutely glowed. She spoke without hesitation: "I never dreamed I would be standing here on this stage. I am so honored that God would use me. I was always the shy girl in the background. I was praying and asking God for boldness, and now I have it!" The audience watched a video clip of Jen cheering at CCA Nationals two years earlier when she won second as a freshman, then saw the story of how her life changed forever only a few months later. Jen spoke from her heart, telling the girls about her love relationship with the Lord and that no matter what happens in this life, no one can take that away from her. The same could be true for each of them.

Jen knew the changes in her life were a blessing from God. He had truly and faithfully given her the desire of her heart. She would never be able to cheer again, but she had a much greater privilege: God was giving her opportunities to speak for Him.

Those opportunities started coming thick and fast that spring and have never slacked off since. In May she was chosen as the

University of Virginia Children's Hospital Comeback Kid of the year. This was a huge surprise and another gift from God. We didn't even know there was such an award. Jen was written up in the local newspaper, which quoted Abena Foreman-Trice of UVA saying they had chosen Jennifer both because of her story and her personality. "Everyone was so impressed by the person that she is, and by her recovery, and her extremely positive attitude that is very grounded within her faith."[5]

The NBC affiliate in Charlottesville interviewed Jen in what had been her ICU room, which no one had expected her to leave alive. The TV news feature recapped the story of the accident and Jen's long road to recovery. "Her miraculous recovery is a testament both to her resiliency and to the committed and caring individuals who work at UVA Children's Hospital," the reporter said.

Dr. John Jane Jr., the neurosurgeon who had done so much to save Jen's life, explained why the hospital chose her for the honor. "She's our Comeback Kid because she was able to overcome what was truly a significant injury and recover from a long hospital stay and from an injury to her brain that many people didn't think she would recover from."[6]

On June 1, Jen appeared on national television during the annual fund drive sponsored by the Children's Miracle Network. The Network is an international nonprofit organization that raises donations for more than 170 children's hospitals, including UVA. It was so exciting to see Jen interviewed live by Laura French on the Children's Miracle Network Telethon and watch as a video of her story was broadcast. From quietly writing journals in her room, Jen was now giving her testimony on national TV to millions of viewers! She had never had an audience anything like it before. Only the Lord could have come up with something that miraculous.

The simple power and broad appeal of her message brought other opportunities to speak for the hospital. She told her story at fund-raising golf tournaments and at the Bad Pants Bash, a dinner and auction attended by the hospital's most generous patrons.

Even as her status as a public speaker grew, Jen faithfully continued writing in her journal, one of the few activities that bridged the chasm between life before the accident and life after. It was no longer the only means for her to express her faith, but it was still very important. Her entries were heartfelt, honest, and incisive, revealing that for all the blessings and improvements God had given her, life was still hard.

> 6/28/08
>
> Going through the storms of life isn't fun at all. I am sorry for ever doubting that it was too hard for You. I know that no one likes going through storms, but at the end of the day when they have finished it is the most beautiful day of all. Trials give us new perspectives on life that increase our faith. Please give me the strength and faith to make the journey. I am trusting in You. Amen.
>
> 6/29/08
>
> Thank you, Lord, for making Yourself so real to me. Please help me to want more of You in everything that I say and do. Please help me just to never be satisfied. Please make my heart available just to be used by You. I know I am weak so I am just begging You to use me just as I am. Amen.

6/30/08
Hey Daddy,
I honestly have had a rough day. I threw up and was
not feeling good so it feels nice to rest in Your presence.
Thank You for always hearing me when I cry out to
You. It means the world to me.

Often I had caught myself wishing desperately that Jen would be normal again one day. But at last I realized that the Comeback Kid would never be normal, yet that was a great blessing. Why should I long for her to be normal when God had chosen her to be extraordinary and miraculous? *Jen is Mine*, God had said to me. *You have to let go and trust Me.* At some level I knew that. Now I was starting to live it.

In June, a couple of weeks after the telethon, Andy and I were able to go to Hawaii to celebrate our twentieth wedding anniversary. Watching the ocean lap up on the beach, I reflected on our incredible journey of the past year and a half and decided I really didn't want to look back. It hurt to think about what had happened to us. So I thought about Jennifer and what God had done in her life. I took out a pad and jotted down some of the miracles of answered prayer:

• Jen has never been bitter or angry at God for what happened, and she praises Him continually. Even when she's sick or tired, she uses every opportunity to share Christ with others. "There isn't much time," Jen says, "and I have so much to do."

- Jen says, "When I'm singing and praising my Savior, nothing else matters because I feel His presence. I feel close to Him."
- Jen has a childlike faith. She has an ability to unconditionally take God at His word and never doubt His plan. She's uninhibited and uncensored in her excitement for the Lord and holds nothing back. Jen is in a whole different dimension with God than the rest of us.
- I'm amazed at how many teenage girls and women say they're jealous of what Jen has. I didn't understand that at first, but now I realize that they mean the freedom and the joy that Jen has in her walk with Jesus Christ.

I closed my eyes and prayed:

Lord, I'm overwhelmed as I sit here looking out at Your beautiful creation. It calls out to me that You are a God of wonder, majesty, and mystery. Father, You are amazing. You give us hope in the midst of the storm. I don't know how we could have survived except for Your loving protection and care. Please forgive my impatience. It's so hard to keep choosing joy when our lives seem so unfair.

Sometimes I feel Jen is being punished for something she didn't do, but then You show me that she has such a pure heart—much purer than mine. And I see now that this vibrant teenager was and is so in love with You. Her face radiates with the joy of the Lord. Her smile and her eyes sparkle. Everyone picks her out of a crowd because she reflects your love and is totally surrendered to you.

She wants her life to make a difference for eternity. I've heard her pray so fervently for boldness to share Christ, and You have answered that prayer in miraculous ways. Jen has big dreams, and she has a big heart for lost people. That's why I can never be bitter over what we have had to endure. It's all part of the plan and opportunity You have given us. Thank You, Jesus. Amen.

CHAPTER 15

BITTER OR BETTER

He will wipe every tear from their eyes, and there will be no more death or sorrow or crying or pain. All these things are gone forever.

REVELATION 21:4

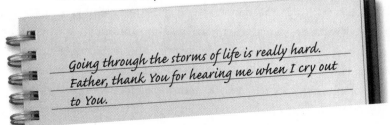

Going through the storms of life is really hard. Father, thank You for hearing me when I cry out to You.

Jen's journal, a year and a half after the crash

JEN LOVED GIVING HER TESTIMONY. When she spoke, she had the same focus and clarity as when she was praying. I asked her questions to help her along, and she moved through her story like a pro, speaking from her heart and sharing wonderful insights God had given her.

Other than the trip to Barry Rice's GO Church in Orlando during Josh's baseball tournament, all of our appearances had been in town in front of friends who knew our story. After Jen was chosen as the UVA Children's Hospital Comeback Kid in May of 2008, our speaking schedule expanded to a whole new level. That May and June the Barrick family spoke twenty-two times to groups ranging from Bible studies and the baseball team to the Fellowship of Christian Athletes and university evangelism classes of five hundred students each.

That fall we spent at home so Jen could concentrate on her schoolwork in hopes of earning a "real" high school diploma in the spring. Then in November we spoke at a state Baptist convention and for a fundraiser at Hershey Christian School in Pennsylvania. Even after all those appearances, I had no plans for any sort of long-term speaking ministry, though I was very comfortable doing it. But what we were talking about now wasn't really my story; it was Jen's.

Except for when she was actually in prayer or sharing her testimony, Jen Barrick remained an anxious, uncomfortable, confused, exhausted, unpredictable, occasionally stubborn, sometimes grumpy young lady who at any given time likely had either a migraine headache or stomach pain or both. I couldn't imagine her on a speaking tour. How could she possibly travel? How could I comfort and corral her when we were away from familiar surroundings and the company of faithful friends?

From the first day I spent with Jen in the hospital after the accident, every day has been an uphill climb. As she became more mobile and self-sufficient, the chances also increased that she would hurt herself. I had to make sure she took her many medications because she couldn't keep track of them. Mealtime remained a battle because after five months of not eating, now Jen couldn't control her appetite and wanted to eat every hour.

Grooming was another source of friction: she didn't like doing it. I would try to help her, but she often didn't want my help. She got upset at me when I tried to fix her hair, saying I was hurting her. She didn't know what season it was and wanted to wear winter boots in the summer or flip-flops in January. Taking a shower was exhausting for her because she would choke and throw up every time. She needed help with her makeup because she couldn't see very well.

Often her eyeliner would be really dark on the right side, which she couldn't see, with a line running down her cheek. When Jen was finally ready, she often needed a nap before going anywhere because she was worn out. People would see us out at a restaurant or a store and think she looked great. They had no idea of the time and effort it took to get her looking good and energized for one hour.

When Jen went to speak somewhere, these behavioral challenges came along too, in ways that were sometimes predictable and sometimes not. If we traveled very far, I always tried to arrive at our speaking venue early enough for Jen to take a nap. Riding in the car often upset her stomach, and she needed some downtime between the trip and her speaking. She struggled with fatigue and a confusion that could veer into irritability.

At home I could scarcely get her to run a comb through her hair. Before she stepped in front of an audience, she would be consumed with how her hair and makeup looked, fiddling with them and being preoccupied until the last instant. Then as soon as she stepped onstage, she was the picture of calm. And once she had the mike, God empowered her to share her testimony and proclaim His truth in a mighty way.

Before and after her presentation I had to keep Jen away from her admirers as much as possible. People wanted to touch her and hug her, which was painful because her body was still hypersensitive. Yet onstage, she connected with each listener like they were in the room alone together.

The fact that I had spent hundreds of days helping Jen and we had been on dozens of trips together didn't make the process any easier for me. Nor did knowing that Jen's condition was part of God's perfect plan for our lives and that her testimony was an inspiration to everybody who heard it. I prayed for patience, stamina, and strength in dealing with my own chronic pain, as well as understanding in dealing with Jen. I believe that God has answered me on every point. But it's still hard.

Though it would be much easier to stay at home, Jen gets a great sense of fulfillment from knowing that her pain has a purpose and that God is using her to encourage others. Her one passion in life is to tell people about Jesus.

This is a very important point in my story. God has blessed us so much, given us so many opportunities, brought Jennifer such miraculous healing. In spite of that, a blessed life doesn't mean an easy life. Every morning I have to make the decision to get out of bed and face the problems I know are going to be there. Some of them will be the same problems I faced the day before, and the day before that, and a hundred days before that, and which I'll face tomorrow and a hundred days afterward. I have always been a positive person, but now joy is a choice—I don't just have it automatically.

There are many days that I want to give up and crawl in a hole and never come out. But I can't because my family needs me. I have to fight for my family. God in His mercy didn't roll the boulders out of my path. What He did was give me light to see them by and the faith that, even when I can't detect it, there's a way through and around them.

That's why the sticky notes and pieces of paper I have scattered around my world are so precious. For two years I kept a big yellow sticky note of verses on my bathroom mirror. Every morning I claimed those Scriptures out loud just to survive. I need constant reminding of the promises in God's Word. That He knows the desires of my heart. That He alone is my rock and my salvation, so I will not be shaken. That God had always been faithful to us in the past and He will not forsake us now. That He has a plan for me, a hope and a future. That His mercies are new every morning; great is His faithfulness. That not a sparrow falls without Him knowing about it. That He will never leave me nor forsake me.[7]

Every morning for three years prior to the accident, I had bowed on my knees in the kitchen while the coffee was brewing to praise God and surrender my day to Him. After I came home from the hospital, Andy brought me coffee in bed, and with my broken ribs and other injuries it had been almost impossible for me to kneel and pray. I had honestly forgotten all about beginning my day that way. Then I saw Jen rolling out of bed every morning and landing on her knees, thanking God, praising Him, dedicating the day to serving Him, asking Him to fill her with His strength to do what she could never do on her own. She realized that the power of prayer is one of the great miracles of life and that it's always available. God is always waiting, always ready to listen. She didn't even take one step without the Lord. I resolved that never again would I give up the privilege of bowing every morning to my Creator. I started praying on my knees again and have done it every day since.

I remained in awe of the power of Jennifer's testimony. There was a part of me that thought public interest in her story might fade after a while. Then as Jen and I began speaking more often, I came to realize that our story isn't the story of a car accident. Our story is the story of God's grace and the working out of His perfect will in our lives. It's the story of faith that allows me to trust God even when I don't understand His plan. It's the story of embracing life one day at a time, letting go of past regrets and leaving tomorrow's problems for tomorrow. It's the story of giving up the dreams I had for the reality I have. It's the story of celebrating the overflowing blessings God has given me rather than mourning what I've lost. It's the story of resting in the Lord and finding contentment in my life today.

And it's one more thing, which is related to the question people ask me more than any other. Of all that has happened, of all the ways God has moved in my life, the number one thing everybody wants to know is this:

"How could you ever forgive that drunk driver for what he did?"

That's a fair question. Not only how could I forgive him, but why? Why should I forgive him? My daughter was innocent. An hour before, she had been singing praises to her Lord. The other driver was fleeing from the police in a truck even though his driver's license had been revoked for more than twenty previous driving violations, including multiple DUIs. That driver was trying to find fulfillment in things that didn't satisfy, and Jennifer and the rest of us paid the price for his mistakes.

Our whole family has suffered because of the sin of someone else. The drunk driver is still alive but essentially brain-dead, unable to function on his own. I wonder if he knew his final drink that November night would be his last? Every day as we watch Jen struggle in pain, Andy has been tormented with the thought that he wasn't able to protect Jen. Now our family will never be the same because of the poor choices made by someone else. In one instant our lives were changed forever.

Actually, I've had an easier time dealing with the drunk driver than with the policeman who questioned him and then let him get away. I believe the officer should have handcuffed him and hauled him in, or at the very least should have taken his keys, because he was obviously extremely intoxicated. Instead, the officer stepped away and left him behind the wheel.

Then there was the ongoing nightmare with our own health and auto insurance companies that we had to battle because the drunk driver was uninsured. Jen was forced out of the hospital after three months even as the drunk driver was still receiving full-time medical treatment. All of these characters and circumstances played a part in robbing my daughter of her future and replacing it with a life of limitations and pain.

See how fast and easy it is to start dwelling on the loss? "Robbing"; "a life of limitations and pain." How quickly Satan can find a foothold! Our real enemy isn't flesh and blood or accidents and disappointments; it's Satan. As John 10:10 says, he comes "only to steal and kill and destroy" (NIV). Those thoughts are never far away, and it would be so easy to give in to them. He wants to destroy my family, my marriage, and my home. He wants to steal my joy. But with strength that can come only from God, I choose not to give in. I say *no*. The evil one will not win! In that same verse, Christ promises us He has come so we may not only have life but "have it to the full." He will never let Satan defeat us if we trust in Him.

Forgiveness is not a feeling; it's a choice I make every day. Some days I make it every hour. I have struggled with being angry at God for allowing all this to happen. As a mom, I prayed faithfully for the Lord to protect my family. After the accident I believed He had let me down. Every time I thought that, Satan saw his opening and whispered, "See what God let happen to that beautiful daughter of yours? She loved the Lord with all her heart. Now look at her! He let a drunk driver going eighty miles an hour hit her head-on!"

In my heart I questioned whether the Lord had been good to my family and whether I could still rely on Him. But if not on God, then on what? I realized there was nowhere else I could turn. God alone is my only hope. And as the old hymn says, "All other ground is sinking sand."[8] Satan wants to keep me bound in bitterness and lies. God offers me freedom to let go and trust Him.

When I was a child, my father taught me that when people hurt me I have a choice to make: I can become bitter, or I can become better. If I don't forgive, it only hurts me. When I don't forgive, the person who is the focus of my anger is all I can think about and consumes my thoughts. That person becomes an idol because he or she is placed in front of God. I agree with people who say holding on to bitterness is like taking poison and hoping the other person will die. The drunk driver is still in a vegetative state and doesn't even know what he did. He doesn't care how I feel. My anger doesn't affect him at all. Nor does it affect the others I'm tempted to condemn. My bitterness hurts only me. And I've been hurt enough already without adding to it myself. So I decide every day to be better, not bitter, and with God's help that's what I do. I had to lay the hurt and bitterness at God's feet. It is impossible to forgive in my own strength. But as Philippians 4:13 reminds us so beautifully, "I can do all things through Christ who strengthens me" (NKJV). Not some things, *all* things. And that includes forgiving others, no matter what they've done.

I'm proud of Josh for his spiritual maturity through all this. He, too, has chosen to forgive. He still prays for the man who hit us. "I'm not mad at him," he says. "I feel sorry for him, even when I look at all that my family has been through. Jen didn't deserve what happened to her. Some days I wish I had the brain injury instead of her."

Josh is also perceptive enough to sense how I still struggle with my old dreams for Jen: "Mom gets sad sometimes because she sees all that Jen has lost and tries to give her as normal a life as possible, then realizes that Jen is not like normal people. God has made her stand out. God has a way more special calling on her life than she had before. God has set her apart for His glory."

Josh and Andy sometimes join Jen and me in our presentations, and also speak on their own. Josh sees these opportunities as part of God's perfect plan for our family. If not for the horrific accident, "we wouldn't be able to witness to people everywhere," he says. "We wouldn't have a story to tell."

Jen has never blamed God, never doubted Him. She has never

been bitter or angry either, though at one stage, she did question if she deserved what had happened. "Why do I have to forgive?" she asked. "What did I do wrong?" Like me, she has often prayed out loud for God to help her forgive. "Sometimes I can only forgive half-heartedly," she admits, then segues effortlessly into prayer as though she were turning to someone else in the room in conversation:

"Help me to see people through Your eyes. I pray for spiritual eyes that God would allow me to see what He wants me to see. Help me to love people the way You love us. Help me to see everyone as an equal chance. Only through Jesus' grace are we capable of total forgiveness."

After she spoke one day, a gentleman in his fifties asked Jen why she wasn't bitter. "I have to forgive because I want God to forgive me," she explained. "I don't want to limit what God wants to do in and through me."

Jen's spiritual perception never ceases to amaze me. After she started noticing her scars, she didn't like them very much, and I didn't blame her. What girl would? Perhaps that's why one of her favorite songs is "Heal the Wound" by Point of Grace. Part of the lyric goes: "Heal the wound but leave the scar, a reminder of how merciful you are."[9]

One day she and I were talking about our scars, as we do from time to time. "But you know, Jen," I said, "I think of them not as scars but as beauty marks of God's faithfulness." We had discussed this before, but she had never expressed herself on the subject with such conviction and God-given insights.

"Everybody has scars," she said. "They may be outside like mine, or they may be deep inside your heart, invisible to the rest of the world. But God wants to redeem every scar and buy back everything that has been taken from us."

Jen continued, "You know, Mom, Jesus has scars too. He has nail prints in His hands that shout, 'I love you, and I died for you!'"

From that moment on Jen and I have never been ashamed of our scars. They remind us of the miracle of God's grace.

CHAPTER 16

REACHING OUT

No eye has seen, no ear has heard, and no mind has imagined what
God has prepared for those who love him.   I CORINTHIANS 2:9

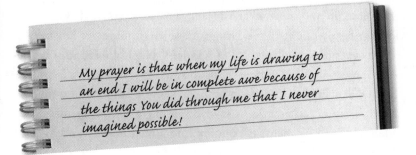

My prayer is that when my life is drawing to an end I will be in complete awe because of the things You did through me that I never imagined possible!

Jen's journal, three weeks before the crash

As we passed the second anniversary of the crash, Jennifer's
enthusiasm for proclaiming Christ and helping others was stronger
than ever. She was absolutely on fire for the Lord! There was no
end to the compassion she felt for others, no limit to her capacity
for reaching out to anyone she felt was hurting or in crisis. Jen had
gradually recovered her emotions, though as her personality emerged
from the fog of the brain injury it was still completely different from
what it had been before the accident. The first glimpses we'd had of
the new Jen showed us an outgoing, sanguine young lady who never
met a stranger. She reinforced that impression as God continued to
heal her.

The quiet, deep thinker was now a bubbly extrovert who could talk to anyone and didn't care what they thought about her. The idea of trying to impress someone never crossed her mind. She spoke the truth from her heart, which was sometimes startling because she didn't have many of the social filters we have. Would what she had to say be embarrassing? Confusing? Seemingly inconsistent? She didn't know and didn't care. Over Christmas dinner, she told my sister with three small children, "I don't mean to be rude, but your kids can definitely be quite a handful. You might want to consider a little stronger discipline, if you know what I mean." Thank goodness it was my sister and everyone got a good laugh out of Jen's unhindered honesty.

Another new challenge for us was Jen's inability to control her emotional swings from one extreme to another. She could be laughing and dancing one minute and crying uncontrollably the next. She might carry on an amazing conversation like a spiritually mature adult and then moments later bump into a table and fall to pieces emotionally and physically like a toddler. I never knew what emotion or "age" I should be prepared to handle next.

Physical pain seemed to send her into a downward spiral more than anything else. Because of her sensitivity, she felt excruciating pain whenever her poor eyesight caused her to hit her head on a cabinet door or walk into a wall. She would cry loudly and say, "I hate my life. Did I deserve this? I've had a headache for weeks. I can't remember what it is like to feel good. No one knows what I am going through."

While these mood swings were—and still are—emotionally exhausting for all of us, they have also been one of the areas where God has shown His power in her weakness most emphatically. I quickly learned that if I quoted a verse, such as "I can do all things through Christ who strengthens me," out loud, Jen's outlook would brighten instantly.

God's strength working through Jen's weakness is also evident in her ability to speak or minister to others for any length of time. In fact, it is nothing short of miraculous. Most people who see Jen publicly have no idea how many miracles are alive and active beneath the surface.

From having no emotions at all during her rehab at Kluge, she became very expressive, showing us her love every chance she had. She told her friends and family how much she loved them dozens of times a day. She meant it with all her heart, and she didn't remember that she'd told the same person the same thing five minutes before. She hugged and kissed us every morning and every night. She got so excited every time she saw us that a stranger watching would have thought she hadn't seen us in a year. Good-natured as always, Josh patiently put up with her kissing him every time she saw him, even if it was in front of his buddies at a ball game.

The way Jen's emotions work now reminds me of the way she initially reacted when she felt water on her skin in the shower: everything is enhanced and magnified. When she's happy, she's the happiest person in the world. When she's moody, she gets very abrupt and insistent, though never mean. When she realizes she has misunderstood or misinterpreted something, she apologizes profusely over and over. I think her sensitivity has a lot to do with how strongly she feels the pain and suffering of others. Her emotions are magnified in her just like the feel of the water was magnified.

As a consequence of that empathy, she's drawn like a magnet to anyone who is struggling or has a special need of some kind. One day Jen asked me, "Do you think I have special needs? Sometimes people look at me funny like they are trying to figure me out."

I smiled and said, "Jen, you have so much wisdom and spiritual insight way beyond your years. You are the person I run to for prayer and advice. But you do have some obvious physical limitations. The good news is that God is still healing you a little more every day."

With conviction in her voice and a big smile on her face, Jen replied, "I hope God is healing me every minute!"

Jen shared her wisdom and spiritual insight with many thousands of people in the months that followed. One of the first outings in 2009 was on Valentine's Day. Jen remembered how she enjoyed our family tradition of going to a hospital on Christmas Eve with a group of friends, singing carols and passing out candy canes to the patients. The opportunity to give instead of receive made it one of our favorite Christmas activities. She decided she wanted to celebrate Valentine's Day with a visit to cancer patients, many of them elderly, in the hospital. Since she was leading a Bible study of middle school cheerleaders at LCA, she invited them to come with her. Some varsity cheerleaders and junior varsity basketball players joined in as well. A dear friend of ours had designed sweet little stuffed bears called Born Again Bears that Jen wanted to hand out. They were fuzzy brown teddy bears with a red heart and a place inside for prayer requests. Each one came with a pocket-size Plan of Salvation.

So two other moms and I loaded up twenty-five Born Again Bears along with Jen plus the ten other girls in their uniforms and headed for the hospital. Jen prayed with the girls in the lobby before we started, asking God to make them a light to the patients and to help the girls share God's love with them. Jen reminded her friends, "Everyone is looking for love in all the wrong places. We forget that God *is love!*"

We went up to the cancer wing where most of the patients were terminally ill. Jen led the way into the first room, holding hands with a cute, spunky little cheerleader sporting a red, white, and blue hair bow. Jen gave the patient a dazzling smile and exclaimed, "Happy Easter!"

Jen's little friend squeezed her hand and reminded her that it was Valentine's Day. "Oh, I'm so sorry," Jen said without a pause. "Happy Valentine's Day!"

She might not have known what day it was, but as soon as Jen started talking to the patients about God's love, the words flowed effortlessly out of her mouth. As she began her testimony she drew from that tower of strength she was always singing about with such joy. She had an immediate connection with every patient on the hall, some of whom were mad at God for their illness and suffering. She understood their pain and how hard it was not to know the future. She told them that God loved them so much that He sent His only Son, Jesus, to die on a cross and pay the price for all of their sins so that they could go to heaven someday. She told them that even if they weren't physically healed, they could be healed in their souls with the peace of God. She asked all the patients if they knew Jesus as their personal Savior, then explained what it meant to be "born again" as she handed them each a bear.

Then she would ask if she could pray over them. Every single patient, even the ones who were angry, welcomed Jen's prayers. In every room, Jen's prayer flowed out with wisdom and discernment from God—exactly what those fragile, hurting men and women needed that day. Every prayer was completely different. It was as if God Himself were praying through her the very message each person needed to hear. The words she spoke were so powerful that the other two moms and I stood in the hallway with tears flowing down our faces. This child, who didn't know what day it was, prayed the glory of heaven down into every hospital room. By the time Jen finished, the patient would be smiling and hugging her and begging her not to leave.

After visiting all the rooms in one hallway, Jen was exhausted and needed to stop. That's when another wonderful transformation took place. The shy cheerleaders and basketball players, emboldened by Jen's example, started going on their own into the hospital rooms in groups of two or three. Then they felt the joy in their own hearts of praying with the patients and giving each one a Born Again Bear. That day Jen lifted the spirits of a hall full of very sick people. And while she was at it, she showed ten younger girls that "It is more blessed to give than to receive" is more than just a Bible verse—it's the truth.

As more people heard our story, speaking invitations increased from a steady stream to a torrent. People who knew of us through the Liberty University community, the LU evangelism classes, the Children's Miracle Network interview, or one of our earlier appearances wanted to meet Jen and hear her story firsthand. I told Jen about these requests but also told her we didn't have to accept them if it was too tiring.

"No," she insisted, "I want to speak. Every soul is important to the Lord." So I never said no to an invitation unless we were already booked or it was impossible to get somewhere at the right time. Sometimes we had two presentations in the same weekend.

During the spring of 2009 we spoke somewhere every weekend, throughout Virginia and in Texas and Georgia. These trips were exhilarating and deeply rewarding. They were also frustrating and exhausting. Though Jen's schedule was busier than ever, her stamina had plateaued, so conserving her energy was a constant challenge.

She thrived on the familiar—whether places, people, food, routines, movies, or music. She loved it when she recognized a song or knew what the next scene in a movie would be.

Traveling required just the opposite. Being surrounded by unfamiliar people in strange places, getting through airports, and staying in hotels were all unsettling for Jen. Not knowing where she was or what was happening made her apprehensive and fidgety. It would have been far easier and less stressful to stay home. But Jen knew God wanted her to go, and she was determined to fulfill what she saw as her responsibility to Him.

I quickly learned that it was best not to prepare Jen ahead of time or preview the questions I was going to ask onstage. When I did that, I would get her best stuff in the car. On the spot she would give an amazing testimony and talk about all the possible ways we could encourage people and what we might say. But she would use her brain too much, so that by the time we got onstage she would be worn out and yawning. Besides—and I should have figured this out sooner—preparing ahead was a waste of time because Jen didn't remember any of it anyway. Her best preparation was to pray and ask God to speak through her when the moment came.

Managing Jen away from home was sometimes almost more than I could do alone. For such a time as this, God brought a new friend into Jen's life. Lauren Moody was a student at LU who started traveling with us every weekend. Just under five feet tall, Lauren exudes energy and enthusiasm, her big, blue eyes framed by light-brown curls. She never got upset with Jen and happily accepted her just the way she was, with no expectations.

Since I've never liked to drive, I asked Lauren to drive to all our Virginia speaking dates. Lauren's trusty GPS unit would help us get everywhere easily and on time. At least that was the theory. In practice, that little screen led us on some crazy adventures. We'd get lost, we'd get confused, we'd end up going the wrong way down a one-way street. Somehow with God's help we always made it to our destination safe and on time.

The process of preparing Jen to speak began as soon as we arrived. The movement of riding in a car usually gave Jen a bad headache, so that she got to the speaking venue tired, grumpy, and in pain. No matter how specific I was in talking to our hosts in advance, sometimes people wanted to meet Jen, talk to her, shake her hand, and hug her right away, all of which made her anxious and uncomfortable. The first order of business was to find a quiet place for her to lie down. If we had a hotel room, we went there. If we were at a church or school, I would scout out somewhere for her to get away and take a nap.

After she rested, I had to fix Jen's hair and do her makeup. Sometimes we were invited to dinner before we spoke, which meant another hurdle for Jen because she often felt ill after eating. Also, from the time we arrived until the time we spoke, Jen never went more than a few minutes without needing to go to the bathroom. The last time would be as close as possible to the moment we walked onstage.

It took all of my and Lauren's attention to keep Jen happy and calm. As I tried to get myself ready and pull my thoughts together, Jen would be asking a hundred rapid-fire questions prompted by her anxiety and anticipation.

"Where will I stand? Who will help me up the steps? Will I have a microphone? When can I eat dinner? What if people touch me too much? Can you please remind them not to touch me unless they ask me first? I love to hug people—it just scares me when they come at me from behind and I can't see them. Sometimes people squeeze my neck and hurt me. Should I wear earplugs? What if the music is too loud? What questions are you going to ask me? What are the plans for tomorrow?"

When I responded to her questions, she remembered my answers for only a minute. The one thing that calmed her was to stop and pray together. Then she would be all right again for a while.

Sometimes Jen's headaches and stomach pain would well up at this point and become almost unbearable. When that happened she would declare out loud, "Satan, you are not going to win! I can do all things through Christ who strengthens me!"

I kept last-minute snacks in my purse because Jen ate only a little at mealtime and was hungry every hour. She couldn't function if she was hungry. Lauren and I were lucky to have five minutes to get ourselves dressed and comb our hair. Sometimes the two of us didn't look so good. One night Lauren had on this cute black dress, and luckily, as she was walking out the door I noticed the tag sticking out—she had her dress on inside out. That was good for a welcome, tension-relieving laugh!

Jen was often the most confused and disoriented right before she spoke. One night she was in the bathroom minutes before we were to go on, already wired up with a head mike. Thank goodness I went in to help her hurry because I caught the microphone/earpiece contraption just as it was about to fall in the toilet. We had another good laugh and thanked the Lord for sparing us that little inconvenience.

Anyone who saw Jen as I did in the hours and minutes before she went onstage would never believe she could hold a room full of people mesmerized by her presence and her testimony. But the moment she got onstage, God would speak through her. Watching her, then and now, is truly amazing for me because I know how fragile and confused and in pain she is, and how there's no way she can be up there doing and saying the things she does. Every time she steps onstage, God shows the world another miracle.

When I once asked Jen why she never got nervous once she started speaking, she told me, "I just picture Jesus standing in the back of the room, and I am talking to Him."

Sometimes she preaches a complete sermon in a prayer, and the whole audience weeps as God speaks to every heart individually. She will quote different verses or tell Bible stories that I didn't even know she knew. They are hidden in her heart, and God reminds her of them at just the right time.

Speaking gives her such joy. I still lead her through her stories with questions, and also speak about my own experience and what it's like as a mom watching Jen's progress. As she has continued improving, I've adjusted my account of Jen's recovery and her limitations. She has become more aware of what I'm talking about when I discuss her day-to-day problems with memory and functioning. While I want the audience to understand and appreciate her struggle, I don't want to say anything that will embarrass her or make her self-conscious.

I could fill another book with stories of Jen and her audiences. She especially loves speaking to young girls. One night after three hundred teenage girls heard her tell her story, eleven of them prayed to receive Christ as their personal Savior. As soon as the event was over, thirty girls got in line to talk to Jen and get her autograph. Usually Jen is completely drained at the end of the presentation and needs to lie down again in a quiet place. Sometimes she will almost hide from people in an effort to relax. This time, her usual weariness and anxiety completely disappeared, and she grabbed a pen to autograph the first girl's folder. But she was so mentally tired after speaking she couldn't remember how to write her name. I saw her pause, look up, and pray out loud, "Lord, please help me remember how to sign my name!" Then in the next breath she exclaimed, "Thank You, Lord, thank You!" She autographed all thirty folders, adding her favorite Bible verse, 1 Corinthians 2:9, at the bottom, the same verse she had quoted when she spoke at the national cheerleading competition only months before the accident.

She prayed one-on-one with the girls, got her picture taken with them, and gave them advice about their problems. One girl asked her how old she was, and she hollered across the room to me, "Mom, how old am I?" It was 11 p.m. by the time she was done. Jen had never functioned that late at night before. She had never been capable of talking to so many people afterwards. On this night God had given Jen the strength to minister to these girls even after everything was over. He was healing her some more!

We spent the night in a beautiful, white Victorian home in the countryside. The owners were out of town and had graciously let us stay there so the church didn't have to pay for a hotel. I was helping Jen get ready for bed when I noticed hundreds of little flying black beetles all over the ceiling and on the bed. Where did they come from? There must have been an open window somewhere. The good news was they didn't seem to sting or bite. I stood on Jen's bed and killed what seemed like a hundred on the ceiling. Lauren and I worried that this would upset Jen and she wouldn't go to sleep. What were we going to do?

While we were battling the bugs, Jen brushed her teeth and climbed into bed despite the fact that bugs were raining down on her from the ceiling. She simply closed her eyes and prayed, "Lord, please help me to sleep with my mouth closed so I don't swallow any bugs," then immediately fell sound asleep. I, on the other hand, slept with my head under the covers, and Lauren stayed up all night swatting at beetles with her slip. That was one trip we will never forget!

The ride home is generally like the ride out, in that it gives Jen a splitting headache and makes her grumpy. It's like the need has been met, the show is over, and she wants to be home. Traveling works best when she knows there's a purpose in the trip. She needs to understand the reason for going somewhere, and then God enables her to embrace all the hardship and make it through the journey.

Another incredible journey for Jen that spring was the process of getting through high school and earning her diploma. Through her daily LCA classes in choir and Bible, we were trying to get Jen back to familiar surroundings and back into her friends' lives. I thought being in a classroom environment would be good for her; however, it was very hard for her to be in crowded hallways or to remember where she was going next.

Also, it didn't take long for her to start figuring out that she no longer fit in. I think some of her old friends felt awkward around her. She wouldn't remember talking to them a few minutes earlier and would say the same things over and over. Her loud, blunt questions could be embarrassing. And for some well-meaning, good-hearted girls, the situation was simply too much.

We were walking in the mall one day and ran into an old soccer teammate. At first she seemed excited to see Jen, and the two of them started talking. Then without warning the friend burst into tears, cried out, "Oh Jen, I'm so sorry!" and hurried away. Jen turned to me and asked, "What's wrong with her?"

It was hard for Jen's peers to have a normal, offhand conversation with her. She didn't care about the things most teenagers obsessed over. While I loved that Jen was on a spiritual high, it deeply pained my heart that after all she'd been through, my daughter felt left out. Students she knew would pass her in the hallway at school without speaking. How could kids be so insensitive and not take time to say hello?

If you are the parent of a physically challenged or special-needs child, I'm guessing this is one of your biggest heartaches: longing for classmates or peers to view your child as "normal" and to take the time and effort to be his or her friend, to talk to your child more than in passing, or to invite him or her to do something—anything at all. I realize most of the kids probably didn't know what to say so they decided to say nothing. I'm sure they wanted to help but didn't know how. Nevertheless, I wanted my daughter to feel some comfort of acceptance in her old stomping grounds. Once again, though, it was Jen who taught me the greater life lesson.

In the car on the way to school, she'd start getting anxious and say, "Tell me I'm beautiful. Tell me you believe in me. Tell me I'm smart. Tell me I can do this." It suddenly dawned on me that every teenage girl must be thinking these things. They just never say them out loud. I had the privilege to glimpse what was really going on in my teenage daughter's heart because of Jen's uninhibited emotions. I remember thinking, *I've got to tell moms what their daughters are thinking.* Then Jen would suddenly start praying out loud, "Lord, help me to encourage someone else today." She calmed her anxieties by focusing on others instead of on the way she felt. I realized that's how we would survive our physical, emotional, and spiritual roller coasters—by helping others find hope.

Jen was at high school only a couple of hours a day and lived for the most part in a completely different world from her peers. But like most girls, she dreamed of wearing a beautiful dress and going to her school's junior-senior banquet. Her friends had been planning and talking about it for months. When Jen asked her good friend Luke Seavers if he would take her, he gladly accepted.

Even though the Seavers lived in Pennsylvania, our families still got together at least twice a year. Luke was a year older than Jen and had been the friend who visited her in the hospital, singing at her bedside and playing his guitar because he knew how much Jen loved praise music. Luke, now a very handsome young man with blond hair and green eyes, was gracious enough to drive five hours from his home to make Jen's dream of going to the formal banquet come true.

Jen looked like a princess in an iridescent purple dress that changed colors in the moonlight, one of those Cinderella styles that puffed out from the waistline and turned every head in the room when she walked in. Jen was so excited, and we knew Luke would take great care of her.

The band at the banquet was too loud for Jen, so at Luke's suggestion, he and Jen walked up and down the streets of downtown Lynchburg in deep conversation as cars honked and onlookers hollered at Jen because she was in such a beautiful dress.

The best part of the night for Jennifer was the huge surprise Luke had waiting for her back at our house: he had written a song about her and recorded it with his band, My Useful Weakness. Jen listened with her eyes closed, enraptured, taking in every word. "Miracles never seemed so true than to see you here and hear you pray. . . . Lives are being changed because one girl was willing to obey."

She especially loved the lyrics at the end of the chorus:

Sometimes we don't understand what's in Your plan
But I'm going to trust,
I'm going to follow You.[10]

Luke recorded Jen's voice that night quoting 1 Corinthians 2:9 and added it to the recording of "Jen's Song." He even put it on iTunes.

Wonderful as it was attending the formal banquet and having a song written in her honor, Jen still faced the challenge of passing her state proficiency tests and earning her high school diploma. Jen's homebound teacher, Kim Cherry, came to the house twice a week to work with her on the core subjects of English, science, math, and history. God also provided two tutors from Liberty University, Samantha and Stephanie, to help her finish school. These two girls loved Jen and over time became her very closest friends. They enjoyed praying, laughing, and having adventures together on the weekends. (Stephanie has remained close to Jen and even lived with us one recent summer. She has spent countless hours taking Jen out to eat, going through the steps of paying for purchases in stores, and otherwise helping integrate Jen back into the real world.)

In order to graduate, Jen had to pass the Standards of Learning tests for Virginia. I was sure this was an impossible task. The closer we came to test time, the more concerned and anxious I became. Jen's memory was improving, but she still had a long way to go. Jen, however, was not the least bit worried.

Mrs. Cherry spent many hours preparing Jen for the SOL tests, encouraging her and telling Jen she believed in her. In order for Jen to graduate with a "real" high school diploma, she had to pass all her state tests, including algebra. I knew there was no way she could pass the algebra exam given to regular high school seniors. All I could do was pray and worry and hope for a miracle. One day I was cleaning Jen's room and found a journal she had written six months before. She was praising God as if graduation had already happened! There was no doubt in her mind that she'd do it. And of course, in the end, she was right. She got her diploma in June.

Hey Daddy!

It's me, Jen! You know, the one with the brain injury. I'm sure You remember me! LOL Well, I don't want to dwell on myself, I want to dwell on You and who You are! I just wanted to thank You for Your healing hand and just for all the hope and encouragement that You give me! I do have some exciting news that You deserve all the credit for. Have I told You that I am graduating this year from high school? Hehe!! Well, I do have to pass the algebra SOL test, but I know with Your help I can do anything!

Lord, I think I am doing pretty good. I am kind of scared about the future and what it holds. I don't want to limit You and what You want to do through me. At times I'm not sure if I have the faith that I am going to need to survive through life. So Father, I am just asking that You will increase my trust and my hope so that I will make the finish line. Lord, help me to never take for granted that You are my escort. Daddy, I know with Your help, the two of us can change this lost and dying world together! I love how You use the weak and incapable for Your glory, so that means You can use me just as I am. Lord, I know I can't do anything without You being by my side.

Father, I would like to pray that You would reveal Yourself to me today! I want You to become greater and me to become less. Lord, help me to make You my one passion and the one reason that I am living for. I give You my all and my everything! Please Lord, order my steps for Your ultimate glory! Thank You so much for listening! Oh, and I almost forgot to say,

I love You!!!

It's in Your wonderful and precious name, Amen

CHAPTER 17

IS ANYTHING THE SAME?

Forgetting the past and looking forward to what lies ahead, I press on
to reach the end of the race and receive the heavenly prize for which
God, through Christ Jesus, is calling us. PHILIPPIANS 3:13-14

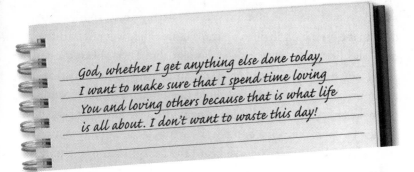

*God, whether I get anything else done today,
I want to make sure that I spend time loving
You and loving others because that is what life
is all about. I don't want to waste this day!*

Written on Jen's homework pad, two days before the crash

GOD HAD GIVEN JEN HER OWN SPECIAL PLACE IN HIS WORLD. And
along with reminding me how extraordinary Jen was, He reminded
me that she lived according to her unique set of standards and not the
world's. I'm ashamed to admit that I worried about what strangers
out in public thought of Jen because she was so uninhibited, almost
boisterous. She still laughed uncontrollably at times. She heard music
in the mall and suddenly started dancing. In church, she answered
the altar call week after week.

When I confessed to the Lord that sometimes I was still consumed
with the idea of Jen getting back to "normal," He again challenged

me: *Why do you want Jen to be normal when I have set her apart to be extraordinary and to walk in the miraculous with me?*

Why was I chasing after my limited, shortsighted goals instead of the ones an all-knowing, all-loving God had in store for me? Why did I wake up anxious and worried in the middle of the night? Where was my faith? Why couldn't I trust God like Jennifer trusted Him? I had to try. The next time I woke up with my nerves in a knot I started singing a praise song—and it worked! It made me focus on God instead of on me and my problems.

Months later during a walk, Jen put words to my thoughts when she said out of the blue, "God is speaking to my heart, and for every door that closes, He will open up three more. They will just be different." She didn't care what anyone thought about her. She only cared about her audience of one, her Lord and Savior Jesus Christ, and about proclaiming His hope out loud to a broken and needy world.

Awkward as they could be, Jen's unguarded reactions could also be tender and precious. One Sunday after church our family went out with some friends for pizza. Jen heard the background music in the restaurant and wanted her father to waltz with her like she'd seen in a movie. She pulled Andy up to dance as we all looked on. At first I cringed in embarrassment to see them waltzing around the salad bar, wondering what the other customers must be thinking, but I didn't ask them to stop. Andy couldn't have cared less what anybody else around them thought. He was enthralled by Jen and accepted her just as she was. He never tired of her or got upset. If she was being silly, he acted silly right along with her. His fatherly love for Jen reminded me of God's grace.

As I watched them dancing around the restaurant, I saw the joy on their faces, both of them glowing and laughing, completely unaware of everyone else in the room. The next thing I knew, tears were streaming down my face as I realized what a beautiful picture it was of how our heavenly Father loves each one of us. He is never embarrassed by us. He loves us unconditionally just as we are. There is nothing we can do to make God love us any less or any more than He does at this very moment. This same powerful, life-changing lesson is what Jen teaches everyone she meets.

Two years after the accident, we went back to UVA for a doctor's appointment. Entering the medical building, we found it sobering to see so many children with brain injuries who would never walk again. Some had severe trauma and disfigurements. Jen looked at them with compassion, overwhelmed with the realization that she could have been in that shape—or worse. It was a startling reminder of how much God had healed Jen and how far she had come. She was functioning at a level all the experts had once thought would be impossible, surpassing even their most optimistic hopes. Yet she still had a long way to go.

We were there to see Dr. Peter Patrick, the psychologist who had told us, just before Jen went home, that we were in a marathon. He had worked with brain-injured patients for more than thirty years.

Dr. Patrick asked Jen about her everyday life and how things were different. He understood that Jen had lost so much: she couldn't drive a car, her personality was completely different, she still had headaches every day, she couldn't play soccer or cheer like she once did.

Abruptly he asked Jen, "Is there anything that is the same as before the accident?"

After pondering a few seconds, Jen smiled and replied, "My love relationship with the Lord. It's stronger than ever!"

That answer was a big reminder to me that no matter what happens in this life, the one thing that can never be taken away is our salvation and love relationship with the Lord.

Then Dr. Patrick asked Jen, "What if you don't heal any more than you are today?"

All of a sudden, Jen turned a little feisty and said, "That is *never* going to happen! My God can do anything, and He is healing me every day."

Dr. Patrick chuckled and said, "Good, that is exactly what I wanted to hear—that you still have hope."

Evidence of that hope and her faith in God's plan for her life poured out of Jen constantly, sometimes in unexpected ways. One day in church we were singing "You Are God Alone," a song made popular by Phillips, Craig & Dean. All of a sudden Jen almost knocked me over in her excitement to start doing sign language for the lyrics. She had learned the signs at cheer camp before the accident. Now, with no filters or self-consciousness about what anyone sitting around her might think, she was beaming from ear to ear as she executed each hand motion perfectly:

Unchangeable, unshakable, unstoppable,
That's what You are.
You are God alone![11]

About a month later Jen and I spoke at a mother/daughter banquet where one of the ladies in the audience was deaf. Moments before we were supposed to go onstage, Jen leaned over and whispered, "Go get the 'You Are God Alone' CD out of the car. God is telling me to do the sign language tonight for that precious lady."

I had learned from past experience that when God was speaking to Jen, I'd better listen. After we spoke I started the CD. Jen stood in the spotlight, and as the music began, her joy was unmistakable. The presence of God was just shining out from her. She was having the time of her life worshiping and praising Him. It reminded me of the times she would sing to CDs in the hospital, completely oblivious to anyone else in the room: she was worshiping for an audience of one.

God moved in many hearts that night. By the time we got home I had an e-mail from the daughter of the deaf woman: "My mother wept the whole way home from the banquet tonight. . . . She said that never before had someone spoken so beautifully in her language, and it thrilled her heart to know that God did that just for her. My mother kept repeating, 'God knows my language!' Jen, please don't ever stop proclaiming Christ."

Since that night Jen has signed "You Are God Alone" hundreds of times at various speaking venues. Whenever she does, her face radiates joy as if she's worshiping at the feet of Jesus.

August 2009 marked another miracle, another new beginning in the life of Jen Barrick, when she started college at Liberty University. I went with her the first week until we could find a friend in each class to help her take notes and go from one class to the next. She enrolled in two classes: an Old Testament survey class taught by Papa Ed and a women's ministry class. I knew she could handle the OT curriculum because her Bible knowledge was completely intact. She probably knew as much Scripture as anybody else in the room. But the women's ministry class presented another level of responsibility and pressure.

The first day of class, the women's ministry teacher went through all of the exams, the required reading, and the papers the students had to write. I was completely overwhelmed at the thought of Jen tackling this course. She could write now, but slowly. Because her vision was so poor, she could barely read. And it took her forever to memorize new information. I knew I would need to devote many hours to helping her read, do research for her papers, and study for tests. As soon as the class ended, I shot Jen a worried look and said, "There's no way *we* can pass this class."

"Mom, where is your faith?" she demanded, almost bristling. "God always enables me to do what He asks me to do."

As the semester got underway, stories from the classroom proved Jen right. A friend who helped her in class said, "Mrs. Barrick, when Jen talks in class, it is amazing! Everyone turns around and listens. The students respect her, and she has so much wisdom."

I waited for Jen after school every day because it was too dangerous for her to walk in a parking lot or across campus alone. With her limited vision, she could easily be hit by a car. One day Jen was so excited when she came out to meet me.

"Mom, you would be so proud of me," she said. "I said something really good in class today, and the teacher was amazed. It was on topic and it made sense and everything."

I could hardly wait to hear this inspired nugget of wisdom. "What did you say?"

"Well, I can't remember—but it was really good, and the teacher was so impressed. It had to be the Lord!"

My college coed was still the unpredictable, tell-it-like-it-is young lady I'd become used to. Another day she said, "You would be so proud of me! We prayed for you in my class today."

"You did? Why?"

"It was prayer request time, and I raised my hand and said, 'Please pray for my mom because she is really stressed.' And the teacher said, 'Oh, yes, we need to pray for your mom.'"

The truth was that I was really struggling and stressed about something, but in my pride I didn't want Jen's whole class to know about it, especially her teacher. I should have known long before then that if you spend much time around Jennifer Barrick, the truth in your life will come out.

And of course, on the question of whether she could pass the class, Jen was right as usual. She got an A.

Meanwhile Andy was going through a transition of his own. His job at LU required a lot of travel, and Andy wanted to spend more time at home. So he went back to work with his good friend Dr. Tim Clinton as director of member relations for the American Association of Christian Counselors (AACC).

This led to an opportunity for Jen and me to attend the AACC World Conference in Nashville in September 2009. That was where we first had the privilege of meeting Joni Eareckson Tada. While Jen had always admired Joni's faith, courage, and perseverance, Joni became even more of a hero to Jen after her brain injury. Though paralyzed from the shoulders down by a diving accident when she was a teenager, Joni has inspired millions with her books, daily radio program, and more than thirty years of Christian ministry to the disabled around the world. Jen saw a kindred spirit in this brave and faithful woman who has lived her life as an encouragement to others and a testament to God's goodness.

Andy arranged for Jen and me to watch Joni on the big TV screen backstage in the speakers' greenroom, away from the noise and commotion. When we went in, we saw Joni across the room preparing to go on but didn't want to bother her.

Tim's daughter, Megan, was Jen's friend who had stood beside her during the choir concert the night of the accident. She saw us there and said, "Don't you want to meet Joni?"

"Yes!" Jen exclaimed, and Megan took us over and introduced us.

Immediately Joni and Jen had a special heart connection. They both knew what it was like to be in pain and totally desperate for God, completely dependent on Him every day. As they talked, Jen asked Joni how she could pray for her.

Joni said, "Well, Jen, I'm getting ready to go onstage and speak, and I'm having trouble breathing. Would you pray over me right now that God will give me the strength and help me breathe?"

We all circled around Joni and held hands as Jen prayed. God gave her the exact words that Joni needed to hear. I can't remember what they were, but I know we were all in tears by the time the prayer was over. We could feel the presence of God. Jen looked at Joni and said, "God wants me to tell you that you are so beautiful!"

While Joni was speaking, Jen whispered in my ear that God was telling her we should give Miss Joni one of her *Miracle for Jen* DVDs, which shows Jen singing in the chior the night of the wreck and tells Jen's story in a breathtaking way. "I think it will encourage her," Jen said. Once again I knew if God was speaking to Jen I had better listen, so I went back to our hotel room in the conference center and got a DVD. I was able to hand it to Joni's assistant.

One week later, Jen received a wonderful letter from Joni. "Jen— the Lord has blessed you with a powerful ministry; I know that because of the way *He encouraged me* through you during our brief time together backstage at the recent AACC conference. I pray every blessing of Psalm 20 over you, asking God to bring much fruit for the Kingdom out of all your hardships."

Later we planned a trip to the Joni and Friends International Disability Center in California. Jen had clearly made quite an impression. "Aside from a few obvious signs of brain injury, I couldn't help but get a spiritual suntan in her presence," Joni said in the e-mail confirming our visit. So Andy, Jen, and I started preparing for a trip out west in March.

It almost didn't happen.

On February 3, 2010, Andy and I dropped Josh off at the movie theater with a group of friends and decided to take Jen on a date. We headed over to one of our favorite restaurants, Shakers, to get our usual cheddar chicken grill sandwich. Andy and I sat side by side, with Jen across from us. When she finished eating, she started to tell us how much she loved us and how she appreciated all the things we had taught her and how she wanted to be just like us. She continued to embellish the thought over and over, as she often did, using different words to say the same thing.

The first sign of trouble was a sudden, ominous quiet. Jen abruptly stopped talking, as if someone had turned off a radio in midsentence. Her head jerked up. She stared vacantly at the far corner of the room. Then a horrible, earsplitting shriek welled up from deep inside her, shattering the silence and sending chills up and down my spine.

I stood and tried to grab her from across the table. Andy jumped over to her side and caught her as she fell to the ground. Her whole body clenched up, and her eyes rolled back into her head. It took all of Andy's strength to hold on to her head to keep her from knocking it against the floor. There was devastation in Andy's eyes: his daughter might be dying in his arms. A nurse who happened to be in the restaurant ran over and told us that Jen was having a seizure.

The restaurant manager called 911, and an ambulance arrived within minutes. As the EMTs tried to get Jen onto the stretcher, she became very combative. She didn't know who anybody was, not even us. I felt sick to my stomach and gripped by fear. *Have we lost everything we worked so hard to gain?* It felt like déjà vu; this was how Jen acted when she was emerging from the coma. Andy helped calm Jen down in the back of the ambulance while I sat up front with the driver. *Could we be starting all over? God, don't let that happen!*

An hour later in the hospital, it was like nothing had ever

happened. Jen seemed to be acting like her sweet self again. However, I noticed that she kept asking the nurses the same questions over and over. Fear flooded over me as I realized that all of her short-term memory was gone once more. *Lord, please don't let Jen lose her memory again. She's come so far.*

Andy and I spent a long night at the hospital, praying continually in our hearts for God to help us. By daybreak the doctors could tell us that though Jen was exhausted, there was no permanent damage from the seizure. They reminded us that seizures were actually pretty common with a brain injury as severe as Jen's and that she could have another one at any time. In fact, she had been on seizure medication in the hospital, but since she'd never had one, it was discontinued before she came home. We had let the possibility of seizures slip to the back of our minds, crowded out by day-to-day struggles and successes.

This was our reminder that we had to be diligent—had to expect the unexpected—from now on. It was a refresher course for us: living with a brain-injured loved one is a lifelong journey. Once again, we were back to relying on God, one day at a time.

There are times when I don't see how I can gather the strength to do this for the rest of my life. That's when Jen reminds me, "Mom, we were chosen for this journey. God handpicked us. And He isn't finished yet."

Jen felt fine as the time approached to visit Joni and Friends. A week before we flew to California, Joni sent an e-mail asking if *Joni and Friends* could do a TV show on Jennifer's story to inspire and encourage others.[12] We were blown away with the honor. Only God could have orchestrated an opportunity like this one. We quickly replied that Jennifer would gladly speak and be on camera, but I would have to speak with her and ask her questions.

When we arrived at the center for Joni and Friends on March 5,

Joni was waiting for us at the front door. Her first words to Jen were, "Give me a hug!" Our first stop in the beautiful new headquarters building was a chapel, where as soon as we walked in the door Joni turned to Jen and said, "Let's sing!" So we sang hymns to the Lord on the spot, a cappella. Then Jen asked Joni if she knew the song "Lord, You're Holy."

"No," Joni said, "but I would love for you to sing it for me." Jen sang her heart out, remembering every word. Even though some of her notes were a little off-key, nobody cared because it was a joyful noise unto the Lord. Joni, just like Jennifer, drew her strength from singing praise songs to God. What a glorious way to begin the day!

When the time came for Jen and me to share our story, there was a TV crew and a room full of staff members, a much bigger crowd than I had imagined. I was worried because the day before Jen had been very tired and disoriented, barely able to function due to the traveling and the three-hour time change.

While the sound crew was adjusting our microphones, Joni wheeled up to Jen and said, "Don't be afraid, Jen. These people are your friends. I will be praying for you." We asked God to speak His words through us, and once again the power of the Holy Spirit filled the room as Jennifer spoke from her heart. She was clearer and more articulate on camera than she had ever been. She even quoted the journal entry that she wrote before the accident from memory: "Anything is possible with you, Lord." I was astounded!

Afterward Jennifer gave Joni a pair of dangly pearl earrings that she had made for her, and Joni had a friend put them in her ears immediately. Then Joni whispered in my ear something that I will never forget. She said, "Linda, when Jen prayed at the end, God spoke directly to my heart. I asked my husband, Ken, and he agreed. Maybe that is what this brain injury is all about. Jen is a vessel that God can speak through."

Joni told Jen that she was speaking the following month at Liberty University in Virginia and wondered if it was close to where Jen lived. Jen smiled and said, "Honey, I go to Liberty University!" God had already orchestrated another detail. Since the film crew would be in Lynchburg with Joni, they would plan to stay several extra days to shoot footage of the crash scene, interview us in our home, and speak with others involved in the story. At dinner that night with Joni and Ken, we enjoyed a wonderful evening of fellowship. By 9 p.m. Jen and Joni were singing praise songs again in the parking lot of an Italian restaurant. What soul mates they were!

Joni spoke a month later, on April 7, at the Liberty University convocation. Known as "convo" to the university community, this weekly assembly each Wednesday in the Vines Center athletic arena is a long-standing campus tradition. In the middle of her talk Joni recognized Jen and the rest of our family in the audience. "Wow," she said. "Has this young woman stirred my heart and prompted me to draw even closer to the Lord Jesus!" Then she asked Jen to stand. As she did, Jen's face was beamed onto the giant TV screens in the arena to the applause of the crowd. Joni told the audience that later in the day she would be taping an interview for a documentary segment on her television show.

That afternoon the video session went well. Jen took a fifteen-minute power nap in the car and then shot a thirty-minute interview with Joni. I was so proud of Jen as she answered each question with confidence and poise. At the end, Joni put her hand on Jen's hand and said, "Jen, let's sing 'I Surrender All.'" The two of them glowed as they sang together. Later, alone in a corner of the studio in the university communications department, Joni, Jen, and I prayed that our story would have power and would change the lives of viewers forever.

Joni's producer, Duane Barnhart, and cameraman Tim Rygh spent four days doing interviews at our house with Andy, Jen, Josh, and me. During that time they also interviewed others who were part of our story: Kristi Vann, the EMT who was at the accident site; the helicopter pilot; friends; doctors and nurses at Kluge. Duane and Tim had no idea what they were getting themselves into. When Jen spoke, God ministered to their hearts so powerfully that they were nearly overwhelmed with emotion, barely able to keep the cameras steady because their hands were shaking.

They put together an incredible two-part documentary on our story for Joni's ministry. At the end of the second segment, Joni closed by quoting Philippians 1:12 (NIV). "Now I want you to know, brothers and sisters, that what has happened to me has actually served to advance the gospel." Looking into the camera with conviction, she added, "Jen can say the same thing. But the question is, can you?"

In December we were interviewed for the program *Cross Examine* produced by Coral Ridge Ministries in Florida. This show focused on the key issue of forgiveness. The invitation came thanks to a suggestion by Tim Rygh, who also handled assignments for Coral Ridge. The program host, Dr. Del Tackett, showed clips of Andy, Jen, and me talking about our struggles to forgive the drunk driver and my own anger at the policeman who let him get away. Del reminded the viewers that none of us can forgive in our own strength. "Only the Lord gives us the power to forgive," he said.

I spoke on camera about the freedom of forgiveness, and how God showed me that when we don't forgive, the target of our anger and bitterness becomes an idol. "The Lord doesn't waste trials," Jen added. "He has a plan and a purpose for everything."

Suffering was part of God's plan for Job, for Paul—who prayed repeatedly but in vain for the Lord to remove the thorn in his flesh—and, most of all, for His Son, Jesus. And suffering was part of His perfect plan for the Barrick family. I don't understand it. I can only hold on to my conviction that, as Del affirmed, God's plan is better than mine, and that in His strength alone I can let go of my plan and embrace His.

Every day I have a choice: hold on to old dreams and be angry and bitter about my loss, or let go of my old plans—what Del called "the script"—for my life and reach forward with joy and faith toward what God in His wisdom has planned for me instead. Del's summary was right on the mark: "One path leads to destruction. The other path leads to life."[13]

It was wonderful to be interviewed for these programs and reach many thousands of people at once. But for every one of these shows we did, there were many more live appearances in front of audiences ranging from a handful to a thousand or more.

By now I knew what parts of our story listeners responded to best, the parts that bared their own hearts to face their particular disappointments and crises and find faith in the Lord to overcome them. I also knew what Jen needed onstage to feel most comfortable sharing her testimony.

I typically started by introducing Jen and myself and explaining how our lives were changed by our accident. "First I begged God to heal Jennifer," I explained. "Then I demanded that He do it. But after a while, I got into the Word of God and saw I'd been going about it all wrong. Instead of crying and begging for God to heal her, I started *thanking* God for healing Jen's vision, her confusion, and her short-term memory, as well as for restoring the dexterity in her hands and her ability to process new information.

"This changed my whole mind-set from begging God and feeling helpless, to praising God and focusing on His power and His promises. In the crucible of our testing, we move from theory to reality as we begin to experience God's power. I was blessed to learn what I believe is a divine thought: *Don't become obsessed with healing. Get lost in the wonder of God.*"

After that I turned the floor over to Jen, who talked about the unfathomable faith and goodness of God. "I want everyone who is broken or hurting to know that God can still use you. He doesn't look down on you. He looks on you more. The weakest people have done the most for God, because in our weakness, He is strong. Don't ever be ashamed of your weakness. God wants you to see the potential of who you are going to be with His help. He wants to bring beauty from your ashes and heal your wounded heart. God wants to use you where you are, as you are. And He promises to carry you on the days you can't see ahead."

Then I concluded our presentation. "My new faith motto is: This life is just a dot on the timeline of eternity. I've said it out loud so many times that Jen has given me the nickname Polka Dot. Maybe our earthly life isn't even as big as a dot. Maybe it's a fraction of a dot, a molecule in a breath of air, compared to forever in heaven with our Lord and Savior. I hope that you will seek the presence of God in your life. Once you have been in the presence of Jesus as Jen has, you'll have a different perspective on life. Jen isn't earthly minded. She isn't distracted by the things that don't matter. There isn't anything she would rather do than proclaim Christ."

Thousands have come to know the Lord as a result of Jen's testimony. Although my fallible, all-too-human heart still grieves at times for what she has lost, she has gained something far more precious in the Lord's sight. She is a witness for Him like never before, winning souls for heaven.

When all is said and done, the only important question is, do our lives bring glory to God? By that standard—God's standard—Jen's life is richer than ever.

CHAPTER 18

THE BEST IS YET TO COME

My life is worth nothing to me unless I use it for finishing the work
assigned me by the Lord Jesus—the work of telling others the Good
News about the wonderful grace of God.   ACTS 20:24

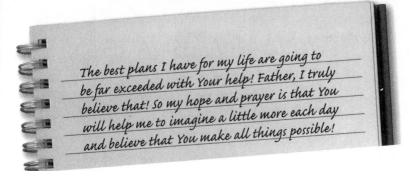

*The best plans I have for my life are going to
be far exceeded with Your help! Father, I truly
believe that! So my hope and prayer is that You
will help me to imagine a little more each day
and believe that You make all things possible!*

Jen's journal, three weeks before the crash

THIS IS NOT A JOURNEY I WOULD EVER HAVE WISHED FOR. I didn't
want it. I didn't like it. I didn't deserve it. I didn't understand it. For
a long time all I could do was endure it. Just surviving from one day
to the next, sometimes from one hour to the next, took every ounce
of energy I had.

Without faith in God's goodness, it would have been a hopeless
effort. I could never have survived or accepted what happened to my
family. God's love lifted me up when nothing else could. It would
have been so easy to give up, to climb into a dark place of bitterness
and anger and disappointment and stay there.

Satan's number one weapon is to get us to doubt God's love. If

God really loved Jennifer, how could He let her suffer the way she has? How could He let me and the rest of my family go through the trial by fire we have endured? What's He doing? Doesn't He care? Is He not paying attention?

Here's where faith makes all the difference. I have faith that God's plan is better than mine. He loves the Barrick family so much that He sent His perfect Son to pay for our sins with His life. A God who has done this could never wish us harm. Whatever happens to us, even if it seems hard and painful by our standards, is part of His flawless plan for the world. From our limited, self-centered, human perspective, the tribulations we face seem devastating and all-consuming. Faith tells us that from the Lord's perspective, those trials are the refiner's fire that show us how helpless we are on our own. They turn our eyes away from the desires and distractions of the world and force us to focus on the power of God in us. It's only when God is all we have that we know for sure God is all we need.

I had to let go of my plans for our family and trust God's plans. I had to have faith that everything that happened was subject to God's power, even when I didn't understand. Faith was there for the taking, but I had to reach out and grab hold of it; I had to choose victory over defeat. Satan had tried to destroy my family by making us doubt the goodness of God, but *I was not going to let him*!

Through faith, you can know that your pain has a purpose and that God never wastes a tear. That's easy to say, but there were times when I thought it was impossible to believe in my heart. I was exhausted from acting like everything was fine when it wasn't. I was so numb, so emotionally fried, that I began putting up walls to protect myself. But I didn't want to continue down that dark path. I wanted to live again! I wanted to feel again!

One day when no one was looking, I crawled up into our big chair in the den. I pictured myself crawling up into God's lap as He wrapped His arms around me and held me tight. Although I didn't have the words to express the emotional pain that I felt, God understood it completely. I sat there and wept while God held me in His arms. Then I remembered something Jen had told me: "Mom, ask God for what you need. Ask Him to whisper hope in your ear." So I did. I asked God to tell me He loved me and that He would take care of me. I asked Him to help me let go and trust Him because I knew I couldn't go on in my own strength. I was completely broken and desperate.

That is exactly how God longs for us to be—broken and desperate for Him. He isn't overwhelmed by our hard questions or our problems. He wants to come to our rescue. God gave me a Scripture passage that day that I had read before, but somehow it jumped off the page as if God were speaking directly to my heart. I have clung to Isaiah 41:9-10 and shared my paraphrase of the passage to audiences many times since: "I have called you. I have chosen you. Fear not! I am with you. I am your God. I will strengthen you. I will help you."

Jennifer senses God and the spiritual world in vivid, intimate ways. This is one of the ways I know the Lord has guided her steps through these last five years of tragedy and struggle. From an earthly perspective Jen has lost so much; yet from God's perspective she and He are closer than ever. She has become His mouthpiece to untold thousands of people who are desperate for Christ in their lives and who hear Him through her when they haven't heard Him any other way. Without the changes in Jen caused by the accident, she could never have done what she's doing for the Lord. She tells me my brain gets in the way, and she's right. The new Jen is "simple minded." Her brain is not clogged with all the things that are fighting for attention and swirling around inside my brain. She has become hardwired to God. She lives and breathes in Him and for Him to the exclusion of anything else.

One morning Jen and I were on the screened porch drinking coffee and enjoying the beauty of God's creation. All around us birds were chirping and flowers were blooming. I asked Jen what her perspective on life is now.

She thought for a minute and said, "I know God is holding me in His hands. I am His. I have moved beyond asking why the Lord allowed this to happen to asking, 'Lord, why did you choose me for this incredible honor? Why did you choose me?' I can't believe what God is doing through me and how He is using me. I am so honored and excited to be His vessel. I am so thankful for where He has me, and I wouldn't change any of it (except I would like to know how long I'm going to have these headaches!).

"I don't feel normal, and I'm okay with that. I never wanted to be normal. And I don't want to be remembered as 'the girl with the brain injury.' I want to be remembered as the girl who loved Jesus with all her heart."

There was a time when Jen thought she wanted to be a missionary. By God's grace she has become a powerful and effective one, though in a completely different way from what she imagined. In her journal the summer before the accident she wrote to God, "Daddy, I know with Your help the two of us can change the lost and dying world together." God has answered that prayer beyond her wildest expectations. Over the past five years Jen and I have spoken to tens of thousands of people and probably reached millions more through radio, television, and the Internet.

Her ministry has grown in other, unexpected ways. When Jen was eleven years old, Andy came home from business trips with gifts of jewelry for her. Jen loved jewelry and decided she could design her own. Within a year, she was making hundreds of bracelets that her father would sell for her at women's conferences across the country. She started her own little business, and creating jewelry was one of her favorite things to do.

After the accident, it seemed impossible that she would ever make jewelry again. Not only was her memory impaired, her vision was bad and she didn't have the necessary dexterity in her hands anymore. As a mom, my heart was broken because there were so many things that Jen couldn't do and the thought that she could no longer make jewelry was devastating. I remember praying, "Lord, please don't take away her ability to make jewelry too. It gives her so much joy! Please let her be able to use her hands again!"

One day about a year after the accident Jen said, "God is speaking to my heart, and I think I am going to make jewelry again. I might even put a Bible verse on it." Miraculously, Jen is doing it. Even though it is hard and takes her a lot longer than before she was injured, this project has given her a new confidence. She loves creating original designs, including beautiful hand-beaded earrings, bracelets, and necklaces made of colored crystals and gemstones. Jen claims the verse Matthew 19:26, "But with God all things are possible" (NIV). Every item comes with a card that features the verse, pictures, and Jen's story.[14]

Her dream for the future is to have a speaking and writing ministry. Jen also has a special desire to write children's books and prayer books. "I don't want to limit what God wants to do in and through me," she says. "I am willing to go wherever He wants me to go and do whatever He wants me to do. I believe God wants me to have a ministry to the world." In fact, our family recently founded a nonprofit ministry called Hope Out Loud to encourage those who are hurting and broken with the hope found in Jesus Christ.

Jen continues to heal. Today her stomach pain is completely gone and, five years after the accident, she has much more energy. Her memory is gradually improving, and she is more independent in taking care of her personal needs. Only God knows how long her progress will continue or how far it will go. Every morning I thank Him for another day of her life and for every new sign of recovery.

I know that everyone reading this book has a story. Even if you haven't experienced anything life-threatening or physically violent, you've likely been through hard times—pain, brokenness, and shattered dreams that have shaken your faith and caused you to doubt God's love and His plans for your life. It could be sickness or death, financial or career crisis, betrayal or divorce, or something else that stops you in your tracks and makes you ask, "Why, God? If You really love me and You're really in charge, how can You let this happen?"

Perhaps your life hasn't turned out like you planned or hoped. You may be on a completely different path than you expected to be. You can choose to spend every day longing for the way things used to be or "should" have been, or you can celebrate the person you are now.

Whatever caused your scars and whoever's fault it was, you have a choice: you can be bitter, or you can be better. I can't share your burden or take away your pain. What I can do is tell you with absolute certainty that God loves you unconditionally and does everything for your ultimate good, even when it doesn't seem that way at the time. With God there is always hope, no matter what. With God you can always forgive and be forgiven, no matter what—not in your own strength, but in His. With God you can learn, as I have, that however heavy your burden, God always stands ready to help you bear it. My prayer for you is that you will know these things in your heart and hold fast to them. They will see you through.

Faith brings assurance that you are becoming exactly the person God wants you to be. God never wastes a pain or a tear—He promises to use everything if we let Him. God wants us to give all our scars and broken pieces to Him so He can put us back together again and make us into something beautiful. Even if the physical scars remain, God can heal all of us in our souls. If you listen to Him, He will assure you that through your sometimes painful, tearful journey of growth and change, He is preparing you for heaven.

Jennifer says that she wouldn't change what happened to her even if she could. That sounds like a crazy statement at first. Until you realize that it's not the old scholar/athlete Jen talking, it's the new Jen, who has accomplished more for the Kingdom of God in a few short years than many "normal" people do in a lifetime. She wakes up every morning ready to serve Him with her whole heart. It's all she needs and all she wants.

This wasn't the miracle that I prayed for, but God has shown me over and over that He has something far greater for Jen. "God whispers 'hope' in my ear," she says with a smile, "and tells me the best is yet to come.

"And that someday, I will understand."

CHAPTER 19

MORE THAN WE IMAGINED

October 2012

Yet what we suffer now is nothing compared to the glory that he will reveal to us later.

ROMANS 8:18

The victory is greater than the suffering. We must have an expectation of what God is going to do.

JEN TO HER MOM, LINDA, JUST AFTER *MIRACLE FOR JEN*
WAS RELEASED

THESE DAYS WHEN I TURN ON MY COMPUTER and discover e-mails from places like South Africa, Israel, Romania, and Portugal, my mind races back to February 2007. Jen had just come home from the hospital. She could barely see. She had no short-term memory. She still received nourishment through a feeding tube. But she marched around the kitchen saying, "I'm going to proclaim Christ to a lost and dying world. I'm gonna have a ministry to the world."

I confess that I looked at her and thought, *You are so confused. You can't even find the bathroom. How are you going to have a ministry to the world?*

I get chills now as I realize Jen was proclaiming out loud the hope of what would happen in the future. Since then, God has used Jen's story to give hope and purpose to people all over the world. I believe it is just the beginning, and it is amazing to watch.

Following the release of *Miracle for Jen*, Jennifer, Josh, Andy, and I were able to tell our story over and over during an extensive speaking tour that included book signing events, national and international radio and television programs, churches, and conferences.

While every engagement was different, each one showed three things: first, God continues to heal Jennifer; second, she still must cope with her disabilities every day; and third, God supplies just what we need in our weakness; there is no limit to what He can do.

God has given Jen the strength and energy she needs to keep up with a traveling and speaking schedule that would wear out most people. She no longer needs a midday nap or chokes on the water when taking a shower, and she can get by on ten hours of sleep. Recently, she even started running! To our astonishment, she ran one and a half miles her first time out. After training for two months, Jen competed in a 5K race and refused to stop even at the water station. She was determined to run the whole way and cross the finish line.

After buying a wireless keypad for her iPad, we discovered another surprise: Jen remembers how to type! She can't use a mouse or see the cursor on the computer screen, but she still has the muscle memory that enables her to type. She has already typed over one hundred new prayer journal entries.

Jen is also able to interact with people who want to talk with her after hearing her speak. At the first event on our speaking tour, I panicked after her talk when I realized I'd forgotten to warn the audience that Jen was so sensitive to touch that even patting her on the back could cause her pain. I started to run over to her, but when I got closer, I realized she was perfectly fine. She was sitting in a chair with a long line of people waiting to talk to her. It was a miracle happening right before my eyes. For the next ninety minutes she signed books, prayed with people, and carried on conversations without any help from me. Nothing seemed to bother her. She didn't shake or get nervous. She was full of wisdom and advice. Since that day, she has never been hypersensitive to touch at ministry events. I believe with all my heart that God healed her a little more that day.

In fact, when we are out speaking and meeting with people, I'm almost tempted to think that she is completely healed. On the road, she's a wise theologian whom God clearly uses to minister to others. When we return home, Jen is weary and she reverts to more of a dependent child. Because she can't drive, she spends a lot of time at home making jewelry and playing memory-building games on her iPad.

One day I returned home after being gone all morning at Bible study. When I greeted Jen and asked how she was, she sighed loudly and said, "Ahh! I'm exhausted! I've done so much today."

"Really?" I asked. "What did you do this morning?"

"Well . . ." She thought hard for a moment and then added, "Well, I got up!" She couldn't remember anything else. Jen, Andy, and I just laughed. The truth was, Andy told me, she had done a lot. She had crocheted a scarf, written a journal entry to the Lord, and gone to lunch with her dad. But by the time I talked with her, her mind had gone blank and she couldn't remember any of it. This underscores one persistent problem: her short-term memory remains poor.

When NBC's *Today* show came to do a story on our family, cameramen captured this deficit when they followed her around Liberty University. As she walked to class, a few of her friends went with her so she wouldn't get lost in the hallways. One of the cameramen caught the moment when Jen turned to me just before entering the room and asked, "Now, what's my teacher's name again?"

Like many people, Jen has hidden disabilities that may not be immediately obvious but that limit her nonetheless. What sets Jen apart is her attitude, as when she told Michelle, the NBC reporter, "I know I am different, and I'm okay with that."

Later that day, Michelle and Robert, NBC's producer, sat down with Jen in our kitchen for an hour-long interview. Her answer to

Robert's final question seemed to stun them. "Jennifer," he asked, "if you could go back and change the wreck, would you do it?"

She immediately said, "No, I would not. I trust God's plan for my life, and I'm thankful that God is using me to make a difference in the lives of others."

While her answer might strike people as naive, Jen often says how honored she feels that God is using her to help others. Her childlike faith enables her to rest in Him, in a spirit of joy and contentment. She seems to have been spared the battle of the mind that the rest of us must wage every day to live with peace.

A little later, Robert asked me the same question. "Linda, would you change what happened the night of the wreck if you could?"

How I wanted to be like Jen! Yet I knew I needed to be honest. "As a mom," I said, "I would do anything to go back and stop the wreck to prevent my child from suffering so much."

Prayer remains a vital link between Jen and her heavenly Father. In fact, just as when Jen was hospitalized, the one time that Jen appears completely uninjured is when she prays. When we speak on stage, I often have to give Jen cues and ask her questions. But she closes every speaking engagement with prayer, and her petitions are so powerful. She has never spoken the same prayer twice; God always seems to bring different verses and words to her mind.

After she spoke at a high school, one of the kids went home and told her mom, "When Jen prays, she's not injured. She speaks clearer and faster and more eloquently." When this mom told me what her daughter had said, I realized she was right. Often she'll preach a whole sermon in her prayer.

God even seems to work through some of her prayers to reenergize

Jen herself. One day we filmed twenty interview segments for the Canadian TV show *100 Huntley Street*. As we finished segment after segment, Jen began to get tired. To offer some relief, we took a lunch break; we changed outfits; we had a chocolate break. Finally, in the midst of filming the seventeenth segment, I was sure Jen had passed her limit. She looked completely worn out, even grumpy, and she seemed confused. Frankly, after talking for about seven hours, we were both getting tongue-tied. *That's it*, I thought. *We are not going to be able to finish. We're done.*

Then Moira Brown, the show's host, closed that segment by asking Jen, "I hope I'm not pushing you too much. But it would be a shame to miss having you pray for someone who would love to know God the way you do. Could I ask you to pray?"

When Jen began to pray, something amazing happened. Her words became clearer and louder, and she gave a beautiful summary of God's plan of salvation before inviting viewers to ask God into their lives. The tears flowed down my face as I realized that God was reenergizing my daughter even as He spoke to countless hurting people through her prayer.

Once we'd finished that segment, Moira Brown said, "Jen, look at you! You've got energy!"

In fact, Jen was smiling and nearly dancing around. I, on the other hand, had to look on quietly as a makeup artist came over to remove the mascara that had smeared from my tears.

Not surprisingly, people with disabilities are especially drawn to Jen. Just after the book came out, we spent a week in California where she spoke to over one hundred men and woman with severe physical or mental disabilities. The audience at John MacArthur's Grace Community Church in Sun Valley also included 90 caregivers and disability ministry volunteers. The room was completely silent as they listened to a video clip that told our story. The audience seemed entranced as they realized that Jen had been through pain and turmoil, just like they had.

When Jen took the stage after the video, everyone began clapping and shouting, "We love you, Jen! We love you!"

Jen responded, "Who loves Jesus?"

"We do!" the audience shouted.

"Do you know the song 'Jesus Loves Me?'" Jen asked to cheers and applause.

"Can you sing it with me?" she said.

With the innocence and excitement of little children, the group began singing, even doing the song's hand motions with Jen. Then Jen had the opportunity to tell them that, in their weakness, God is strong and that He has a special plan for each one of them.

Jen spoke from experience. During that same trip to California, Jen taped a national radio show with Joni Eareckson Tada. After singing a few hymns to invite God's power and presence into our day, we headed to the studio, where Jen was given a twenty-five-page script. Since her vision is so poor, Jen can barely read, so the script was nearly useless to her. Unintentionally, I complicated things even more by trying to jump in and give her cues. That just made things harder for Joni since I was giving away details I wasn't supposed to reveal yet.

Meanwhile, Joni was struggling too. She was exhausted and her voice was weak because she had returned from an out-of-town trip late the night before. It was hard for her to clear her lungs and get a deep breath so she could speak. Finally Joni stopped and prayed, "Lord Jesus, please give me your voice. Please help me." Then she asked Jen if she would sing a praise song. So Jennifer, Andy, and I sang "Lord, You're Holy" in the little taping room. It was beautiful and humbling all at the same time; beautiful because we knew God was moving but humbling because we don't have the best singing voices!

Joni then asked Jen if she would pray for her. As she did, I realized that because Joni has a physical weakness and Jen has a mental weakness, they are both forced to rely on God's strength to get through the relatively simple task of reading through a radio script.

It's hard to describe what happened next, other than to say we could feel God's presence in that little studio. Joni's voice was strong again, and Jen's mind was sharp and clear. Joni started giving Jen cues to help Jen know what to say next. By the time they finished, Joni and Jen were so full of energy that they taped two more short radio shows, along with a video blog.

It was another reminder that, in our weakest moments, we have a choice. We can give up, isolating ourselves and dying a little inside. Or we can realize that God has a plan and purpose for everything we go through and then reach out to help others. When we call out to Him, we find the healing that comes from knowing our pain has a purpose.

In fact, the most thrilling part of Jen's book has been reading the thousands of e-mails from readers. The book is impacting people in very different ways. One person wrote to say she now views her scars as beauty marks. Another told us she is praying out loud for the first time. Still another said that he prayed and accepted Christ as his personal Savior. And there are so many more responses:

- "I'm now writing my prayers to God."
- "I'm bowing and surrendering my day to the Lord every morning."
- "I'm refusing to give up on my dreams because of my deficits."
- "My family is praying together."
- "I'm viewing my disabilities as gifts instead of burdens."
- "I'm letting go of bitterness toward my broken family."
- "God healed me after I read *Miracle for Jen*. I am able to focus and remember what I read for the first time in fourteen years."

But the most astonishing—and meaningful—personal connection we made happened at a book signing right in our own hometown. Thanks to an article in our local paper, a huge crowd showed up to meet us at the bookstore. About an hour after we'd started talking with people and signing books, I glanced up to see the woman next in line. She was shaking and crying, hardly able to meet my eyes. I could never have anticipated the words she finally choked out to me.

"I'm Carl's sister," she said.

For a moment, Jen and I sat there stunned, looking at the sister of the man whose truck had hit us head-on. The one whose choices that night had caused so much pain and suffering to our family . . . and, as I saw clearly in her face, had torn hers apart as well.

Jen never hesitated. She got up and embraced her, and I joined her as we all wept.

Finally, the woman said, "I didn't know if you would want to meet me, but I read the newspaper article this morning and decided to come."

Looking intently at Carl's sister, Jen asked, "Is he in pain? Can he talk? Does he understand what you're saying?"

Carl's sister told us that her brother was still being cared for in a long-term medical facility nearby. He still cannot talk or eat, though he is breathing on his own.

After we had talked for a few minutes, we exchanged e-mails and phone numbers and have stayed in touch. Someday we'd like to meet Carl and extend our forgiveness to him in a way that will bring more healing both to our family and his. While I hope our meeting with Carl's sister gave his family some measure of peace, I now realize God orchestrated our meeting at least as much for me as for them.

When I've asked God why it is taking so long for us to meet Carl, He has said to my heart, *You're not ready yet, Linda. You need to pray every day for Carl, his mom, and his sister. You need to come to the place where you can love them unconditionally.*

In other words, I need to learn what forgiveness truly means. As I've e-mailed his sister, I've learned that Carl grew up in church but eventually made some poor choices and became an alcoholic. While he's still incapacitated after all these years, his family is left to deal with the pain and hurt. Even on the day of the book signing, his sister said, Satan was tormenting her with thoughts like, *You shouldn't go. They're not going to want to see you.*

The more I pray for Carl, I am reminded that any one of us is just one decision away from a bad choice. God doesn't condemn us when we mess up; He is waiting with open arms to redeem us and give us a second chance. I've also come to understand that forgiveness is not a quick thing, it's a process. I won't be ready to meet Carl and the rest of his family until I am no longer worried that it might cause me more emotional pain but am concerned only with reaching out and encouraging them.

Jen, on the other hand, is excited about meeting Carl. She holds no bitterness toward him and hopes to have the opportunity to visit and pray over him in person. That unconditional love and acceptance, I think, is what draws so many people to her. Even when we're not on the road, many people call and ask to meet with her. As Jen talks and prays with hurting people, it's clear the Lord gives her His wisdom and insight to share. With that in mind, Andy and I are planning to move the ministry we started, Hope Out Loud, out of our home and into its own space. It's obvious that God is growing our ministry to serve more people and purposes than we could have ever imagined.

Hope Out Loud, we believe, is Jen's future, and we want to have a place where she can meet with others, have prayer groups and Bible studies, continue to make jewelry, answer e-mails, and extend her outreach. Our family's passion is to share Christ and to help people who are hurting and broken. We are excited to see how God will use and grow Hope Out Loud. We have already seen God transform thousands of lives as we continue to travel and speak in venues all over the country, and Jen never lets us forget that He has big plans to work through us.

"When I look at my life," Jen says, "it's not that I get to choose what I want to do, but it's what I do with what I've been given. That's what really matters."

Among other things for Jen, that meant finishing high school. It also meant completing all of her Bible and women's ministry classes to earn a biblical studies diploma from Liberty University. In May 2012, she walked with the graduates from Liberty's seminary and Bible institute at commencement, which was held at Thomas Road Baptist Church . . . on the very same stage where Jen had performed in her first choir concert, just hours before the wreck.

After watching the graduates file in, I waited to hear Jen's name called. They had saved hers for last. As the student before her was called, I ran to the front (making a bit of a scene, I must admit) so I could videotape Jen while she walked across the stage.

Dr. Harold Wilmington, head of the Bible institute, told the audience, "We saved a special girl for the end because she has an amazing story. Her grandfather happens to be one of the professors sitting on stage today. When she comes across the stage, I'm going to ask him, Dr. Ed Hindson, to say a word."

My heart was about to pound its way out of my chest. *Can she walk all that distance in front of so many people without tripping?* I was so proud of her I could hardly stand it. I thought back to that terrible night when the doctors told me she had no hope. She would probably die before morning, and if she lived, she'd be comatose for the rest of her life. If only they could see her now!

Five and a half years and a lifetime ago, when she stood on that stage singing her heart out with her high school choir, she had no idea how her world was about to change. Part of me longed for the chance to go back in time to that moment; to grab her and hold her close and stop her from riding home in the van. *Sure, Jen, you can ride home with Brandon's family. We'll see you at the house.*

I was jerked back to reality as Jen and my dad stepped onto the podium. After briefly introducing her, Dad said, "Better than me saying a word—Jen, why don't you?" I prayed instinctively, *Lord Jesus, give her the words.*

She beamed her megawatt smile. "Hi! My name is Jen Barrick." The big auditorium was absolutely silent as she spoke. No one moved or made a sound. Jen continued, "God has been so faithful and true to my family over these past five years. He doesn't always promise to take away the trial but to help you through the trial. He promises to be there for you and with you every step of the way. He is the one who has sustained my family, and we have held on to the verse Philippians 4:13, 'I can do all things through Christ who strengthens me.' Thank you." [15]

Jen's words were as clear and strong as if she'd been practicing for weeks, when in fact she'd had no warning at all she would be asked to speak. When she finished, the room erupted with cheers, the roar of applause echoing off the distant walls. Everyone jumped to their feet, including the distinguished professors onstage. My heart was filled to overflowing as I felt warm tears running down my face.

Get a grip, Linda, I told myself. *Jen's coming off the stage and she'll need your help.* I ran to the steps to meet her so she wouldn't feel lost or afraid. I shouldn't have worried. By the time I got there she was posing for pictures and smiling from ear to ear. She looked up and saw my tears.

"Don't worry, Mom, we're going to make it," Jen said, smiling.

Then her smile broadened into a mischievous giggle. "God is speaking to my heart. He says this is only the beginning. He's just getting started, and it's about time to pick up the pace. You better get your rollerblades on!"

Me on rollerblades would definitely add another miracle to our incredible experience. But based on our journey so far, if the Lord tells Jen it will happen, I have complete faith that it will. Their relationship is characterized by a closeness and power unlike anything I've ever seen. It's proof every day that God can use anyone—you, me, the brain injured, the honor student, the least of His people—to do great works in His name.

It will be amazing to see what God has in store for Jen and the rest of us. I'm lacing up my skates and I'm ready to go. I just hope I can keep up with her!

a word from Jen

I WAS JUST AN ORDINARY GIRL WITH BIG DREAMS. Now my dreams have changed. My one desire is to tell the world that true hope is found in Christ alone and that with Him you can do anything.

God's love is not reserved for perfect people. In fact, His greatest miracles often come through the weak and broken. His power is made perfect through human weakness. I still wear my MIRACLE 4 JEN bracelet today because I never want to forget that. I believe that God's miracles will continue to unfold. His promise that "no eye has seen, no ear has heard, no mind has conceived what God has prepared for those who love him" (1 Corinthians 2:9) isn't just describing what we'll experience in heaven. Instead, I believe God's plans for each of us on this earth surpass our wildest dreams!

Maybe you've been through some terrible hardships and feel that your life will never be the same again. Regardless of your circumstances, you can be healed in your soul with the peace of God, and your life may never be the same again—it may be better than you ever imagined possible.

None of us can heal on our own. For that we need a Savior. The good news is that God is ready to rescue you. Ready to offer the free gift of salvation in His Son, Jesus Christ—the gift of redemption and a new life. Once you pray and invite Him into your heart, His spirit lives in you and fills you with His power and strength. "If you confess with your mouth that Jesus is Lord and believe in your heart that God raised him from the dead, you will be saved" (Romans 10:9).

If I didn't have a personal relationship with the Lord, my story would be completely different. If you are broken and hurting today, cry out to God. He doesn't want you to be afraid or ashamed. He wants to come to your rescue and take the pain and fear away. He is the only one in this world who will never disappoint you or desert you. He wants to redeem everything that is past and make all things new.

The Lord is the writer of my story, and I can't wait to see how it ends!

Forever hoping,

Jennifer Barrick

Notes

1. Eddie James, "Lord, You're Holy," copyright 2001 New Spring (ASCAP)/Fresh Vine Publishing. Used with permission.
2. Ibid.
3. Eventually we went to court and settled with our insurance company. A suit filed against the deputy sheriff was later dismissed.
4 Beth Moore, *Believing God* (Nashville: Broadman and Holman, 2004), 22-23.
5. Dave Thompson, "Bedford Teen Featured in University of Virginia Children's Hospital Telethon," *News and Advance*, June 1, 2008, http://www2.newsadvance.com/m/news/2008/jun/01/bedford_teen_featured_in_university_of_virginia-ch-ar-223273/.
6. "Comeback Kid of the Year: Jen Barrick," http://www.nbc29.com/story/8301963/comeback-kid-of-the-year-jen-barrick?redirected=true.
7. See Psalm 37:4; Psalm 62:2; Jeremiah 29:11; Lamentations 3:22-23; Matthew 10:29; Hebrews 13:5.
8. "The Solid Rock" by Edward Mote (1797—1874).
9. Clint Lagerberg and Nichole Nordeman, "Heal the Wound," copyright 2007 Birdwing Music/Bird Boy Songs (adm. by EMI CMG Publishing), Word Music LLC.
10. Luke Seavers, "Jen's Song," from the album *Do Not Listen*, My Useful Weakness, 2009.
11. Billy and Cindy Foote, "You Are God Alone," copyright 2004, Billy Foote Music.
12. To view the video, go to http://www.hopeoutloud.com/video.html or more directly at http://www.joniandfriends.org/television/jennifer-barrick-story-part-1/.
13. You can also see the "Forgiving When It Hurts" program produced by *Cross Examine* as well as other videos on our story at http://www.hopeoutloud.com/video.html.
14. To see Jen's original creations, visit http://www.hopeoutloud.com/store/store-main.html.
15. The link to Jen's graduation speech is http://hopeoutloud.com/Jen_graduating.html. In her remarks, Jen quoted from the NKJV Bible.

About the Author

LINDA BARRICK is an inspirational speaker with a broad record of media experience in radio, television, and writing. Linda leads a weekly Bible study of 500 women at Thomas Road Baptist Church, and cohosts a Christian television program called *Lighting the Way* with her father, Dr. Ed Hindson. She and her daughter, Jennifer, are accomplished speakers and share the platform at various venues. The Barrick family lives in Lynchburg, Virginia, and has founded a nonprofit ministry called Hope Out Loud. For updates on the Barricks and their ministry, visit www.hopeoutloud.com.

HoPE OUTLoUD

- Watch Video Clips
- Order Jen's Original Jewelry
- Purchase a *Miracle for Jen* DVD
- Schedule Speaking Events
- Join the Facebook Page

For the latest news on
the Barrick family and their ministry,
visit www.hopeoutloud.com.

Online Discussion *guide*

Take *your* TYNDALE READING EXPERIENCE *to the* NEXT LEVEL

A FREE discussion guide for this book
is available at bookclubhub.net, perfect
for sparking conversations in your book
group or for digging deeper into the text
on your own.

www.bookclubhub.net

*You'll also find free discussion guides for
other Tyndale books, e-newsletters, e-mail
devotionals, virtual book tours, and more!*